WOMEN
AT WAR

WOMEN AT WAR

IRAQ, AFGHANISTAN, AND OTHER CONFLICTS

* * *

James E. Wise Jr. and Scott Baron

NAVAL INSTITUTE PRESS
Annapolis, Maryland

Naval Institute Press
291 Wood Road
Annapolis, MD 21402

Library of Congress Cataloging-in-Publication Data

Wise, James E., 1930–
Women at war : Iraq, Afghanistan, and other conflicts—James E. Wise Jr.,
and Scott Baron.
     p. cm.
Includes bibliographical references and index.
ISBN 1-59114-939-8 (alk. paper)
    1. Women soldiers—United States—Biography. 2. Women sailors—United
States—Biography. 3. Iraq War, 2003—Women—United States—Biography.
4. AfghanWar, 2001—Women—United States—Biography.   I. Baron,
Scott, 1954–   II. Title.
U52.W578 2006
355.0092'273—dc22
[B]

                                                                2006018561

Printed in the United States of America on acid-free paper ⊛

12 11 10 09 08 07 06   8 7 6 5 4 3 2

First printing

Legend for photo credits: U.S. Army (USA); U.S. Navy (USN); U.S. Marine Corps
(USMC); U.S. Air Force (USAF); U.S. Coast Guard (USCG); Army Nurse Corps
collection (ANCC); U.S. Naval Historical Center (NHC); Women In Military Service
For America Memorial Foundation, Inc. (The Women's Memorial); U.S. Navy
Bureau of Medicine and Surgery Archives (NBMSA); and U.S. National Archives and
Records Administration (NARA). Photographs from private collections are so noted
in the given credit line.

Dedicated to the American military women
who have served and continue to serve our nation
with steadfast patriotism, courage, and valor,
and to those who are left behind
to pray for the safe return of their loved ones.
May their many sacrifices,
in peace and war, never be forgotten.

Contents

Preface

WOMEN AT WAR: IRAQ, AFGHANISTAN, AND OTHER CONFLICTS contains a series of interviews with, and stories about, U.S. women who have served and continue to serve in the global war on terror. The insurgency war in Iraq, which has no front lines, has made the debate regarding women in combat irrelevant. In such a war zone, anyone can be killed or injured at any moment.

Today women in all military services are involved in the war as fighter, bomber, helicopter, and transport pilots; as physicians, medics, and nurses; and as crew members ashore and afloat. Servicewomen are frequently engaged in firefights with enemy insurgents while guarding convoys, traveling in hostile territory, or performing military police duties and other vital support functions. Unique to this war is the role of "searchers," played by female military women as they pat down Muslim women, checking for weapons and harnessed suicide bombs before they cross through checkpoints.

Like their male counterparts in these conflicts, many have been killed and wounded, some with grievous loss of limbs. They continue to carry out their missions with determination and great courage. During interviews with them they displayed extraordinary dedication to their tasks and the military men and women with whom they serve; they are truly inspiring. Perhaps this military force of American men and women volunteers may someday be called America's "Second Greatest Generation."

Women at War: Iraq, Afghanistan, and Other Conflicts will give the reader a new and perhaps underreported perspective of just how valiantly our women have served in the global war on terror. As in past wars, American women serving in uniform or as members of such civilian agencies as the American Red Cross, Catholic Relief Services, the Central Intelligence Agency, the U.S. Agency for International Development, among others, have proven to be vital to America's war efforts.

Note: The military women included in this book were selected for their diversity of wartime experiences and courageous service. It was hoped that more women could have been included, but the authors were unable to contact many active duty and discharged servicewomen. The active duty personnel were deployed, being redeployed, changing duty stations, etc. and were not available to participate in this project. Also, it should be noted that the chapters vary in length because no literary restraints were placed on the women who related their compelling experiences. The voices of these women deserve to be heard.

Acknowledgments

THERE ARE MANY TO THANK FOR assisting us in this comprehensive work. As in all of our writing efforts, we must first recognize the exceptional research and administrative work done by our chief research assistant, Natalie Hall. She is an indispensable member of our team.

Women at War could not have been written without the invaluable assistance of Kate Scott, the oral historian of The Women's Memorial. It was her tireless work in interviewing the many servicewomen included in this book and sharing the transcripts of these interviews that make up the core of this work. Kate is an extremely dedicated historian, and her enthusiasm and professional demeanor make it a joy to work with her.

Another member of The Women's Memorial staff who supported this effort was Britta Granrud, Curator of Collections. Britta maintains the organization's photographic files and memorabilia collection. Many of the photos contained in the book are from Britta's extensive archival files. Other staff members who shared their administrative and contact files were Judith Bellafaire, chief historian; and Lee Ann Ghajar, historian.

Additionally, we would like to thank Hanna Cunliffe, Glenn Helm, Jack Green, Diane Dellatorre Stevens, Roger Cirillo, and the editors and production staff of the Naval Institute Press.

Acronyms

I MEF—I Marine Expeditionary Force
AAA—Anti-Aircraft Artillery
ADA—Air Defense Artillery
AFB—Air Force Base
AFNC—Air Force Nurse Corps
AIT—Advanced Individual Training
AIT—Advanced Infantry Training
ANC—Army Nurse Corps
AO—Area of Operation
API—Aviation Preflight Indoctrination
ARVN—Army of the Republic of Vietnam
ATARS—Advanced Tactical Airborne Reconnaissance System
AWACS—Airborne Warning and Control Systems
BEQ—Bachelor Enlisted Quarters
BOQ—Bachelor Officers Quarters
BWI—Baltimore Washington International Airport
CAG—Civil Affairs Group
CAS—Close Air Support
CCC—Civilian Conservation Corps
CG—Commanding General
CJ SOTF—Combined Joint Special Operations Task Force
CONUS—Continental United States
CPA—Coalition Provisional Authority
CPV—Chinese People's Volunteers
CRC—Continental Replacement Center
CWO—Chief Warrant Officer
DCU—Desert Camouflage Uniform
DoD—Department of Defense
DSC—Distinguished Service Cross
DSM—Distinguished Service Medal
ECMO—Electronic Countermeasures Officer

ECP—Entry Control Point
EM—Enlisted Men
EPW—Enemy Prisoner of War
ETS—End of Time in Service
FAC(A)—Forward Air Controller Airborne
FANY—First Aid Nursing Yeomanry
FEC—Far East Command
FLIR—Forward Looking Infrared Radar
FRS—Fleet Replacement Squadron
HARM—High-Speed Anti-Radiation Missiles
HHC—Headquarters Company
IED—Improvised Explosive Device
ISF—Iraqi Security Forces
JCOC—Joint Civilian Orientation Committee
MAAG—Military Assistance Advisory Group
MAES—Medical Air Evacuation Squadron
MAGTF—Marine Air Ground Task Force
MARPAT—Marine Pattern
MEF—Marine Expeditionary Force
MEPS—Military Entrance Program Station
MO—Morale Operations
MOS—Military Occupation Specialty
MRE—Meal Ready to Eat
NATS—Naval Air Transport Service
NBC—Nuclear Biological Chemical
NFO—Naval Flight Officer
NLF—National Liberation Front
NNC—Navy Nurse Corps
NORAD—North American Air Defense Command
OCS—Officer Candidates School
OEF—Operation Enduring Freedom
OEF-A—Operation Enduring Freedom Afghanistan
OEF-HOA—Operation Enduring Freedom the Horn of Africa
OEF-P—Operation Enduring Freedom the Philippines
OJCS—Office of the Joint Chiefs of Staff
OPS—Operations Officer
OSO—Officer Selection Officer
OSS—Office of Strategic Services
OWI—Office of War Information
PATFOR SWA—Patrol Forces Southwest Asia

PDSS—Pre-Deployment Site Survey
PMO—Provost Marshal's Office
POM/POR—Processing for Overseas Movement/
            Processing for Overseas Replacement
POW—Prisoner of War
PROFIS—Professional Filler System
PSD—Personal Security Detachment
PTI—Physical Training Instructor
PX—Post Exchange
ROK—Republic of Korea
ROTC—Reserve Officers Training Corps
RPG—Rocket-Propelled Grenade
SERE—Survival, Evasion, Resistance, Escape
SOR—Statement of Request
SPARS—Semper Paratus—Always Ready
SPC—Staff Platoon Commanders
TAC(A)—Tactical Air Controller Airborne
TBS—The Basic School
TTP—Techniques, Tactics, and Procedures
USAHAC—United States Army Headquarters Area Command
VADs—Voluntary Aid Detachments
VC—Viet Cong
VJ—Victory in Japan
WAAC—Women's Army Auxiliary Corps
WAC—Women's Army Corps
WAF—Women in the Air Force
WASP—Women's Airforce Service Pilots
WAVES—Women Accepted for Voluntary Emergency Service
WRAF—Women's Royal Air Force
WSO—Weapons Systems Officer
XO—Executive Officer

Ranks and Ratings

1st Lt.—First lieutenant
1st Sgt.—First sergeant
2nd Lt.—Second lieutenant
Adm.—Admiral
Capt.—Captain
Cdr.—Commander
Col.—Colonel
Commo.—Commodore
Cpl.—Corporal
CWO—Chief warrant officer
Ens.—Ensign
Gen.—General
GySgt.—Gunnery sergeant
Hon.—Honorable
LCpl.—Lance corporal
Lt.—Lieutenant
Lt. Cdr.—Lieutenant Commander
Lt. Col.—Lieutenant colonel
Lt. (jg)—Lieutenant junior grade
Maj.—Major
Maj. Gen.—Major general
MGySgt.—Master gunnery sergeant
Pfc.—Private first class
Pvt.—Private
Rear Adm.—Rear admiral
Sgt.—Sergeant
Spc.—Specialist
Spc4—Specialist 4
Spc5—Specialist 5
SSgt.—Staff sergeant

PART I

* * *

Iraq, Afghanistan, and the Persian Gulf

As the twenty-first century approached, the role of women in combat was in transition. Prior to World War II, the only women allowed near a battlefield were nurses. During World War II, servicewomen, as well as nurses, served overseas with distinction; this continued during the Korean and Vietnam wars. Despite serving in combat zones, they were not given firearms training, and were dependent on males for protection.

After the Vietnam War and the end of the draft, the military began a more active recruitment of women to fill the ranks vacated by a decline in enlistments. Although service opportunities increased, women were still excluded from combat aircraft, ships of war, and ground combat units.

In the intervening years, bureaucrats at the Pentagon wrestled with such abstract concepts as what constituted "close combat" and how that differentiated from "direct combat." They developed complicated classification and rating systems, and "risk rules." The result was more women in units classified as "combat support."

During the American intervention in Panama in 1989, women flew Blackhawk helicopters under fire, and female MPs operated under combat conditions. During the Persian Gulf War (1990–91) the U.S. military deployed more than forty thousand women; fifteen were killed and the other women became POWs for the first time since World War II.

By 1993, women could serve in all branches of combat aviation and the Secretary of Defense repealed the ban on women aboard military ships (with the exception of submarines). When the risk rule was rescinded the following year, it opened the way for women to serve with peacekeeping missions in Haiti (1995) and Bosnia (1996–2001).

Women participated in combat air operations during Operation Desert Fox (1998), a three-day bombing operation to gain Iraq's compliance with United Nations inspections; Operation Allied Force (1999) against Yugoslavia; and Operation Enduring Freedom (OEF), a response to the terrorist attack on 11 September 2001, which was actually a three-prong operation against Afghanistan (OEF-A), the Philippines (OEF-P), and the Horn of Africa (OEF-HOA). "My fellow citizens, at this hour, American and coalition forces are in the early stages of military operations to disarm Iraq, to free its people, and to defend the world from grave danger." With those words, on 19 March 2003, President George W. Bush committed the American people to Operation Iraqi Freedom, the first major war of the twenty-first century.

As more than two hundred fifty thousand American troops from all services began operations against the regime of Saddam Hussein, historians estimate that about thirty-seven thousand of those troops, roughly 15 percent, were women. Following Operation Desert Storm (1991), the U.S. military had opened 90 percent of all military career fields to women, with those prohibited relating primarily to positions involved with ground combat. So it was that as American military forces invaded north into Iraq, women were positioned within all elements throughout the area of operations.

At this writing, three years since the start of Operation Iraqi Freedom, the character of the war has changed into an insurgency bordering on civil war as the Iraqi people struggle to establish democracy, and the United States struggles to find its role. As politicians and citizens debate, American servicemen and servicewomen continue to serve with distinction in harm's way, in a combat environment without front lines. Women are still, in theory, excluded from combat. The reality in Iraq is that women are in combat, and continue to prove that gender distinctions are irrelevant.

Pfc. Sam W. Huff, USA

A mother's letter to her daughter as she departed for army boot camp and war:

Dearest Sam,

As you leave our protection today I want you to know some things that may help you in your grown-up life. First of all you have chosen a great challenge. I salute you for that. The best way is generally not the easiest. Remember, particularly through boot camp, that the worst days are still only twenty-four hours long and the time you spend there will bring you great rewards. I want you to work hard, keep your goals in sight and NEVER give up. Everyone fails at something but real failures are people who simply quit trying. The next five years are an investment that will pay you for the rest of your life and you need to believe that. I know it is the truth. Don't look back, now that you have made this decision only you can make it the right decision. Give yourself to it wholly and realize that not just the ARMY but your whole life is only what you make it.

I have some advice for you, also. All the choices you make are yours alone now. Choose to live your life guilt free and with much joy. Find your passion and build on that. Start each day with a smile and a hopeful attitude and do your job with the very best you have to offer. I wish for you many moments of happiness that take your breath away. Make your life count in small ways and it will add up to a great life that you can relive in memories that make you smile. You will see wonderful things and unspeakable horrors . . . choose to forget the horrors. Don't let a bad act (yours or anyone else's) ruin even one day of your life. If you do something you are ashamed of, take responsibility for it, make amends as soon as possible and move on. Learn to forgive yourself. Give and accept apologies gracefully. SAY YOUR PRAYERS EVERY DAY AT LEAST ONCE.

And last, know that I am with you. My wishes for you include a relationship like the one Dad and I have and a child as wonderful as you. No matter what else happens in our lives, nothing will compare to the joy you have brought to us. The mists of age and illness will never dull the wonderful memories we have of you. REMEMBER no amount of space or time can separate our hearts. I have thought about you every day of your life and I will think about you every day for the rest of my life with a smile in my heart. You have made me very proud. My prayers are with you.

—Mommy

Eighteen-year-old Pfc. Sam W. Huff was assigned to the 170th Military Police Company, 504th Military Police Battalion, 42nd Military Police Brigade, Fort Lewis, Washington. She died on 18 April 2005, in Baghdad, Iraq, of injuries sustained when an IED detonated near her vehicle.

Private Huff's mother graciously gave oral historian Kate Scott of The Women's Memorial permission to reprint this letter and to reproduce the photo of her daughter.

Lt. Cdr. Holly R. Harrison, USCG

Lt. Cdr. Holly R. Harrison is the first woman in the history of the United States Coast Guard to be awarded the Bronze Star medal for her service in Operation Iraqi Freedom. She just completed her tour as executive officer of the Coast Guard's Maritime Law Enforcement Academy in Charleston, South Carolina, and will become the executive officer of USCGC Legare (WMEC-912), which is homeported in Portsmouth, Virginia.

* * *

I was born in 1972 in Tucson, Arizona. My dad was in the Marine Corps at the time, flying F-4 Phantoms over in Vietnam. My mom, who was in the U.S. Navy, had been stationed with him at Kaneohe Marine Corps Air Station, Hawaii, but when her unit deployed to Vietnam, she wasn't allowed to go with her unit due to the difficulty accommodating women overseas. Then, of course, she realized she was pregnant and in those days the Navy had no idea what to do with a pregnant officer. So, basically, that ended her military career; she occasionally likes to tease me that I'm the cause of that. With my dad deployed to Vietnam, she went back to Arizona, which is where my grandparents are from, and had me in Tucson while my dad was overseas.

Holly R. Harrison was interviewed by Kate Scott in Arlington, Virginia, on 11 November 2005. The tape and transcript are deposited at The Women's Memorial in Arlington. *Photo courtesy of USCG*

My mom's side of the family, particularly, is very heavy military. My grandfather was in the Navy, graduated from the Naval Academy, and became a fighter pilot. My great-grandfather, Rear Adm. Robert H. English, served in World War II and was Commander of Submarine Forces, Pacific Fleet, when he was killed in a plane crash. My family has an Air Force base named after great-great uncle Oscar Monthan (Davis-Monthan Air Force Base) in Tucson, Arizona. My great-aunt was a WAVE in World War II, two aunts served in the Navy, and I have a cousin at the Air Force Academy. On my dad's side, my grandfather served in the U.S. Army in World War II and a cousin served in the Marine Corps.

One fateful day when I was in high school, an announcement over the public address system mentioned that someone from the U.S. Naval Sea Cadet Corps was going to be visiting the career center that day. I had no clue what it was, had never heard about it, but thought I'd check it out. I spoke to the representative, signed up, and they threw a uniform on me. I was assigned to a unit that met one Saturday a month for drills and training. It's sponsored by the Navy League of the United States and cadets work through the enlisted Navy ranks. Part of the way you get advanced is to complete basic military requirements courses, pass advancement tests, and get hands-on experience with the military out in the field. I spent some time on several Navy ships, with Navy flight squadrons, and even went on an exchange with Canada's Sea Cadet Corps.

Planning to get further advanced, I began looking for training I could attend during two summer weeks I had free, but nothing was available. Because it was local and easy to arrange on my own, I ended up spending two weeks down at the Coast Guard recruiting office in Alexandria, Virginia. For two weeks, I was surrounded by Coast Guard recruiting paraphernalia, which made everything look cool and glamorous and pretty interesting. So the next time I needed some training, I specifically chose training with the Coast Guard and ended up at what was then Coast Guard Reserve Training Center, Yorktown, Virginia, and spent two weeks at the small-boat station there. Later I went to Coast Guard Station Miami in Florida for another two weeks.

I went down to Miami by myself for Coast Guard training even though I was still in high school and a teenager. My parents thought it was great; of course, any parents who have a high school kid actually interested in something think it's great. I had a wonderful time with it; they let me go out on patrols aboard the 41 footers. We conducted underway drills and training while patrolling around the Miami area. In just two weeks, I got to help rescue a couple adrift offshore after their boat's engine failed, observe a joint U.S. Coast Guard/U.S. Customs seizure of a suspected drug-smuggling vessel, and search for a missing scuba diver we then recovered three days later. Mom hid it well, but years later admitted she was a little worried with some of the stuff I came across, but she watched how

I reacted to the things I encountered and figured, "Okay, I guess this is what she wants to do."

Looking past high school, there was only one place I wanted to go: the Coast Guard Academy. I applied for the Academy but they turned me down because I was blind as a bat and didn't meet their eyesight requirements. At the time, enlisted personnel could have 20/500 vision, as long as you could correct it to 20/20, but for officers, the standard was no worse than 20/200. I had heard that they were going to adjust the standard for officers and increase it to match the 20/500 enlisted standard so I figured I'd go to college and apply the next year.

After graduating from Thomas Jefferson High School for Science and Technology in 1990, I went to a small college called Pfeiffer College, now Pfeiffer University, in Misenheimer, North Carolina. I picked a school with a good reputation where I could continue to get good grades while playing in sports and participating in other activities. While I was at Pfeiffer College, the Persian Gulf War erupted. My friends and I all sat around in our dorm rooms watching the war halfway around the world. I had no idea at the time I would be there years later for Operation Iraqi Freedom. Right after the Persian Gulf War ended, I learned I had been accepted to the Coast Guard Academy. In May 1995, after four years of military academy training, I graduated as a new ensign with a bachelor of science degree in government and orders to USCGC *Storis* (WMEC-38) in Kodiak, Alaska.

USCGC *Storis* was a 230-foot prototype, a World War II era, one-of-a-kind icebreaker designed to handle heavy weather. Every patrol was in the Bering Sea, and every patrol was spent boarding fishing vessels in cold weather and rough sea conditions. That was actually a great vessel on which to learn how to drive ships. She had one screw, one rudder, and you couldn't just power your way out of a mistake. You couldn't just use a bow thruster to kick the bow over, or to adjust at the last minute. I learned the fundamentals of ship driving on *Storis*, and got my feet wet as a law enforcement boarding officer doing tons of boardings, and as a junior officer in general.

The only way the Coast Guard can enforce laws and regulations at sea is to go to the other vessel and see what's going on. A small boat would be launched, we'd crawl in and cruise over to the other vessel; somehow we'd have to find a way to get on board, and then depending on the nature of what the vessel was doing, we'd have to inspect it, inspect their paperwork, and inspect their safety equipment. If it was fisheries, we had to see what they were catching, what nets they were using, where they were fishing, and determine if they were catching anything they weren't supposed to be catching to see if any laws or regulations had been violated.

For the most part, the crews on the fishing vessels were compliant and just wanted the boardings to go well so they could get back to fishing, so boardings typically went smoothly. However, every once in a while things would get tense.

The closest I ever came to someone not complying with my tasking, which would have escalated the level of force I needed to use to compel compliance, was on one of those fishing vessels in Alaska, and some fishermen weren't used to being boarded by female Coast Guard personnel. I hadn't given it much thought, until after one boarding in particular. I had completed all of my qualifications to become a law enforcement boarding officer, the leader of the boarding team, and the final step for me to earn full qualification was to lead a boarding under the supervision of my OPS. I was nervous from the get go, because it was my first time as boarding officer and OPS was there evaluating me.

I went up on the bridge to find the master of the vessel and discovered him to be a burly guy who just wanted us to get the boarding over with as quickly as possible. I introduced myself, explained why we were there, and my team and I began the boarding. As things progressed, I asked him for his halibut log, where he was required to log details about the halibut he was catching, but he wouldn't give it to me. I tried to reason with him, but still he would not give it to me. Knowing I had to inspect the log, and with OPS watching from the corner, things were growing more tense as the master refused to show me his log.

At the time, halibut regulations simply required fishermen to record specific information about their fishing activities, but did not require any specific form or format. Fishermen could write it on a roll of paper towels or toilet paper if they wanted to, as long as the correct information was there.

I finally convinced the master we were running out of options for a resolution without consequences, and he reluctantly handed me a simple plain-looking notebook. When I opened it I immediately noticed white pages with data logged on it, and then my eyes flashed to the inside front cover and only then did I fully understand the reason he didn't want to give it to me. Taped to the inside front cover was a graphic full-color picture from, shall we say, one of your finer men's magazines. At that point, the entire tone of the boarding changed, because instead of him being defiant and resistant, his demeanor changed to one of defeat. He knew I had seen the picture and was waiting for my reaction to it, obviously expecting a less-than-positive response from me. I ignored the picture and went to work inspecting his halibut log, which turned out to be in compliance.

Meanwhile, OPS was in the corner maintaining a professional demeanor and I'm sure doing everything he could not to laugh at the situation. That boarding was one of many that taught me how to interact with different people, who didn't necessarily have the same objectives I did.

So while *Storis* was all about fisheries boardings, my next ship, USCGC *Kiska* (WPB-1336) a 110-foot patrol board homeported out of Hilo, Hawaii, was a whole hodgepodge of miscellaneous things. We'd board some of the "six packs," the local charter fishing boats licensed to take out up to six tourists on fishing trips. A lot of the local Hawaiian fishermen worked on everything from tuna boats to big long-liners to tiny jig boats to unique native Hawaiian vessels. It was very interesting dealing with some of the native Hawaiians when we'd board them. Being of northern European descent, one look at me and you know I'm not a native Hawaiian, and at first, I had a hard time understanding some of the local slang and lingo they'd use. Those boardings were another good lesson in how to deal with different people and just get along with them, even when they weren't so happy you were there. After two great years patrolling the mid-Pacific from Midway Island down to the Republic of Kiribati, I left *Kiska* and was assigned as the protocol officer for the Commandant of the Coast Guard.

Protocol officer is a unique position in the Coast Guard; we have only one. It was my job to ensure the commandant, Adm. James Loy, was prepared for all of the ceremonial and social events he was to attend, and ensure they were conducted in an appropriate manner befitting the Commandant of the Coast Guard and in keeping with military and governmental traditions, customs, and courtesies. A major benefit of being on the commandant's personal staff was that it gave me an awesome vantage point from where I could learn from and interact with some of the top leaders in the Coast Guard, people I personally admire and respect and who taught me a lot about how to take on a challenging issue and achieve success.

After two years, my tour was up and I asked to screen for command afloat. Basically, you request to be selected for command and a screening panel meets to review the records of all those wanting command to select the best qualified. A list of people would be released in December and if you were on it, it meant that you had successfully screened and might get a ship. The panel always screened more than they needed, so there was no guarantee. I put in my list, with USCGC *Aquidneck* (WPB-1309) in Atlantic Beach, North Carolina, as my first choice.

As happens around assignment season, people began to hear rumors from the detailers, and everyone at headquarters was talking and speculating about who would get what assignment. Rumors were flying, and yet I hadn't heard anything from the detailer. I thought great, he's talking to the people he's giving ships to, and I'm down on the list. At best, he's going to offer me one or two of the ships that nobody wants, and I began to think of ways that I could sell him that he should still give me one of these ships.

He finally called me up one day and basically said, "You've got *Aquidneck.* Have a good one."

I was so surprised that I replied, "Say that again?"

To this day, I don't know how I got picked for *Aquidneck,* if the admiral made a special phone call on my behalf, or if the detailer just assigned me there based on my record. But it worked out and I'm grateful for it.

After taking command of *Aquidneck* on 1 June 2001, we spent the next few months on patrol and were down in the Caribbean for a counter-narcotics patrol when the 9/11 attacks occurred. For about a year after 9/11, we patrolled up and down the East Coast escorting any and everything in and out of port, and protecting facilities. In late October 2002, we had been told we were going to have to escort a cruise ship out of Philadelphia. Because cruise ships didn't normally leave from Philadelphia, many people, including the media, were pretty excited about this event because it could signal a new industry for Philadelphia. Knowing there was increased media coverage, we knew the threat of a terrorist attack on this particular vessel would be higher than normal.

As we were getting ready to begin our escort, I got a call telling us to cancel our escort and return to home port immediately. I asked which unit was taking the escort for us and was told none. At this point I was puzzled. I'd never been called off a mission to return to port so I knew something was up. I contacted my operational commander to figure out where this was coming from. Basically, he told me, "You need to get back to home port because we've got a new patrol for you that you need to prepare for." Curious about this new patrol, I asked if he had any details so we could start planning for the new patrol. He told me it would be a lengthy patrol and that we would not be sailing there.

I immediately knew. When I heard that we wouldn't be sailing [to Philadelphia], I knew where we were going. I had been watching the news and knew about the escalating tension with Iraq, that President Bush and Saddam Hussein were trading comments about each other and weapons of mass destruction. I knew military personnel from other services were already being sent to the Middle East. I knew the 110-foot patrol boats came with a custom-designed cradle to allow them to be lifted out of the water, placed on a bigger ship, and shipped anywhere around the world, and I knew the Coast Guard had intended to send 110-foot patrol boats overseas for the Persian Gulf War but it ended before the boats left the United States. In an instant, I knew.

When we got to home port, everyone on base had heard about our new assignment. Everyone pitched in and gave us whatever we needed. We spent the next few days crawling over every inch of the cutter, removing gear we wouldn't need, loading spare parts and supplies, and repairing any malfunctioning equipment. We threw all the cold weather stuff off the ship, because we knew we wouldn't need it in the Arabian Gulf. We brought lawyers in so the crew could do powers of attorney and take care of their families. I cancelled all my utilities, battened down the hatches of my house, and put my car in storage because I knew I wasn't coming back any time soon.

The seas around Cape Hatteras were nasty and the ship pounded into the seas for most of our transit North, but we finally made it up to Portsmouth, Virginia, and met up with three other patrol boats headed with us overseas: Coast Guard cutters *Adak, Wrangell,* and *Baranoff.* The next morning we had an initial meeting with all crews and personnel from *Lantarea.* The excitement in the room was palpable. They couldn't give us many details because they didn't know how soon we were going to be needed, if at all. Although no one told us where we were going, no one had to; we all knew where we were headed. I think everyone had their focus in place. No one in the crew tried to get out of it. Everyone knew we were going, they were worried about their families but they said, "Okay, let's do it."

After the meeting, one of the commanders from *Lantarea* approached me and said they had no problems with the fact that I was a female in command of a vessel headed to a combat zone. I was pleasantly pleased because I knew women in the naval services have been blocked from combat assignments. I would have fought like hell to stay in command of my ship with my crew, but thankfully the Coast Guard recognized that I was a commanding officer first and foremost, who as an afterthought just happened to be female.

It was a once-in-a-lifetime opportunity, and we knew it. Other cutter commanding officers and crews were begging to go too. We knew we were being handed a very special mission, and we took it very seriously. We trained hard for it. The initial plan called for the cutters to be loaded in about ten days and there was so much to do. We had maintenance teams crawl all over the ships and fix absolutely any and everything that was broken, because they wanted these ships in pristine condition when they went over. We had to order new classified material and codes so we could communicate in theater, order new charts, install new equipment, make room for four additional crew members, get physicals and shots, not to mention a ton of training.

After ten days our departure was delayed another week or so, and then delayed again and again. We ended up spending about four months in Portsmouth and kept using the additional time to work on the cutters, conduct more training, and prepare for what we were about to face.

I wasn't really nervous since I was going over with my crew that had been together for a year. We'd been training for this. We'd been going over scenarios, what-ifs, the big issues. The big uncertainty at the beginning of the war was chemical/biological weapons, because Saddam had used them on his own people, what if he used them on us? Unfortunately a 110 has no capabilities to defend against a chemical biological attack, so we were coming up with all kinds of ways we could do it. What if this happened? What's the best we can do? We'd run those drills in port with the entire crew, and before we even had the real gear, we simulated it. We used our rain suits and rubber gloves and must have looked like idiots running around on deck in yellow rain gear, with blue latex medical gloves and face masks, but it was as close as we could get to simulate the gear we would use in theater and that was the time to figure out what worked/didn't work, not later on in theater during an actual attack.

The first month of the war we received several alerts about possible inbound missiles with chemical or biological agents and had to put our practice to actual use. Thank goodness we practiced because everyone was prepared and knew what to do. Luckily the alerts turned out to be false alarms, but at the time there was no way to know that.

By January 2003 we knew we were deploying because the cutters were loaded aboard a large cargo vessel and shipped overseas. Because it took a while for the ships to actually sail overseas, we had some time from the time the ships left port to wrap up some loose ends on our end. They gave us a few days to go spend time with family, then we all met back in Portsmouth, and we flew over to Bahrain. It was a very interesting flight, a chartered US Airways flight. I don't think the US Airways flight crews were used to these types of charter flights, and they knew where we were going, so they played any movie we wanted and let the crews eat all the food off the snack cart. Everyone was excited and anxious at the same time.

We didn't know what the mission was for the longest time; we didn't know until we got in theater. We didn't really even know who to ask until we met our operational commander, and even then he couldn't tell us much because our potential future missions were highly classified, and plans were still being made. If we were going to invade, how were we going to do it?

When we got in Bahrain, we started to get our feet wet and figure out what's where. The four commanding officers of the cutters went to meet with our new operational commander, Commo. John Peterson, Commander of Destroyer Squadron 50 (DESRON 50). As it turned out, Commodore Peterson had been the one who initiated the request for Coast Guard 110s to support the Department of Defense. When tasked with putting together resources for a possible invasion of Iraq, he recognized a need for smaller ships that could get up the Iraqi rivers and patrol, because the bigger U.S. Navy ships couldn't operate in waters that shallow or confined, and yet he needed something big enough to be self-sustained, unlike smaller rigid-hull inflatable boats.

The Navy had some small ships capable of operating in a littoral environment; they are 179-foot patrol craft, nicknamed PC170s, that are similar to the Coast Guard's 110 patrol boats and typically used to deliver SEAL teams ashore. The Navy sent USS *Firebolt* and USS *Chinook* to join *DESRON 50*, but it needed additional vessels. When the commodore was a junior officer, he had done some joint operations with Coast Guard patrol boats in the Caribbean and knew their capabilities.

While the commodore had a very good understanding about our capabilities and limitations, his staff didn't have that same background. The four Coast Guard 110 commanding officers had to explain to the *DESRON 50* staff what our cutters could and could not do. If they wanted us to do a particular mission, we had to explain how long we could sustain it, when we'd need to refuel and resupply, when the crew would need to rest, and how quickly we could be back up to speed for the next mission. That was very interesting, because I don't think they knew quite how to handle us, particularly at first.

We, meaning the Coast Guard personnel, also had a somewhat different operational culture than the Navy personnel. For example, the Coast Guard gives cutters patrol orders and missions, and then gives the commanding officers of those cutters broad authority to make decisions and accomplish the missions. We are very good at operating independently, where there seems to be more command and control involved in the execution of U.S. Navy missions. There are pros and cons to both approaches, and while I think the commodore understood this difference between us very well, judging by some of the responses and tasking we received, I suspect his staff wasn't sure what to make of us at times. Overall, we just had to get on the same page, learn to speak the same language, and learn the operating rules.

As soon as we thought we had figured that out, and before we had any time to let everything we had learned sink in, the cutters arrived. *Aquidneck* was the first cutter offloaded. As soon as it was placed in the water and tugs pushed it against the pier, we jumped aboard, unsecured everything, inspected the ship, loaded fuel, water, food, and our personal effects, and headed out for sea trials to make sure everything was operational. The next day, *Adak* and *Aquidneck* set out for patrols of the Northern Arabian Gulf. Ten days later coalition forces invaded Iraq.

From the start, we never knew what new challenge would be thrown at us, many missions were things we had never trained for, and we had to improvise on the spot. We worked grueling hours 'round the clock, day after day. We had great highs and terrible lows. The first day of the war is a prime example. That evening the majority of the crew and I manned the rails topside as we watched USS *Higgins* two miles away launching Tomahawk missiles toward Iraq. The sea was as flat as glass, and we disengaged the engines to sit and watch the missiles. It was an incredibly patriotic moment because we were there. We were on the front line, watching, heck, making history. That was a great high and we all shared that moment together.

A few hours later brought the other extreme; I was asleep in my cabin when I got a call from my officer of the deck. To this day I have no clue exactly what he said to me, but I flew up to the bridge as fast as I could only to find the sea directly off the bow of the ship on fire. Two British helicopters from HMS *Arc Royal* had collided in midair and exploded. We were at the crash site in minutes and spent the next few hours looking for survivors, and combing through the wreckage. The winds kicked up, the seas turned choppy, and the search became difficult, but no one complained, no one wanted to quit looking. Despite our best efforts, there were no survivors; eleven British and American military personnel lost their lives in that crash. That was a terrible low. And that was just one day.

Over the next few months, we boarded any and everything moving in Iraqi waters, cleared Iraqi observation posts watching coalition operations in the rivers, sent personnel ashore to clear bunkers that were inaccessible from land due to mines, and guarded critical infrastructure and military assets. We guarded the British and American minesweepers as they entered the Khawr Abd Allah River to detect and clear mines, kept Iranian patrol boats out of Iraqi waters, and escorted ships carrying humanitarian supplies to the Iraqi port of Umm Qasr. There were several tense situations where we almost ended up in a firefight, but luckily found other ways to resolve them. Many operations similar to ones we conducted are still ongoing, and therefore the details about them need to remain untold to protect personnel over there performing those missions today. Whatever needed to get done, we would do it.

As far as I know, no coalition ship has been struck by mines during Operation Iraqi Freedom, primarily because coalition forces were able to capture vessels carrying mines before they could be deployed. At the beginning of the war, there had been a fleet of Iraqi ships, or dhows, trying to export oil in violation of the United Nations oil embargo loitering at the mouth of the Khawr Abd Allah River. Since the Persian Gulf War, U.S. naval forces had been keeping the dhows from leaving, although from time to time a group would try to escape.

At the beginning of the war, we were part of a large operation to screen and clear each of the dhows to ensure no Iraqi leadership was trying to sneak out and that the dhows weren't carrying explosives, then get them away from Iraqi waters so we could conduct operations. The down side was that with the dhows in there, it was difficult for anyone to lay mines because the dhows would hit them. With the dhows gone, there was concern the Iraqi military could set mines for the coalition ships. As soon as the dhows were cleared, coalition forces, including the Coast Guard 110s, patrolled the river. Coalition forces did capture several vessels carrying mines.

One of the neat things I heard later on was that after some of our forces captured a tug and barge carrying mines, the Iraqi crew was debriefed and asked why they hadn't deployed their mines when they were in the river for several days and had time to do it. The response from one of the Iraqis was that they didn't "because the white boats were there," meaning the Coast Guard 110s. Because we were actively patrolling the river, and keeping a close eye on everything that happened, we made them nervous enough that they didn't want to start laying mines because they were concerned we'd see them doing it. With us nearby, they didn't have an opportunity to deploy their mines, which would have threatened the lives of every person on any vessel operating in the Arabian Gulf for years to come. You know how when you're driving down the highway and you see a police car and take your foot off the gas? The police car's very presence is enough to make you behave; the presence of the Coast Guard 110s was enough to keep the Iraqis from laying mines.

Navigating in Iraqi waters was difficult at best. The charts we had were years out of date, charted depths did not match actual depths, most aids to navigation were not in the positions indicated on the chart or missing all together, there were wrecked vessels sitting in the middle of the navigable channel where they had been bombed and sunk during the Persian Gulf War years earlier, and the currents in the upper part of the river made navigating in tight areas tricky. Normally, Coast Guard cutters would navigate waters like these with fully manned navigation teams, but because we had to operate in the river for many days while conducting other operations, we had to do it with our normal watch section. We used every skill we had to keep the cutter in good water. We would go in and take a look at new areas, sending the small boat in ahead if possible, we'd pick off landmarks, and reference points, and update the charts with our information. We had to use a tremendous amount of "seaman's eye" to correlate everything and figure out what was accurate and what was not.

Most of our interaction with the Iraqis was with the crews on the dhows. There were generally two types: big steel dhows used to carry cargo or oil, and a smaller, wooden dhow used primarily for fishing. The wooden dhows are a very unique, traditional ship design and they are everywhere in that region. Part of our mission over there was to maintain control of the river and offshore Iraqi waters. We wanted to know who and what was moving on the river. We wanted to allow the Iraqi populace to fish and get food for their families, yet at the same time had to prevent any potential attacks. We also had humanitarian ships delivering supplies up to the port of Umm Qasr that we'd have to protect all the way up to the Iraqi port, where other security forces would take over. To maintain control over what was happening on the river, we were constantly boarding dhows and any other vessel coming in and out of port. We had to constantly change our operations, because you could see how even the fishing vessels would learn what to expect and adapt their fishing operations in response to ours over time.

In addition to the dhows, we also had to board the wrecks littering the river because they were great observation posts for anyone wanting to know what we were up to. The first one we discovered had a couple of prayer rugs, a couple of rifles, gas masks, and a little notebook with drawings of the profiles of the different military ships in the area; people had been sitting there watching what was going on, who was moving up and down the river, and taking notes. We had to constantly sweep these wrecks to make sure that people couldn't keep tabs on what we were doing.

We had no interaction with Iraqi women, because there were no women on the dhows. But there was an interesting reaction by the Iraqi crews about my being a woman on the cutter. When my boarding teams would board vessels, I'd often be the one on the bridge talking on the radio with my team, while my executive officer led the boarding team. He told me that when the Iraqi crews would hear a female voice over the radio, the Iraqis would all ask him why the cook was on the radio. He'd tell them that it wasn't the cook, it was the captain and they wouldn't believe him. They'd say, "No, no, the cook, why is the cook on the radio?" He tried to explain but I don't think some of the Iraqis ever believed him; they thought he was kidding.

When we had occasion to return to Bahrain, I had a chance to interact with the local people. We always went out in groups and did not wear any Islamic attire while ashore. We wore Western attire, but it needed to be conservative in nature, loose fitting, full-length slacks and full-length sleeves. Whenever I went out in public, I always tied my hair back in a knot to minimize the attention I brought. I'd be in the local souq, which is a market covering several city blocks where you can buy anything, and got stares. Obviously I stood out because I'm a Western woman, but I'm also taller than a lot of the local women over there, and they'd just kind of look at me. The little kids would be holding on to their moms, looking and staring. No one ever said anything odd or did anything disrespectful, but it was kind of like, who is this strange woman?

Our time in Bahrain was a much-needed break because conditions underway were cramped. Living arrangements on the ship were designed for sixteen. It could hold eighteen, but we packed twenty-two onto it so living arrangements were tight. The executive officer and I had our own separate staterooms, but for the crew it was tight. We had to put four tiny portable cots in our aft berthing area, no one wanted to share racks, and it was just packed. Tons of uniforms, protective chemical biological gear, flak jackets, battle helmets, and personal effects. We didn't have laundry machines on *Aquidneck* so we had to get creative to do laundry, otherwise things would get really nasty in those hot temperatures. There were times the crew would run out of clean clothes, and have to hand wash uniforms in tubs on the back of the cutter, and then we'd be sailing around with laundry drying off the back of the ship on lines. With our cramped living conditions and outdoor temperatures exceeding over 129 degrees Fahrenheit (the thermometer didn't go any higher), if we didn't do laundry, it was going to get really smelly and nasty for the crew.

They had us on a very aggressive operational schedule, so when we did finally make it back to Bahrain, we'd all pile off the ship, get our mail, get some sleep, and maybe wander out into the souq one or two nights just to see people other than the twenty-one faces we'd been staring at for weeks on end.

While we were catching our breaths and taking a much-needed break, personnel from the Coast Guard's PATFOR SWA would swarm on board the cutter and fix anything that was broken. We'd send them a list ahead of time as we were heading into port so they knew what to work on. It gave us a chance to relax while the ship was getting some much-needed maintenance. Because there were so many of us on the ship, we couldn't all stay on board while in port with repairs going on. While the ship was tied up, we stayed in a local hotel and took a few days to unwind and gear up for the next deployment, when everything would start all over again.

People ask me why I was awarded the Bronze Star. Simply put, it was because of what we did over there from start to finish, all the various operations and missions. The award citation details what the ship and its dedicated team did to accomplish our missions. Because I was the commanding officer, I represented the crew and the entire command, so that's why I got it. But really it was awarded for what we as a close-knit group of Coast Guard professionals accomplished over there. It was for what we did as a team, day after day from day one.

Lt. Cdr. Holly R. Harrison, USCG, receives applause and recognition at the 2005 Veterans Day Observance at The Women's Memorial, Arlington National Cemetery. Lieutenant Commander Harrison (third from left) is the first woman in Coast Guard history to earn the Bronze Star for her service as commander of the cutter USCGC *Aquidneck* in Operation Iraqi Freedom. *Courtesy of Donna H. Parry Collection*

There are three things that I learned from my Iraqi Freedom experience:

1. You can't do it by yourself; you have to rely on your team.
2. Anyone who thinks that they've got something mastered, that they're the expert, you know, "I'm the Captain. I know everything," is wrong. I relied heavily on my XO and my chief to sanity check me, because I'd never done some of those things before. I'd say, "XO, what do you think of this idea? Do you like it?" And sometimes he'd tell me, "No" and recommend an alternative idea. Being able to foster an environment where my crew could speak up and bring ideas forward was invaluable.
3. Regardless of the uniform or rank, you're all people. My most junior seaman was just as important, just as valuable and deserves just as much respect for what he did over there as I did as the captain. Yes, I got the Bronze Star, and if I could, I wish I could give it to every one of my guys. They contributed just as much, and they got the job done and worked just as hard, so regardless of rate or rank, everyone contributed to our success.

On a personal note, I'm proud of everything I've accomplished. I'm even proud of some of my not-so-sharp moments, because I learned a lot from them and that in turn has made me a better person and officer. And as far as the uniform goes, I love wearing this uniform. People always ask me, how long are you staying in the Coast Guard? Are you going to make it a career? I always tell them, "I'm going to stay in until they throw me out, or I stop having fun." And that's not the party line. I'm having fun. I enjoy my assignments doing different things and working with different people. Believe me, there are days that are not much fun, but overall, it's challenging, and I like the challenge. So I'm going to stick with it until the very end, and they're going to have to drag me away kicking and screaming.

Pfc. Teresa Broadwell Grace, USA

The military police mission in Iraq, previously considered "combat support," has broadened almost to the point of being a branch of the combat arms. Besides traditional roles, such as custody and care of enemy prisoners and basic law enforcement operation, military police units in Iraq and Afghanistan have engaged in reconnaissance and patrol missions, provided convoy and route security, set up roadblocks and manned checkpoints, and supported police intelligence operations. Additionally, they have assisted in the training of the new Iraqi police officers and manning Iraqi police stations. As a result of these new roles, military police training now includes a greater emphasis on combat survival skills.

Because Army women were not allowed to serve in combat arms (as of spring 2006), serving in the military police was the closest women could get to the infantry, and women have enlisted in large numbers. By spring 2006, five female MPs had given their life in Iraq; nine had been wounded.

The 194th Military Police Company, commanded by Capt. Terri Dorn, served in Karbala, south of Baghdad, providing force protection for the police station and patrolling the city. Of the 171 Soldiers in the 194th, 34 were female, including Pfc. Teresa Broadwell Grace.

Teresa Broadwell Grace was interviewed by Scott Baron in Arlington, Virginia, on 19 April 2006. The tape and transcript are deposited at The Women's Memorial in Arlington. *Photo courtesy of the Washington Post*

On 16 October 2003, Grace was in the middle of a fierce firefight in the streets of Karbala. Iraqis fired at her vehicle from rooftops and alleys along Highway 9 in the heart of the city. Before the day ended, three Americans were dead, and another seven wounded. Grace's actions, however, saved the lives of many of her comrades.

★ ★ ★

Teresa Lynn Broadwell was born in Lewisville, Texas, on 19 July 1983, the oldest of three. Her parents divorced when she was two, but she remained close to her father, an Air Force veteran, and even tried to enlist in the Air Force, but "they took too long." A friend enlisted, and her recruiter convinced Grace that the Army would allow her both to travel and serve her country, two of her ambitions. She chose the military police with the goal of later entering law enforcement.[1]

On 22 November 2002, Private Grace reported to Fort Leonard Wood, Missouri, for basic training and military police training, graduating on 11 April 2003, the same day as the 194th MP Company left for Iraq. She was assigned to the 194th, arriving at Fort Campbell, Kentucky, on 26 April and departing to join her unit in July. She flew to Kuwait, where she was met by a member of her unit and transported to Al Kut, about three hours southeast of Baghdad. In September, relieved by Ukrainian troops, the unit deployed to Karbala.

"When we first got there, we were the only U.S. troops there," Grace recalled. "It was mostly Polish troops, and we worked to learn the city, then patrolled and provided force protection." It was a dangerous job.

Sheik Mahmoud Hassani had recently moved his forces from Najaf and set up his headquarters in Karbala. The Shiite religious leader let it be known that he was against the U.S. presence in Iraq. Because of recent run-ins with Hassani's men, American commanders had banned Hassani's forces from carrying weapons in the street. MP vehicles patrolled the streets enforcing the ban.

On 16 October, Grace was working the swing shift (1400–2200 hours) with the 2nd squad/2nd platoon. Her patrol consisted of three trucks (Humvees), each with a team leader, gunner, and driver. She rode with Lt. Guerrero, the platoon leader, and Pfc. Rape, the driver. Grace manned the turret position in the Humvee. At five feet four inches, she had to stand on tiptoe to see through the sight of her M-249 machine gun.

"We got ready for patrol, maintained our weapons, got the trucks ready. The city was quiet. We observed some armed men on the street carrying weapons in the open. We told them to take it inside, and they complied, but soon were out on the street again." She remembered, "Our battalion commander was out with the first squad, and the call came in, 'Soldier down.' Our truck was the first to respond, and we were taking fire even before we arrived in the area."[2]

The commander of the 716th Military Police Battalion, Lt. Col. Kim S. Orlando, had traveled to Karbala that day to verify information that tensions in the city were about to ignite after a recent shootout between religious groups. Orlando's group had spotted some of Hassani's men openly defying the weapons ban, and stopped their vehicles. Orlando and several of his Soldiers had left their Humvees and walked toward a guard who motioned to the Americans to lay down their arms before coming any closer. As the guard motioned to the Americans, he'd lifted his AK-47 into a firing position and either he or another guard fired a shot. Orlando fell to the ground, critically wounded. Sgt. Troy Wallen, who was standing next to Orlando, stated that "all hell broke loose" after that first shot was fired. The Americans found themselves in an ambush; Iraqis started firing on them from the rooftops, store-fronts, and alleys. Wallen later reported that if Grace and her comrades "hadn't fired that night, none of us would have made it out."[3]

When the fighting started, Grace's three-truck patrol was a short distance away. Orlando's troops immediately transmitted a call for help and within three minutes Grace's patrol arrived on the scene, driving right into the killing zone. Lt. Guerrero, who led Grace's patrol, jumped from his Humvee and took cover. He heard short, controlled bursts from Grace's turret machine gun. This forced the Iraqis to run for cover.

Since Grace wasn't quite tall enough to see through her weapon's sight, she stood atop a TOW missile mount and gauged the accuracy of her fire with tracer rounds. Every fifth round in an M-249's ammunition belt ignites a phosphoric compound that leaves a luminescent trail to help gunners see where they are firing. She recalled being terrified through it all and "walking tracer rounds" into targets. Fortunately, Lt. Guerrero wasn't hit during the shooting; however, Grace suffered a severely bruised back when she was thrown back in the turret following explosions that hit the front of her truck. Guerrero credits Grace's action with saving his life. "She was up there doing what we trained her to do as a gunner. She kept their heads down."[4]

"The firefight lasted fifteen to twenty minutes, but it seemed like hours. I stayed on the gun as the driver and the lieutenant brought in the wounded. I helped drag him inside, then returned to my gun. We withdrew to the PMO and I pulled security while they checked his condition. Then we took him to the base hospital at Camp Lima, mostly Polish troops. He survived, but we lost three, including the battalion commander."[5]

Other women saw combat that day. Pvt. Tracie Sanchez, a mother of four, in the same group as Orlando, failed to get a shot off. As soon as the firing started, her Kevlar helmet was cracked by a round, then a grenade blew up a few feet from her truck and she was knocked from the turret down inside the vehicle. She credits her driver, Spc. Woodrow Lyell, with treating her wounds and keeping her calm. Meanwhile, a combat medic, Sgt. Misty Frazier of Hayden Lake, Idaho, was out on the street running from one fallen comrade to another, all the while dodging a hail of bullets. Thinking back on the action she could hardly believe what she had done. "That's the first time I had ever heard gunfire and rocket-propelled grenades go off that close, knowing they were shooting at us. I was very lucky."[6]

The last woman to see action that night was Spc. Corrie Jones, 27, of Shreveport, Louisiana. Her three-vehicle patrol moved in to back up Grace's patrol, which was in the middle of the firefight. Jones began firing at the Iraqis immediately and, outgunned, the enemy withdrew. In those moments of battle, Jones found the answer to the question in the minds of Soldiers who have yet to experience combat: How will I react under fire? "I don't think it's something anybody knows," Jones recalled. "Now, I know how strong I am."[7]

Her commanders estimate that Grace and her fellow MPs killed more than twenty Iraqis during the encounter. Grace says, "That was something I never thought I would have to do. I never thought I would have to take somebody's life, but I had to. It was kind of a shock; I wish there was something we could have done differently, but there was nothing we could have done."[8]

On 18 March 2004, the 194th moved to Kuwait for processing and customs, and returned to the United States on 2 April. That same day she met her future husband, Spc. Jake Grace, also a military policeman. She took two weeks leave, and the couple began dating on 8 May. They married the following 31 July, 2004 and Grace returned to regular patrol duties at Fort Campbell.

On 17 January 2005, she was redeployed to Iraq, this time to Mosul, the city where Saddam Hussein's sons, Uday and Qusay, had been killed by coalition forces on 22 July 2003. Three months into her second tour, in early April, while on a three-and-a-half-mile run, Grace felt dizzy. She rested and the symptoms passed, but she blacked out while guarding prisoners at the hospital the following day. She was flown by Blackhawk helicopter to Teqriq, where a cardiologist discovered a hole in her heart. She was flown to Balad, then to Germany, before arriving at Walter Reed Army Medical Center on 12 April, where she had open-heart surgery to correct the defect.

At present, she is at Fort Campbell, assigned to Echo Company, the rear detachment company, while she recovers. She delivered a son in early April 2006. She will remain in the Army if the medical board allows. "If not, I'll be a stay-at-home mom. Or I might go back to school, and teach elementary school."

For her part in the 16 October 2003 firefight, Grace was awarded the Bronze Star with V for Valor, and the Purple Heart. Maj. Gen. David Petraeus, commander of the 101st Airborne, presented the medals during a memorial ceremony honoring Colonel Orlando and the two other Soldiers killed during the firefight, Staff Sgt. Joseph P. Bellavia, 28, of Wakefield, Massachusetts, and

Cpl. Sean R. Grilley, 24, of San Bernardino, California. Grace was close friends with both men. One officer recalled how Grace stood in the front row and cried the whole time. The unit's first sergeant added, "The whole damn unit did!"[9]

ENDNOTES

1. Teresa Broadwell Grace, interview by Scott Baron, 19 April 2006, transcript, The Women's Memorial, Arlington, Va.
2. Ibid.
3. Loeb, Vernon, "Combat Heroine: Teresa Broadwell Found Herself in the Army—Under Fire in Iraq," *Washington Post*, 23 November 2003.
4. Ibid.
5. Teresa Broadwell Grace, interview by Scott Baron.
6. Loeb, Vernon, "Combat Heroine."
7. Ibid.
8. Ibid.
9. Ibid.

Pfc. Michelle Loftus Fisher, USA

Michelle Loftus Fisher recalls nothing extraordinary about the morning of 23 July 2003. It was a day much like every other since they'd crossed over into Iraq. She remembers her unit was excited at the prospect of moving to Kuwait in three days, and then returning to the United States.

Her unit, the 581st Area Medical Support Company, was preparing to depart Iraq, and Fisher had volunteered with six others for a two-vehicle convoy to provide route reconnaissance prior to the unit's departure. "We were checking out the road prior to a Baghdad-to-Kuwait convoy. I remember arguing with Danny Smith over the seat behind the driver in our Humvee. I won!"[1] It would be a fateful choice. The Humvees were unarmored and without doors.

"We were basically just checking how safe the road was. We went about twenty miles out from the base without incident. We were on our way back, about five minutes from the gate, when the explosion happened." The convoy had been ambushed by a roadside IED and small-arms fire, and Fisher returned fire, momentarily unaware that she'd been wounded, as the convoy rushed to exit the kill zone.

Fisher was not unaware of the risk when she enlisted. Both her parents are Navy veterans, and one older sister, Shannon, is an Air Force nurse with a husband

Michelle Loftus Fisher was interviewed by Scott Baron in Arlington, Virginia, on 15 February 2006. The tape and transcript are deposited at The Women's Memorial in Arlington. *Photo courtesy of Loftus Fisher* in the Navy. Another older sister, Chris, was a civil engineer in the Air Force, where she met her husband. A cousin is in the Marines. "I always knew I wanted to serve."

Born Michelle Lee Loftus in Rochester, Minnesota, on 23 March 1984, the fourth of seven children to Debra and Eugene Loftus, she grew up on the family farm with her five sisters and a brother. She was a good student and athlete, and was popular at Dover-Eyota High School from which she graduated in June 2002.

Fisher enlisted a month later, on 10 July 2002, with the multiple goals of getting an education, training in the medical field, and continuing the family tradition of serving her country. She planned to eventually become a large animal veterinarian.

After nine weeks of basic training at Fort Leonard Wood, Missouri, she was sent for AIT to Fort Sam Houston in Texas where she remained from September until January 2003, learning the skills of a combat medic. Her first assignment was to the 581st Area Medical Support Company, 61st Area Medical Support Battalion at Fort Hood, Texas.

The unit was already under orders for Kuwait on her arrival, and they departed on 17 March, arriving in Kuwait on the nineteenth, the day British and American warplanes attacked targets in Iraq, the beginning of Operation Iraqi Freedom.

Fisher has vivid memories of her entry into Iraq from Kuwait: "It was a reconnaissance all the way up to Baghdad. The morning we crossed [the border], the sun was coming up, and we could hear prayers echoing in the distance. It was eerie! I turned nineteen in Kuwait."[2]

She further recalled, "As soon as we crossed over [into Iraq], we were greeted by a bunch of smiling and waving children making peace signs. There were a few adults, but mostly children, and they all seemed so happy to see us."

Their ten-day journey north to Baghdad ended the day after the city was secured, and they were the first medical unit to enter Baghdad. They set up a clinic at Baghdad International Airport. "Everything was still smoking," Fisher remembered. She described a typical day:

"Our company set up in a number of areas, and I worked an aid station at the airport. We set up cots in the terminal. We would see patients; high-value Iraqis, EPWs, and contractors. We'd also deal with any trauma cases. We had MREs for lunch, and we would return to the main body for hot chow in the evening. If we didn't have duty, we'd read or play cards. We worked a minimum of twelve to fourteen hours a day."

She recalled the capriciousness of logistics: "We came in well supplied, but there were soon shortages as some supplies weren't replenished. We had a surplus of some items and a shortage of others." Working as best they could, they provided medical services as needed. And on that day in July, it was Fisher who needed them.

"It was surprising. . . . I mean we didn't see it coming at all because of where it [the IED] was positioned on the road. I kind of felt it and heard it at the same time . . . (my) reflexes just kicked in."[3] She was rushed back to the airport where doctors from her own unit treated her. After she was stabilized, she was flown to Dogwood, a hospital sixty miles south of Baghdad, where she spent the night. Then she was flown to Baghdad, then to Landstuhl, Germany, and finally on to Fort Hood.

Fisher's injuries were severe: "The top part of my lip and between my nose and top lip, that area was peeled open. There was a gaping wound between the top of my lip and the bottom of my nose. I had shrapnel cuts across my face. I lost three teeth, and there was bone and gum damage. And there was a gash across my left cheek."[4]

Despite her injuries, Fisher has good memories of Iraq. "I loved my job, and we helped a lot of people. Once, an old woman came up and kissed my hand. There was no fear, only appreciation. That was my greatest reward."

Private Loftus met and married Sgt. Anthony Fisher, U.S. Army, in 2004. The couple and their daughter Sydney are pictured here in November 2005 before Sergeant Fisher deployed to Iraq. *Courtesy of Loftus Fisher*

She remains in the Army at Fort Hood and is "pretty much healed." Her teeth have been replaced and she is awaiting one more surgery. Her ETS is 31 January 2007. There have been other changes in her life since her return. She met Sgt. Anthony Fisher in April of 2004 and the two were married a year later, on 23 April 2005. They have a four-month-old daughter, Sydney, and hope to move to Wyoming after her husband ends his military service in 2008. He hopes to work as a firefighter, and she plans a career in nursing.

As for her choice of seats that July morning, Fisher says, "I'm pretty religious! I think I was put in that seat because God knew I could handle it. Any other road, and I wouldn't be where I am."[5]

ENDNOTES

1. Michelle Loftus Fisher, interview by Scott Baron, 15 February 2006, transcript, The Women's Memorial, Arlington, Va.
2. Ibid.
3. Zdechlik, Mark. "Soldier Wounded in Iraq on the Mend Back Home in Minnesota." Minnesota Public Radio, 6 August 2003.
4. Michelle Loftus Fisher, interview by Scott Baron.
5. Ibid.

SSgt. Jessica Lee Clements, USAR

There was nothing unusual about the morning of 5 May 2004 as members of the 706th Transportation Company rose in the early morning to prepare for their departure from Taji, about fifteen miles north of Baghdad. SSgt. Jessica Clements moved among her Soldiers, supervising the loading of eight members of the 706th and their gear onto the rear bed of an unarmored five-ton truck for the trip to Baghdad International Airport. From there, they would fly to Kuwait to pick up new fuel tankers and drive them back to Baghdad. Also along, hitching a ride to the airport, was Russ Contractor, a DoD civilian employee.

There was nothing especially hazardous about the mission, but roadside bombs were becoming more common as the weapon of choice of the insurgents, and Clements understood the importance of staying on guard. "It was scary. Other convoys had been hit, so it was important not to become complacent, and stay alert."[1]

Clements has no memory of the convoy, or the blast of the IED hidden in a guardrail that almost took her life, or of the extraordinary measures taken to save her life. Her first memories are of slowly coming out of a coma almost three

Jessica Lee Clements was interviewed by Scott Baron in Arlington, Virginia, on 27 February 2006. The tape and transcript are deposited at The Women's Memorial in Arlington. *Photo courtesy of Clements Collection* weeks later at Walter Reed Medical Center in D.C. It is a story of a Soldier's fight to survive and return to duty.

Jessica Lee Clements was born in Barberton, Ohio, on 27 November 1976, the middle of three girls raised by her mother. She enlisted in the Army Reserve on 2 May 1995, a month before graduating from Green High School in Akron, Ohio. She was hoping to find some direction for her life and also had a strong desire to serve her country, so she met with her recruiter and signed up.

After taking gender-integrated basic training at Fort Jackson, South Carolina, Clements was assigned to the Transportation Corps and sent to Fort Eustis, Virginia, for three months of training as a cargo specialist, where she learned how to load planes and trains. Released from active duty, she was assigned to the 706th, a reserve unit from Mansfield, Ohio. In her civilian life, she worked as a bartender and sometimes as a model while she attended college to earn a degree in massage therapy. In 1997, her MOS was reclassified as truck driver.

In April 2003, when her enlistment was up, Clements reenlisted. With the war in Iraq, no one was getting out, anyway, she told her mother. "If I go, I go," she recalled telling her mother. Clements's unit was called to active duty on 7 December 2003 and sent to Fort Campbell, Kentucky, prior to deployment overseas. She recalled that her family was apprehensive about her activation. "They were nervous wrecks, but I had a job to do."

The 706th arrived in Kuwait on 18 January 2004, and spent a month in preparation and training before deploying to Iraq on 7 February. Clements, now a staff sergeant, was a squad leader in command of seven Soldiers responsible for supervision, assignment of details, and preparing convoys that transported fuel to different units across Iraq. "We'd prepare the night before, then we'd depart early, around 0600 hours, and we'd try to be back before dark . . . we usually didn't travel after dark."[2]

The 706th relieved a unit in place, and took over their equipment, which was in "bad shape" and required "lots of maintenance." As a result, Clements was tasked with picking up and transporting new fuel tankers from Kuwait in early May.

The only thing she knows about the convoy, explosion, and aftermath is what she has been told by others. Russ Contractor, the DoD employee along on the convoy, visited her in the hospital, and believes she saved his life. They'd been sitting together on the floorboard chatting and joking when the bomb went off when the convoy was about three miles from the airport. At first it was thought that there were no injuries, until Clements fell over in Contractor's lap. "At first, she didn't have a pulse," reports Contractor. "Then she opened her eyes and asked 'Are you OK?'" She has no memory of talking to Contractor.[3] Contractor held her in his lap until medics arrived.

Clements was severely wounded along her left side, with injuries to her hip, lower back, and damage to both sides of her head and brain, caused by shrapnel and "blast overpressure," waves produced when explosives are detonated. No one else was injured. She was rushed to the 31st Combat Support Hospital in the fortified Baghdad compound known as the Green Zone. Within an hour, she was on life-support, comatose and under the care of Lt. Col. Jeff Poffenbarger.[4]

Poffenbarger, a neurosurgeon, performed a craniotomy, removing a sizable piece of bone from the right side of the skull, exposing the traumatized part of her brain. This allowed him to control the bleeding and clean the wounds. Additionally, if any blood vessels weakened by the trauma-induced injury burst, they would have ready access to the brain to control the bleeding. The extra room and soft closure of skin covering the area of removed portion of bone also allowed the brain to relax after the swelling subsided and quicken the healing process.[5]

Poffenbarger removed only the largest piece of shrapnel, leaving the smaller pieces, which were numerous and deeply embedded in her brain. Any attempt to remove them at that point would have been too risky. Rather than replacing the bone removed from her skull, since her swelling brain would need the space, Poffenbarger opened a space in her lower right abdomen to store and preserve the fragment until it could be reattached later, after she had sufficiently recovered. That she *would* recover was optimistic at best. As Poffenbarger stated, "The bleeding was ongoing, the brain was swelling and I really had a lot of concern that potentially she might die on the operating table."[6] It was as tough a fight as any Soldier faced in Iraq.

On 13 May, still in a coma, Clements was flown to the Regional Military Hospital at Landstuhl, Germany, where she remained for seventeen hours until she was sufficiently stabilized for the flight to Walter Reed Army Medical Center in D.C., where she arrived on 15 May. On her arrival, her mother was told that Clements had only a 2 percent chance of surviving, but Clements was a Soldier who refused to surrender.

On 3 June, Clements awoke to find her mother at her side. She had no recollection of the events that had brought her there, and was shocked when she saw her image in the mirror. The flesh on the right side of her head was flat, and there was a bulge on the right side of her abdomen. Her doctors explained that the bulge was a fragment of her skull, awaiting replacement when her strength returned.

What followed was a recovery that can only be called miraculous. A strict regime of physical therapy followed, causing exhaustion, dizziness, and severe headaches. Because of the injury to her brain, there were times when she became agitated, but eventually these episodes subsided, and her strength returned, surprising her doctors. By late June, she was able to stand and walk a few steps with

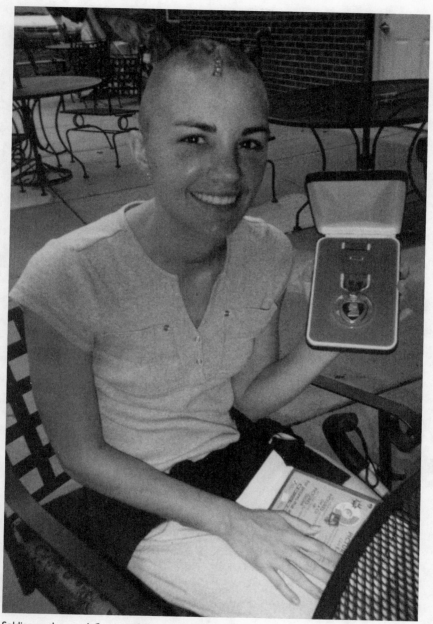

Soldier on the mend. *Courtesy of Clements Collection*

assistance, and was flown to the Minneapolis VA Medical Center to begin a program of rehabilitation for survivors of severe brain injuries.

In mid-August, Lt.Col. Armonda, Clements's physician at Walter Reed, reattached the skull fragment. After six months, she left Walter Reed for good, and returned to the Louis Stokes VA Medical Center in Cleveland, Ohio, where she continues to work toward 100 percent recovery. Clements currently experiences dizzy spells. A CT scan revealed that fluid has collected under her skull and her neurologist has ordered monthly scans.

On 12 February 2005, she was medically discharged from the Army with the caveat "temporarily retired," which requires an annual reevaluation. "I was discharged for my injuries, it wasn't by choice."[7] Presently the army rates her 80 percent disabled, and the VA rates her at 100 percent. If in subsequent physicals she shows improvement, her disability rate could drop, resulting in less pay.

Clements has nothing but praise for the medics who saved her life and will be forever grateful for their care and professional skills, but remains angry at the Army for their treatment of her after she emerged from the coma. Their constant demands that she sign discharge papers, despite the fact that she was facing several surgeries and extensive rehabilitation, made her feel as if they wanted her out of the Army and did not wish to provide further care. "I felt like the Army was trying to get rid of me, pass me on," she said.[8]

In the meantime, Clements, still the Soldier, has her eyes focused on her next objective. She values her Bronze Star, Purple Heart, and Army Achievement Medal, but looks forward to earning a degree and getting into social work, perhaps as a counselor to wounded and injured veterans.

The doctors who treated—and continue to treat—her call her, "Miracle Girl," but Clements prefers a more modest honorific: "Soldier."[9]

ENDNOTES

1. Jessica Lee Clements, interview by Scott Baron, 27 February 2006, transcript, The Women's Memorial, Arlington, Va.
2. Ibid.
3. Lerner, Maura, "Back from Iraq One Step at a Time," *Minneapolis Star Tribune,* 8 August 2004.
4. Claus, C. Todd, "Injury Fails to Impede Clements' Zeal for Life," *The Journal,* 26 August 2004.
5. Ibid.
6. Potter, Ned. "Female Soldier's Recovery Called a 'Miracle.'" ABC News, 28 November 2004.
7. Jessica Lee Clements, interview by Scott Baron.
8. Ibid.
9. Ibid.

Capt. Kellie McCoy, USA

Capt. Kellie Mccoy, USA, an engineer officer in the Corps of Engineers, is currently assigned to the United States Army Special Operations Command 8th Corps located at Fort Bragg, Fayetteville, North Carolina. Among the various ribbons she wears is the Bronze Star with "V" device, denoting a medal she earned for valor while serving in Iraq. In fact, she is the first female Soldier in the 82nd Airborne to be awarded the coveted medal. During her interview for The Women's Memorial Oral History Program on 21 January 2005, she talked about the episode that led to her being awarded the Bronze Star.

"As the Headquarters Company (NOTE: I was assigned to HHC, 307th Engineer Battalion [Airborne] in the 82nd Airborne Division) our mission in general is to provide logistical support to . . . other engineer companies. To do that in Iraq is very difficult because companies are split up, and so my company ended up being sent to several different locations. I had Soldiers in ten camps all over Iraq. To me that meant that I had to travel a lot. My driver and I drove almost twenty thousand miles in six months.

"The majority of the camps we went to were in and around Fallujah. That was at a time when Fallujah was growing as a stronghold for insurgents, and so it

Kellie McCoy was interviewed by Kate Scott in Arlington, Virginia, on 21 January 2005. The tape and transcript are deposited at The Women's Memorial in Arlington. *Photo courtesy of Donna H. Parry Collection* was becoming very dangerous to drive around there. On my third day in country (I arrived in Iraq on 15 September 2003) . . . I was driving toward Fallujah from the town of Ramadi to see my first sergeant and some of my other Soldiers. And on my way back we were ambushed on a highway that connects Fallujah and Ramadi. We traveled in a four-vehicle convoy and I was in the second vehicle because the urban legend was that that was the vehicle that was the most susceptible of being hit by an IED, so I always rode second. We encountered two what they call daisy-chained IEDs, which are two roadside bombs that are linked together to go off one right after another, to increase the odds of hitting vehicles. So the first one went off about fifteen feet in front of my vehicle and then the second one went off and disabled my first vehicle.

"At the same time, however, we were attacked by insurgents with small-arms fire and RPGs at very close range. They were within twenty-five feet of us at some points. Because of the small arms fire and the RPGs, my third and fourth vehicles were rapidly disabled in succession and couldn't move. So that meant that I had three vehicles strung out along the road that couldn't move, and I had ten Soldiers that I was trying to find in all of the smoke and commotion. So I drove up and down the road . . . to get my Soldiers. I had three Soldiers wounded that we had to get and treat. Eventually I loaded eleven people (including myself) into my command Humvee, which looks much like a commercial Hummer. . . . I'm sure it was a pretty interesting sight when we drove back through . . . Ramadi with eleven people hanging out of the Humvee.

"All of the wounded recovered. They had shrapnel injuries from the roadside bombs, and two of them had some pretty serious concussion injuries, both had their eardrums completely blown out.

"With regard to how quickly I was able to recover and react, I think it was a combination of our training and my own self-confidence. I would always tell my Soldiers that they needed to pay attention at training events because you can't wait until something like that happens. Our reaction needs to be automatic. My mother used to ask me if I was afraid. And I really wasn't afraid. I think I just had some internal confidence that if something happened I would be able to handle it. And they say that, you know, luck is where opportunity meets preparation, and in our case that was definitely true. We had the preparation, but there's always a little luck involved, too, in situations like that; I was just glad all my Soldiers came back."

When asked about perhaps being overwhelmed by being responsible for her Soldiers in a dangerous wartime environment, McCoy answered:

"Yes the burden of command can be heavy in general, and especially when I had Soldiers traveling those roads daily, I was always worried for their well being and what was going on. And even though we worked really long days I would try and make a little time out to go run or do something by myself. That's normally my main outlet for stress in general, and I try and keep that up on deployments, I think it helps.

"The Army has two different standards for the physical fitness test for men and women, and that's the same for all units, including the 82nd Airborne. But in the 82nd we do a lot of things that are individual skills and tasks. No one else can carry a parachute for you, or everything else you might carry when you jump out of an airplane. You don't have any assistance when you're doing a road march and carrying your rucksack with your radio in it. So in that regard I had to stay in probably what was relatively much better shape so I could keep up.

"On the subject of women in combat, I think we are using that phrase incorrectly now. When we say women in combat, I think what is really meant, and this is how the legislation is written, is that women don't serve in what we used to call front-line units in the Army, that's what we call the combat arms, the infantry armor branch and field artillery. There are very few women in the field artillery. And so in that regard I think that's the intention of the policy, in that we're not going to integrate women into all-male infantry units. The military police is a different story: women are included in MP units. Are women in combat? They most definitely are. There are women who drive the same roads men do. Roadside

"AIRBORNE!" *Courtesy of McCoy Collection*

bombs aren't discriminatory. There are no safe areas in Iraq to drive. There [are] really no front lines in Iraq."

During the interview Captain McCoy labeled paratroopers as a unique breed.

"Anyone who has served in the 82nd Airborne Division would understand that it's a special place, and it's because of the mentality of the paratrooper that no matter what the mission is, no matter how difficult it is, regardless of rank, that you will do your best to make it happen. There's a story from World War II about a paratrooper, a young Soldier who found himself alone during the Battle of the Bulge with a group of Germans approaching him . . . and they've put this on posters all over the division over the years . . . and he said, 'I am the 82nd Airborne Division, and this is as far as the bastards are going.' You also have just the mentality of just being airborne. And like I said it's an individual task, whether you're a private or a general you have to carry your own parachute. That's what makes paratroopers special.

"Regarding the Army in general, it is very people-based. Some other branches of service may be more technically orsiented but the Army's greatest asset is that you develop people skills. You learn a lot about your own strengths and weaknesses when it comes to interacting with people, as a leader, a subordinate and a peer. I've met a lot of great people in the Army."

Captain McCoy was born in Akron, Ohio, and grew up in and around St. Louis, Missouri. After graduating from high school, she was accepted into the U.S. Military Academy at West Point and was commissioned a second lieutenant upon graduation in 1996. That summer she went through airborne training and then completed the Basic Engineer Course at Fort Leonard Wood, Missouri. McCoy next went overseas to Germany for three-and-a-half years, assigned to a combat-heavy battalion in Bavaria. She later deployed as a platoon leader to Bosnia, as an executive officer to Albania, and then as a member of a battalion staff in Kosovo. In July 2000 she returned to the United States and attended the Army's Officer Advanced course. She then earned a master's degree in environmental engineering at the University of Missouri and was ordered to Fort Bragg. She intends to make the Army a career.

Capt. Jaden J. Kim, USMC

Capt. Jaden J. Kim, USMC, a NFO and an F/A-18D WSO, was the first Asian-American female Marine to fly in combat when she deployed with Marine Fighter Attack Squadron 121. She flew missions over Afghanistan and Iraq during Operations Enduring Freedom and Iraqi Freedom. She also served a ground combat tour as the protocol officer for I Marine Expeditionary Force in Fallujah, Iraq.

In her interview with Eleanor Wilson, Kim spoke about women in the military, Marine Corps training, her love of flight, and her admiration and respect for Marines, especially the ground crews who work tirelessly to maintain squadron aircraft ready for combat missions and put themselves in harm's way in places like Fallujah. She cited these Marines as "unsung heroes." Kim was awarded seven Air Medals and a Navy Commendation Medal during her various combat tours.

★   ★   ★

I was born in Seoul, Republic of Korea, on 13 May 1974 to Won and Susie Kim. We immigrated to the United States in 1977 and set up residence in Chicago, Illinois. My younger sister was born in 1978. She graduated from University of San Diego

Jaden J. Kim was interviewed by Eleanor Wilson in Camp Pendleton, California, on 14 October 2003 and January 2006. The tapes and transcripts are deposited at The Women's Memorial in Arlington. *Photo courtesy of USMC* law school in 2005 and remains in southern California. Both of my parents continue to reside in Chicago, where my father is a pediatrician. My mother devoted herself to parenting when my sister and I were young, herding us from lesson to lesson, practice to practice, and supervising our high-maintenance personalities! I don't know how she ever did it.

I attended grade school and high school in Chicago. In 1992 I matriculated at Princeton University and graduated in 1996 with a bachelor's degree in politics. At the time I was in the Army ROTC program, because I had planned to serve in the military and there was no Naval ROTC program at Princeton. I also didn't have a very clear concept of what the differences were between services; my priority was to serve on active duty in any service branch. However, the Army downsized during my latter college years and by the time I was a senior, there was no room for me on active duty as an Army officer. When I asked for a conditional release so that I could try for active duty in the Marine Corps via OCS, the Army refused to let me go. I chose to disenroll completely from the program and turned down my commission, for the opportunity to apply for Marine OCS.

There were no guarantees when I disenrolled from the Army, only the chance to go prove myself at Marine OCS. If I was washed out of OCS I would end up with nothing—no commission, no turning back, only a very large tuition debt to the Department of the Army. It took about a year to get officially discharged from the Army. In the meanwhile I moved from New Jersey to D.C. and worked part-time jobs from temp agencies and tended bar in Georgetown.

When my Army discharge papers finally came through in early 1997, I submitted my Marine OCS application package and was accepted into the Women's Officer Candidate Class for June 1997. My Marine OSO told me that I had better be in top physical condition, but I had no idea what I was in for! I did my best to work out regularly before I reported to Marine Corps Base Quantico that summer, but I was admittedly in average shape and would pay for it the entire summer. If someone were to ask me now how to best prepare for OCS, I would tell him/her to start working out like it was the end of the world. Run, run, run . . . and work up to a couple of sessions per day. And if you can't climb a rope, learn. At the end of my first week I tripped and twisted my ankle very badly during a trail run. That put me on crutches for a week with one ankle three times the size of the other, bruises halfway up my thigh, and bloody bandages to change out every night. It never really healed properly, because I wasn't willing to quit and get recycled for the next class. I refused to go home. I had given up too much to get this far.

We had five platoons in Charlie Company that summer. Four of the platoons were male with approximately fifty candidates per platoon. Fifth platoon was a female-only platoon. At the time there were only two OCS classes per year that had a female platoon, the June and October classes.

In Fifth Platoon we started with sixty-five female candidates and were left with about twenty on graduation day, three months later. In the beginning, it wasn't too bad. We woke up at 0500 (5:00 AM) and went lights out at 2200 (10:00 PM) every day. At dawn we'd stand in line at the foot of our bunks, dressed in the uniform of the day, each girl hoping that her area was organized and squared away. The drill instructors would arrive in a storm, tearing up and down the line, highlighting every hair and piece of lint out of place. It might be good to note here that some girls didn't even sleep in their beds, rather, on top of them, in order to keep their racks perfectly tucked for inspection.

In the classroom, we covered Marine Corps basics, from organizational structure to fire-team tactics. In the field we got practical training and experience. We'd sit through lectures in bleachers, followed by a demonstration, and then have our own hands-on time. We assembled and disassembled M16s and M9s, which we'd fire later during TBS. We also received classes on NBC warfare issues. Again, we sat through lectures, demonstrations, and then our own practical exercise. The practical exercise for this particular phase of instruction, however, meant a little trip to the gas chamber. You'd wear your mask and walk into a concrete room pumped full of CS (tear) gas.

When I first joined the Marine Corps we actually ran around the room and did exercises, pulled off our masks, and had to wait until we were cleared to leave the room (which wasn't until everyone was maskless and had taken at least one good whiff of the gas). I remember finally escaping the room and everyone coughing, tearing, sneezing, sniffling, throwing up snot everywhere trying to breathe, and pouring canteens of water into their eyes. It's meant to be an unforgettable experience, so that you (a) learn to trust your gear, and (b) realize the importance of maintaining a serviceable gas mask. Unfortunately, it isn't like that anymore. Now you just file into the room, break the seal on your mask, reseal it right away, and then walk back out of the room.

Our platoon sergeant at the time was SSgt. Mannis. Last time I heard, she'd been promoted to gunnery sergeant. At any rate, she was the first female PTI in the Marine Corps. She was the stuff of Amazonian legends that both men and women worshiped. She was a hard, hard woman! And I say this with the utmost respect. She loomed over us at close to six feet tall, with a slender waist and broad shoulders. She could haul herself up the obstacle course rope hand over hand, and most of us were having difficulty using all of our limbs! The male and female candidates alike thought the world of her.

I think that being in an all-female platoon was really important for our initial Marine Corps training. Male drill instructors were quite frankly a little dodgy and standoffish when dealing with female candidates, which was entirely understandable given the climate and some negative Army publicity in the past. The female drill instructors, on the other hand, were able to address any issue openly without worrying about scandal looming over their shoulder at every potentially misspoken or misunderstood statement. If they thought you were screwed up, they didn't have a problem telling you that. I think the value of this kind of honesty is overlooked and unappreciated. I don't deny that there have been incidents in the past where hazing went too far, but I think that to swing the pendulum to the other extreme where we're too afraid to even correct a wayward person is the worse of two evils.

I'm therefore a big fan of separating genders for boot camp and initial military training. Though we had our own platoon at OCS, we did everything side by side with the male platoons. They could see us, we could see them, and we knew that we were all receiving the same training. They also observed every time female candidates were processed out for not meeting the standards, which was very important, since in the end we were all joining the same Corps.

Upon completion of OCS I received my commission as a second lieutenant and reported to TBS, also at Quantico. TBS is like an extended and more in-depth version of OCS, where the premise is to train every new Marine lieutenant in the fundamentals of an infantry platoon leader (actual officers assigned to the infantry attend a separate Infantry Officers Course following TBS). There is less outright physical training, but you spend a lot more time in the field, up to seven or eight days at a time. I remember Virginia weather being miserable that time of year and my impression of TBS is a lot of time spent digging holes in the freezing rain.

We were divided in my company by six platoons, with approximately forty Marines in each platoon. Each platoon had two SPCs, captains who ran the training programs and were in charge of the lieutenants under them. TBS was six months long, from August 1997 to March 1998. I think I slept through every lecture in the classroom. We were all tired, all the time, but I had a particular knack for not being able to stay awake and passing out even while standing!

We didn't live in the barracks because they were undergoing renovations. I lived out in town with two roommates, Rachel Barney and Naomi Boyum, also from my TBS company. I believe Naomi eventually became an ECMO for the EA-6B Prowler. As for Rachel, she became the second female AH-1W Cobra helicopter pilot in the Marine Corps, and has made several combat deployments. I was the only one in the house who didn't have an aviation contract prior to joining the Marine Corps; I got my flying slot out of TBS.

When you're at TBS, MOS billets vary depending on the needs of the Marine Corps. For my company, we had two NFO billets available (we had about two hundred fifty lieutenants). Prior to MOS assignment, the staff announced that if anyone was interested in competing for one of the aviation slots, there were four pilot and two NFO slots available. To compete, you have to pass an aviation exam and a full flight physical. The exam is interesting. The basic English and Math sections are straightforward and unchallenging, but there are a couple of sections that are aviation/ maritime specific. For example, what color is the buoy on the inward side of the channel? There's no way to figure out the answers to this portion of the exam if you don't already know them. Since I didn't really grow up with a passion for aviation as a child, this was my weakest section.

Another section on the exam dealt purely with spatial perception. There are 150–200 multiple-choice questions in this section. It gives you pictures of aircraft at different attitudes and your task is to pair them with the proper depiction from inside the aircraft cockpit. This was a speed exam and highly entertaining, in my opinion.

At any rate, I didn't know aviation was open to women until I arrived at TBS. As a kid I'd always read that only men flew combat aircraft, and since all Marine Corps aircraft are considered combat platforms, there were no female Marine aviators until the ban on women flying in combat was lifted.

MOS assignment is mostly by order of merit in the company, but when there are only two NFO billets, you should probably make it clear if you want one of them. Luckily, I had a fantastic SPC who had the foresight to know I was never going to be great at digging foxholes and decided to go to bat for me. Capt. Peterson (he's either a major or out of the Marine Corps by now) was responsible for shaping a lot of my early philosophy as a Marine officer. I'll never forget his opening words to us. "Do what's right, don't do what's wrong." I've borrowed them often in my career! So simple and yet so perfect.

By March 1998 I was headed down to Pensacola, Florida, and checking into flight school. There are three phases to flight school: primary, intermediate, and advanced. Before primary you go through a six-week academic syllabus called API. This is to help prepare you with a general background in aviation. There are classes on the fundamentals of aerodynamics, engines, flight rules and regulations, and meteorology. There are also pool sessions and a couple of events in the bay for aviation water survival training. Once you complete this phase successfully, you begin primary.

Primary training for an NFO begins in the front seat of the T-34C. The point is to give you a familiarity from the pilot's perspective. You learn some basic takeoff, inflight, and landing skills. After about a dozen flights from the front seat, you transition to the back seat and begin focusing on navigation and systems operations.

During intermediate training you get into more detailed planning. You plot strike routes on charts with notional targets and become responsible for mission planning, targeting, and briefing. It was usually a thirty-minute flight to the selected target, but we had to hit en-route checkpoints visually and ultimately arrive "on target, on time." It isn't just a matter of getting there at the right time without getting lost, however. There are wind, speed, and fuel calculations and corrections made continually on the route. Your success is determined by how quickly you can gain situational awareness, recognize deviations, and make corrections "on the fly."

The advanced portion of training is where you make your money as an NFO candidate. You are given more responsibility for all aspects of training. In the beginning you do more complicated strike routes, now incorporating radar legs with the visual legs. I selected F/A-18s, so after the first strike portion of advanced I entered the fighter phase and began many long months of air-to-air training. During this time I flew the T-39 and the T-2.

Home was Perdido Key, just outside the back gate of NAS Pensacola. They also called it "NFO row," because it was mostly NFO candidates who lived out on the strand. We'd zip out the back gate and race home sometimes, seeing who could get on the beach and into the water first. Perdido Key was this very narrow but interesting strip of land between the Gulf of Mexico and another channel. Alabama was about one hundred feet from my house and the ocean was just a stone's throw across the street. I lived with Capt. (then lieutenant) Ty Westinghouse, who was going through flight training as well. I always viewed her as the all-American girl—smart, pretty, fun, super athletic, and to this day, one of the kindest people I have ever known. She flies the CH-46 helicopter for the Marine Corps and has made several combat deployments.

In the fall of 1999 I received my wings of gold. By now I was a first lieutenant as well. I packed my things once more and drove from Pensacola, Florida, to San Diego, California. There I checked into VMFAT-101, the "Sharpshooters," at Marine Corps Air Station Miramar. VMFAT-101 is one of the F/A-18 FRS where new pilots and NFOs are trained for the first time in the F/A-18, before being assigned to their fleet squadrons. Once you complete the FRS as an NFO, you are a designated WSO (also known as "wizzo"). By the time you check into your fleet squadron you'll be expected to know all your aircraft systems and basic employment and tactics. I took twelve months to complete FRS, which was pretty average at the time. Now I think they've sped up the process and it's only taking eight or nine months to complete.

While I was waiting to start FRS training, I drew the lucky lotto ticket for SERE school. It's basically POW training. So in January 2000 I spent two weeks learning how to handle myself as a downed aviator and POW, should my aircraft ever be shot down in enemy territory. It was definitely some of the best training I received during my career, despite the beatings(!). Afterwards I returned to MCAS Miramar for my FRS training in the F/A-18D.

As far as the aircraft goes, F/A-18Ds are mostly used for air-to-ground missions in the Marine Corps. They are strike-fighters and therefore air-to-air capable as well, of course, but in this day and age there are not too many applications of the fighter role. The United States simply has overwhelming superiority of air power in any conflict. Some specific missions assigned to the D (two-seat) model are FAC(A), TAC(A), and employment of the ATARS. All versions of the F/A-18 are capable of CAS, a critical element of the MAGTF concept.

Inside, front and rear cockpits in the two-seat model are almost identical. The front has stick and throttle, of course, which are missing in the rear cockpit, and in back we have some extra bells and whistles more specific to the WSO's mission. Sensors found in both cockpits include radar, FLIR, three main screen displays, and all avionics/communication controls. It's the roles played by pilot and WSO and their division of responsibility that differentiate the two. There are both independent and overlapping responsibilities between pilot and WSO, depending on the scenario and mission, and a smoothly running team can make the wizzo a combat multiplier, vice, a liability, and burden.

While at the FRS for training, I met Maj. Matthew "Sam" Tolliver. A wizzo who had transitioned to the front seat and become a Hornet pilot, he was going through the FRS a second time from the front instead of backseat. It isn't easy to make that transition. It is a long application process with many blessings from very senior people required (on top of your own requisite experience and skill level of course), and Major Tolliver was one of the first. As a mentor and friend, he helped me avoid several of the early pitfalls as a Marine aviator, and then allowed me to fall headfirst into others(!). I learned my lessons and appreciate his guidance to this day. To my philosophy that one should "do what's right and don't do what's wrong," he added that "birds may flock together, but eagles soar alone." He intuitively understood the challenges I would face because of who I was, and did his best to prepare me to walk tall even when completely alone. And it is the same guidance I would pass on to any other young woman making the decision to take this path. Decide what it is you want and then pursue it single-mindedly. Do not let the naysayers get you down. Follow your own instincts, your own heart, and keep your head up, your eyes on the horizon. As for the rest of them and their negativity? Whenever the murmuring around me got too loud and started to weigh on me, Major Tolliver loved to say to me, "water off a duck's back . . . it's all just water off a duck's back." It annoyed me to no end at the time, because I felt like he was trivializing what I felt were serious issues! But now I use the phrase all the time, and I don't feel any differently about the phrase. In fact, I am even more convinced that it does exactly that—it trivializes what I may feel are serious issues. It puts things in perspective. And the things that are just fluff, they do just slide right off of you. It really can't be any other way.

After about a year in the FRS, I was assigned to VMFA(AW)-121, the Green Knights, out of MCAS Miramar. I checked into my fleet squadron in March

2001. With the Green Knights I made three deployments overseas and several minor short detachments within the United States for training. Our three major deployments were Operation Bright Star (Egypt, October 2001), Operation Enduring Freedom (Kyrgyzstan, April 2002), and Operation Iraqi Freedom (January 2003).

Captain Kim standing next to her F/A-18 Hornet aircraft. *Courtesy of USMC*

Operation Bright Star is an ongoing annual exercise. After 9/11 it had a little more gravity than usual because of circumstances and its location in Egypt. We spent a month fighting Egyptian F-16s out of Beni Suef Air Base and watching a lot of bad television. It was a small base and we weren't allowed anywhere off the camp, so the thirty days dragged by pretty slowly. Some of the guys took to making "weights" out of differently shaped rocks and would "lift" them for exercise. At night a little truck would drive up and down the streets of our camp, spraying diesel fumes into the air to fumigate the mosquitoes. I never saw any of these alleged super-mosquitoes while I was there, but considering the method for keeping them under control, I'm glad I never had an encounter! There were about six to eight of us in each two-bedroom/one-bathroom ranch-style house on this Air Force base. We slept on cots in not only the bedrooms, but also the kitchens and living rooms. Mostly I napped this deployment away.

Once we came home we knew something was going to happen soon. I'm not sure anyone in the squadron unpacked quite everything. And sure enough, with operations kicking off in Afghanistan, we deployed to Peter J. Ganci Air Base (located at Manas International Airport) in Bishkek, Kyrgyzstan. It was a truly multinational effort in support of Operation Enduring Freedom. We had representation aboard camp from the United States, France, Australia, South Korea, Denmark, Spain, the Netherlands, and Norway. At the field we had a detachment of six French Air Force Mirage 2000D fighters and three Spanish PUMA helicopters. We were supported by American, French, and Australian tanker aircraft.

The base itself was named Ganci Air Base in honor of Chief Peter J. Ganci, Jr., chief of the New York City Fire Department, who gave his life during the terrorist attacks on 9/11. From the airfield it took just over an hour to fly down to the northern border of Afghanistan. For OEF we flew missions over Afghanistan during the period April to October 2002. On rare occasions we employed ordnance, but for the most part our missions consisted of reconnaissance and escort. I describe it to people as kind of an airborne police effort. We would cover periods of time on station, let's say, a three-hour time block over the eastern part of the country. If any of the ground units ran into trouble, they gave us a call and we lent assistance in whatever form was most appropriate.

In order to maximize our time on station we typically air refueled and swapped back and forth from the tanker with our wingman, so that someone was always on call. One afternoon I was flying with Capt. "Doogie" Andress, and we received a distress call just as our wingman was headed to the tanker. A special operations team on the ground was in town clearing out a weapons cache and the townspeople had come out en masse. The crowd was building to several hundred, surrounding the team, and the tension was rising.

Because it was a civilian crowd, we wanted to disrupt them without actually causing any harm. The team requested a low pass. We pulled a split-S maneuver from about fifteen thousand feet down to a few thousand off the ground and flew over the crowd with full afterburners. I don't know how to describe it to anyone who asks me what it's like, other than to say, "it's fun!" In all seriousness though, the team relayed to us soon after that "although the people aren't afraid of our .50cals on the trucks in front of them, they're definitely scattering at the sound of your jet engines!" The crowd dispersed peacefully without incident.

We came home in mid-October 2002. This time, we knew better than to unpack more than a toothbrush. Activity in the Mideast was ramping up and we received a warning order to stand by for another deployment. Sure enough, by the end of January 2003 we were on the road again.

When we arrived at Al-Jaber Air Base, Kuwait, it was very, very cold. It was about three or four in the morning, pitch dark. They unloaded our bags onto the gravel in one large pile and after digging around and finding our seabags, we then faced the task of figuring out which tent we'd be living in for the next several months. Row after row of tents faced us in "tent city." They were dark green and black heavy tarps on wooden frames, erected on wooden platforms, each tent a foot and a half from the next one. There were several hundred of these ten- to twelve- man tents.

I'm sure we were a bit of a clown show, balancing heavy seabags, stumbling over gravel and falling into ditches in the dark, going from tent to tent. Well, when I first arrived, there were no cots. It was by then five in the morning, I was freezing, there was certainly no heat or light in the tents, and we were all pretty tired. I ended up just piling into my tent, putting on every layer of clothing I could find readily accessible in my bags, and falling asleep at dawn on the wooden floor. A couple hours later I woke up wanting to use the head, but of course the closest one was about a half mile away and I had no idea where anything really was yet.

In January and February we flew under Operation Southern Watch, patrol flights on the southern side of the no-fly zone. Once the war kicked off we went to twenty-four-hour operations, seven days a week. We had day fliers and night fliers. You generally didn't swap from one page to the other because you would mess up the crew day and crew rest schedules. That's one thing that a lot of folks don't understand about aviators. There's a natural sibling rivalry between the air and ground elements of the Marine Corps.

One of the favorite ground complaints against the air wing is our mandatory crew rest. The idea of crew rest is to have a minimum number of hours between your last flight and your next brief. But I think unless you're an aviator it's hard to fully appreciate how crucial it is for your brain to be firing on all cylinders at all times! I wouldn't have understood it before I started flying either.

But the truth of the matter is, you can't just "nod off for a few seconds" while you're flying. There are too many things happening all at once, and a few precious seconds could easily mean the difference between life and death. And this doesn't even take into account the effect of fatigue on a pilot's judgment. He or she has several thousand pounds of ordnance on that aircraft. Even with mandated crew rest hours, it was hard to get any true sleep. As a night flier I was required to sleep during the day heat, but by the time we left the desert it was over 110 degrees Fahrenheit during the day.

I pretty much flew one sortie per night. My typical schedule was to get back from flying around 0530, eat breakfast, hit the rack around 0700 and try to sleep for an hour or two. It would get so hot by 0830 that I couldn't stay still anymore. I'd get up and wander around the camp or go work out, depending on how terrible I was feeling that day or how hot it was by 9:00 AM. I'd read for several hours at a time; I read about forty books in the last thirty days of this particular deployment. My tentmates would make fun of me, because exhaustion would finally overtake me at times and I'd fall asleep in some odd position on my cot, with my head propped up by one elbow, a book open, and a half-eaten candy bar still halfway to my mouth! After dinner the temperature would cool just a little, so I'd get something to eat and check into the squadron and arrive at the mission-planning center by seven or eight at night.

Mission planning was held in a huge tent, the only tent that had air conditioning. You would set up your charts, figure out if there were any preplanned targets for the night, go talk to the intel guys, basically get the whole mission scenario and find out what you're going to be doing for the night. Are you going to be a mission commander for a reconnaissance run, or a tactical commander for a hunter-killer mission? You'd figure it out, plan the plan, then brief the plan with the rest of your flight for about an hour.

If there was a very large strike early on in the war, it might involve three different squadrons, eight or more aircraft. Small typical missions only involved two aircraft. So you'd brief, get your bags together, drive out to the flight line, put your gear on, walk out to the line, preflight your jet, make sure the ordnance was set correctly, climb in, start it up, and check out all your systems. If anything was wrong and couldn't be fixed right away, you'd have to shut down and get into the spare aircraft.

Finally, you get airborne and head out to execute your mission. From Kuwait to Baghdad it was about an hour's flight. They usually threw a few AAA rounds your way when you crossed the border, which, by the way, didn't look anything like I expected it to look. I'm not sure what I expected, but the first time I saw puffy little white clouds appear around us, the first thought in my mind was not that they were shooting at us.

Captain Kim with U.S. Senator John McCain. *Courtesy of USMC*

Finding and taking out enemy targets was my job as a wizzo. Whether I had preplanned target coordinates or was out there actively looking for something to bomb, it was my job to use the sensors on board to locate and verify the targets. Cooperation and coordination between pilot and wizzo are essential. The pilot is responsible for the aircraft and crew. His eyes are generally outside making sure he neither runs us into a tree nor allows a surface-to-air missile to park itself on our wing! My job as a wizzo tends to keep my eyes inside a great deal, playing with buttons and knobs, manipulating what gadgets we have aboard the aircraft.

People often ask if I ever felt fear. I think that given the high level of activity inside the cockpit, there's almost not enough time to feel much fear. There's definitely a tension, an anticipation, an excitement even. But I wouldn't call it fear. When you're planning, you're concentrating; when you're preflighting and starting up, you're focusing; when you're in the air you're more concerned about safe flight, target acquisition, and ordnance employment. So it's not bravado or machismo to say there isn't room for fear. There really isn't!

I also feel that one of the most important roles of Marine aviation is as a support element to the ground units. When you're in a CAS role, your job is to make sure you knock out targets so they don't harm your Marines on the ground. And this can sometimes feel very personal, because you inevitably know some of those Marines down there. They are your brothers crossing the line of departure and fighting towards Baghdad. And neither hell nor high water will stop a Marine pilot from being there when the call comes in, short of a broken jet or no fuel.

It is thus particularly frustrating when you do have a broken jet or lack the fuel to support a call. One night after we had dropped our bombs and taken out our targets, we began heading back home when we received a call on guard frequency. It was an American unit, reporting troops in contact (i.e., receiving hostile fire), requesting air support. And it turns into a very frustrating situation very quickly. We're the only ones talking to them, but we're out of ordnance, we're in a specially configured aircraft so we have no bullets in the nose, and we don't have the fuel to get to their location. Home base was still over one hundred nautical miles away and we had no divert options for fuel. The call was about seventy nautical miles in the opposite direction.

I spoke to the ground unit and had to inform them we couldn't support them, due to lack of fuel and ordnance. Meanwhile I started checking various radio frequencies, trying to find other aircraft in the area that might be able to reach these guys. I found a couple of F-16s that were carrying HARM; they didn't have any rounds, they didn't have any regular bombs, only the AGM-88, a missile good for knocking out SAM sites but not equipped for close air support. On the other hand, they did have sufficient fuel. So they flew over to the unit and executed some low passes, trying to at least put forth a good show of force. We passed a message with the coordinates back to Al-Jaber, relaying the situation and requesting immediate air support.

With air support you always run into a timing issue. It takes a jet maybe thirty minutes to launch if the pilots are already on standby, and then there's the transit time. To me in the aircraft, ten minutes is nothing. To a guy on the ground taking fire, the fight could be over in ten minutes. The entire time I was out there flying combat missions, the only real emotion I experienced was wishing I could do more. I'm absolutely certain this feeling was shared by all the aviators I served with. Our major concern and first priority was supporting those units on the ground who needed our assets. There was a real sense of failure if we couldn't do what we needed to do, because we realized the impact our failure could possibly have on them.

After a mission was complete and we flew home, it'd be about 0400. We'd take another hour to get out of gear and debrief the intel folks (i.e., let them know what we did, where we did it, turn in any imagery we may have). Then we'd go back to the briefing spaces and debrief the mission with the flight crew. Then it's time for breakfast and bed; it's now 0600 or 0700 and the day starts all over again.

I would complain about the living conditions all the time in Al-Jaber, but of course it was nothing compared to how the ground guys were living. I don't think they had running water most places they camped, so they'd visit us at Al-Jaber on R&R and be amazed by hot food other than MREs and the ability to do laundry. There were ten of us living in our tent. All the women in my squadron lived together in one tent. We had running water in the head and shower trailers, so it wasn't too bad. In fact, we actually had decent food and even a pool on base, though that was entirely because it was an Air Force base! They certainly know how to set up camp when they deploy.

Most of my social time during either deployment was spent with the other female officers in my squadron. Lt. Julie Morgan was our intel officer, Lt. Tegan Owen was the assistant aviation maintenance officer, and Capt. Amy "Krusty" McGrath was the other female wizzo. So I was super lucky to have such great gals on the team, both because of their contributions to the fight and because they were all-around just wonderful people.

We returned home from OIF in May 2003. As a Marine aviator in a fixed-wing squadron, you're expected to spend about three to four years flying before you go on to a nonflying tour. I left the squadron in the fall of 2003 to serve my nonflying duties as the protocol officer to the CG of MEF. As the protocol officer I was mostly an event planner. Any VIPs who wanted to visit with Marines or Sailors under I MEF coordinated through my office. I handled everything from initial contact to itinerary development to billeting/transportation arrangements, press conferences, high-level briefings, and kept the CG up to date on what was sometimes a very fluid schedule.

As luck would have it, not even a ground tour could keep me stateside for too long. By August 2004, the new CG I MEF had checked in (Lt. Gen. John F. Sattler) and we were off to Fallujah, Iraq, for Operation Iraqi Freedom II (OIF II). With the support of some outstanding Marines on my staff, we planned and executed over three hundred VIP events in seven months. Some people are surprised when they learn how many visitors we had to our AO. However, the I MEF AO included all of western Iraq and was the parent command for 3rd Marine Aircraft Wing,

1st Marine Division, and 1st Force Service Support Group, as well as several other units who tactically fell under I MEF command. I was the one protocol officer for I MEF and all visits to any of the subordinate commands at any of the outlying bases had to work through me, so I was ridiculously busy from the time I set foot on the ground.

There were moments of comedy. Less than twelve hours after arriving in Fallujah, I traveled with the CG to a nearby checkpoint so he could visit the Marines there and begin getting a feel for the layout of the land. About thirty minutes after our arrival, mortars started landing near our position. Then came the rapid report of machine-gun fire and the not-so-pleasant echo of rounds ricocheting off things around me. We were already moving and taking cover, but I think the last straw was when an unfamiliar zinging sound went right over my head and Capt. "Dex" Hanley yelled "RPG!" It landed about eleven feet away in the sand.

We all booked it over to the vehicles, but since the door had been open when I initially boarded, I'd never had to actually open it, and I suddenly discovered that I couldn't open the door! If you ask someone off the street to describe how he would open a door, he'd likely answer that you either turn it to the right if it's a knob, or press down on the lever if it's a handle. Well, in a Humvee you actually have to lift the lever *up*. So there I was, three-time combat veteran and fighter pilot, standing at the door of my Humvee while mortars and machine gun fire are raining down upon us, and I'm trying to figure out how to open the door. I spoke to one of the original Marines of the CG's PSD just the other day, and he is still laughing about it.

I cannot even begin to do justice to all that happened during this deployment. During those seven months in Iraq, I MEF executed major operations in An Najaf and Fallujah, oversaw the first national public elections, and assisted in the development of the ISF. I was even standing in the back of the room when Iraqi Prime Minister Allawi suggested to Lt. Gen. Sattler that the name of Operation Phantom Fury be changed to Operation Al Fajr. We supported visits from ambassadors, cabinet members, congressional delegations, famous press personalities, and high-ranking military officers.

But throughout my career, it has been more about the people who have supported me in so many ways, than the job itself. I have worked for and with some really fantastic people. Col. John C. Coleman was the I MEF Chief of Staff and as far as I was concerned, walked on water. For as demanding and outrageously outspoken as he could be, he was ultimately fair and only expected you to perform your absolute best. He trusted me to do my job and left it to me, to decide how to go about doing it. The Marines around me would have followed him into battle any day at a moment's notice, and the kind of leadership that has this effect is a hard thing to put into words. It is a combination of intelligence, integrity, courage, and compassion. In his own way, he took me under his wing. And I owed much of my success during this deployment to his tough guidance.

Again, in my few spare moments I was surrounded by some really fantastic female Marines as well. Maj. Naomi Hawkins, the public affairs officer for 4th CAG, Capt. Jodie Sweezey, the logistics officer for 4th CAG, and Capt. Jennifer Morris, the information operations watch officer for I MEF. They were a fundamental part of what made the deployment more than just a job; on a regular basis they reminded me of the reasons I loved being a Marine and what we were trying to accomplish. They were also a comic relief. No matter how motivated and committed you are as a Marine, there comes a point where you need to take off the hat and relax and play.

I was very blessed in my career; finding a good group of girlfriends was never difficult for me. It's not to say that you couldn't have good male friends, I certainly met some great male Marines along the way. But when you're a woman so far outnumbered, there is something very special about being able to bond with and relate to other women "on your boat."

I had four Marines who worked for me the duration of the deployment (which means they took a lot of abuse), and they ran the actual compound that we used for visitors bureau headquarters. In addition to supporting the events themselves, they were also responsible for the maintenance of the two billeting buildings, the rotunda that served as a secondary operations center, and the grounds. There was always a project waiting on the list between events. From fixing fences and windows to replacing heaters and painting rooms, they stayed busy. One night before a major operations brief was to take place the next morning (involving the CG), a controlled detonation just outside the camp shattered the windows on one side of the rotunda, behind the briefing screen. We stayed up all night sweeping shards of glass, nailing plywood boards to the walls, and trying to coordinate with base maintenance Marines to get the windows replaced in a timely fashion.

In addition to my Marines I had three Iraqis on my staff who were exceptionally hard-working, kind-hearted, and brave. They had friends who had been executed for cooperating with Americans, and yet they continued to drive in and out of the camp main gate regularly to make money and support their families. They were also firm believers in the cause; they were grateful for the Coalition presence and for the downfall of Saddam Hussein. Their only hope was that some day there would be no need for the Coalition's security forces and the terrorists would no longer run rampant in their country. They all went to the polls and voted in January 2005, despite threats against them and their loved ones. They truly humbled me and I will always be grateful for the lesson.

In between these deployments, I did several speaking engagements, accepted awards, and was twice even on national television (once to announce a teaching award and a second time on ESPN to wave at football fans in Tampa, Florida). But I would be remiss if I didn't give credit to the Marines who have always supported the aviators and the protocol officers out there. They are the true unsung heroes, not me, and this is my personal soapbox when it comes to the Marine Corps.

As an aviator, you get a lot of attention for the job you do. You're a fighter pilot, there are guts and glory involved, so on and so forth. A lot of people pay attention to you and are impressed because it's a sexy and glamorous-sounding job. And there are definitely days when you feel that way, for sure. But we couldn't even get off the ground if it weren't for the Marines in the squadron. In a squadron you've got twenty to forty pilots and almost two hundred enlisted Marines, supervised by two or three maintenance officers. They work their tails off on the flight line to make sure your jet is good to go. They support twenty-four-hour operations during combat, which means day and night crews working fourteen-plus hour shifts because overlap is inevitable. Oftentimes maintenance is shorthanded in certain departments, they don't have crew day or crew rest, and yet they are solely responsible for ensuring my jet will safely bring me home, each and every time.

I will never forget sitting on the flight line in Al-Jaber, engines on line, waiting for a replacement part before takeoff, and seeing one of the Marines literally run across the flight line with the part. It was a large boxy shape and heavy, it was over 100 degrees outside, and he was running. These guys went out of their way on a daily basis and showed such incredible commitment to the job, one couldn't help but be inspired by their example.

As the protocol officer, I had the task of juggling many tricky and sharp objects in the air at once. There were so many things racing through my mind during a visit, I had to know that when I turned around and looked at a Marine, he already knew why I was looking at him! Every Marine involved in one of my visits had to be fully aware of the responsibilities of his role and then execute the plan, often using his own judgment when changes came down the line. And they really were fantastic. A couple of months into the deployment, my crew could pretty much run on autopilot. And between two gunnery sergeants, Juan Morales and Paul Zogg, I could rely on the PSD team to cover everything from taking a bullet for a VIP and arranging a fifty-person convoy into downtown Fallujah, to making sure the pigeons were fed (okay, not really, but they did have a pretty wide range of jobs assigned to them). They made even the worst goat rodeos appear seamless.

I decided to leave the Marine Corps in December of 2005 and pursue my civilian career, but the one thing that made it a truly difficult decision was the caliber of Marines I met during my tours. In the beginning, there were definitely some hardships. At five feet six inches and 130 lbs, I am not a physically intimidating figure anyway, and as a woman in a man's world, I didn't fit in very well. I stuck out like a sore thumb and attracted a lot of attention. And when you're constantly under the spotlight, people are bound to start tearing you apart, piece by piece.

But as the deployments went on, I began to realize that despite the insanity of flying and going to war and daily politics, there were still some really great things happening behind the scenes. It's easy to get wrapped up in the daily weeds of who's doing what, who's flying where, why isn't there any hot water for the showers, gosh I'm really tired, and focus entirely on myself. This is especially true in a closed environment. I really had to take a step back once in a while in order to see that despite the things that may go wrong and the people who may disappoint, there are sources of inspiration, too. They are always there, somewhere, and you may have to go out of your way to find them, but they are worthwhile and will help you keep your chin up when things turn the wrong way.

The ups and downs of my career are varied, but the true highlights have nothing to do with me. My strongest memories are of the mentors, friends, and fellow Marines whose company I am proud to have shared. Be it as an aviator or as a protocol officer, I entrusted my life to the Marines who worked with me and I respected the hell out of them for their true dedication and courage.

As a final note, I would also be remiss if I didn't give credit to my family for their love and support throughout my endeavors. I could not have accomplished anything that I have, without their encouragement and wisdom to sustain and guide me every step of the way.

Note: As of this writing Jaden Kim is undergoing civilian flight training and hopes to someday become an airline pilot.

MGySgt. Rosemarie Weber, USMC (Ret.)

MGySgt. Rosemarie Weber retired from the U.S. Marine Corps on 31 January 2006. Coauthor Wise, who attended her retirement ceremony at The Women's Memorial building located at the gateway to Arlington National Cemetery, witnessed a truly remarkable farewell to one of the Corps' finest. Those attending the ceremony included military representatives of three countries and all U.S. services. Noteworthy Marines on hand included: Lt. Gen. Mike Hough, the former Deputy Commandant for Aviation; Lt. Gen. James Amos, Commander, 2nd Marine Expeditionary Force; Vice Adm. Patricia Tracey; and 13th sergeant major of the Marine Corps (Ret.) Sgt. Maj. Lewis Lee.

Additionally, the hall was filled with Weber's family and Marines, active and retired, who had served with Weber during her illustrious twenty-six-year career. Lieutenant General Amos extolled her many outstanding achievements during her service and awarded her the Meritorious Service Medal, third Award during the ceremony. Among the many personal decorations she wore was the French National Defense Medal, Silver Award, presented to her by the French Defense Attaché to the French embassy in D.C. Weber was the first American noncommissioned officer to receive the medal since World War II.

MGySgt. Rosemarie Weber was interviewed by Kate Scott in Arlington, Virginia, on 27 July 2005. The tape and transcript are deposited at The Women's Memorial in Arlington. *Photo courtesy of USMC*

With the exception of a few early assignments as a heavy equipment operator, Weber served as an administrator throughout her career. Following basic training she was ordered to the First Force Service Support Group at Camp Pendleton, California, and after changing her occupational specialty to administration she did a tour in Okinawa, Japan. She next went to Parris Island, South Carolina, where she was assigned as an administrative chief; she also served a tour as a drill instructor and a depot inspector.

Weber was then transferred to Marine Air Group 31, VMFA-312 (F-18 Squadron) at the Marine Corps Air Station in Beaufort, South Carolina. She was senior Marine of the group of the first woman Marines to deploy with a Marine aviation squadron, which gave her the opportunity to visit many countries in the Western Pacific and participate in numerous subsequent deployments. She then served a tour of inspector-instructor duty with the Fourth Force Service Support Group in Massachusetts and then was ordered back to Beaufort and again assigned to MAG-31, with VMFA-451 and VMFA-533.

In 1996, at the personal request of the 13th sergeant major of the Marine Corps, Weber was assigned to the 31st commandant's staff in Washington, DC. She also served with the 14th sergeant major of the Marine Corps before being reassigned to the deputy commandant for aviation. In March of 2000 she was assigned to the Office of the Under Secretary of Defense for Personnel and Readiness, Military Personnel Policy, where she served as the assistant executive officer. In April 2003 Weber was selected to serve with the Coalition Provisional Authority (CPA) in Baghdad, Iraq, where she worked in the Ministry of Defense for the Hon. Walter Slocombe, building the new Iraqi Army. Weber described this tour of duty as probably the most interesting and challenging of her career.

★   ★   ★

While attached to the CPA, I was not part of a regular military unit. There were very few uniformed members in the CPA at the time. Fewer still enlisted. What happened was that because there were so many civilians and we were military and armed (though we weren't infantry, only administrators, supply personnel, logisticians, all support people) we truly felt that we were honor-bound to be responsible for the civilians who worked around us. My job was to go in first and find our spaces in an Iraqi palace. We set up offices, found usable furniture and worked with the communications officer to get computers in order to have everything set up so that when the folks that were going to build the new Iraqi Army came over everything would be in place and ready to go. We also set up office procedures for people who would be attached to us, anything you take for granted in an office. We had to start from scratch. In addition to that, when we got there in

April 2003, we had to clean the palace, there was still no glass in the windows. So we had to make all these very rudimentary things happen.

My first impression of the Iraqi people was, if one took the politics out of it, they're just people. They're like you and me. They want a better life, just like we do. We went through it in our country with discrimination. Anything you can imagine, we have done it on a small scale in our country, and we have come out the better for it. That's all they want. And as people they deserve the same thing. And you see it most when you see the kids. You know, it's not all about soldiers and terrorists and all that. They're just people looking for something better.

With regard to traveling to the country, I must admit I had a big advantage over most of the Marines that were there. I flew over first class. I recall our flying into Kuwait and it was surreal. Here you are in a land that's incredibly old with a history that's so beyond anything you could fathom from what you grew up with. You know it's a history book. But it's moving and breathing around you. It smells different. It feels different. But you've arrived with people you have something in common with and it makes the whole experience a little less shocking. We had to wait in Kuwait for about three days because at the time only military planes could fly into Baghdad. We finally boarded a KC-130 transport plane. I had, of course, done plenty of travel in KC-130s sitting in nets for seats. Though it was not new for us, it was very new to civilians. We watched them groan because the seats were uncomfortable. So as they struggled, we helped them get settled. In addition to what they found inside the plane, they were a bit apprehensive about even boarding the plane.

We flew into Baghdad International Airport and the experience is hard to explain. First of all, as you come in to land, you get your first sight of bomb damage, wreckage, planes blown up on the runway, and also that Steven King-like quality where everything is just dead. You could see the civilian portion of the airport where there was no movement, no people, commercial planes just stopped and abandoned on the tarmac. It was extremely eerie. Of course then you disembark and you're hit with 145-degree heat. And it's at this point that you put on your helmet, flack vest, all your protective gear. Inside, your body temperature under the jacket is about 150 degrees. You can feel yourself losing weight almost immediately.

We grabbed our gear and got on a bus and we drove into Baghdad proper to a palace compound. It took about twenty or thirty minutes and along the way we saw deserted highways, bombed-out buildings, and rubble; you could see where there were cities and civilization, but the air was filled with a dead quiet. I didn't notice any of the local people at the time. You'd occasionally see a military patrol drive by. At this point I began to fear who was out there watching us and wondering if we were a target. You think about all the things you've learned about terrorism. But we arrived safely at the palace compound (which was more or less a gated community) without incident. The buildings were very different in structure but very nice. All of a sudden it seemed that our forces were everywhere. Offices were being set up, checkpoints established and in a short time an operational compound was taking shape. When we first got there, trailers that were to serve as living quarters were not ready for use. Some had been set up but very few were inhabited at the time. They consisted of small buildings that one might see at a construction site: four-man trailers, two sided—two rooms with a shared bathroom in the middle, two people to each room.

Eventually they were all up and running and they were very posh. It's the only time that you go from a palace to a trailer, and you've actually gone up a notch in the social hierarchy. But when we first got there we slept on the palace floor, in any nook or cranny. People were just camped out everywhere. Initially, there were four people there from my group, a colonel, two lieutenant colonels, and me. Eventually our staff fleshed out, but the core staff was about thirteen people to get this whole ministry, the Ministry of Defense, established and functioning again. Within the palace itself it was a kind of a mini-Pentagon.

The Army Fifth Corps military police provided all our exterior guard support and security. Those kids did an incredible job. I can't imagine standing posts out there in the sun. We were working inside and at least had the option of

MGySgt. Rosemarie Weber, USMC, enjoys the view from atop one of Saddam Hussein's palaces in Baghdad. *Courtesy of USMC*

moving around and stopping to pour water over our heads to cool off. These guys were on post and they were there for eight hours at a time in that beating, blazing sun. I don't know how they stood it. Our palace compound was the first place that was established as a safe zone that had adequate security on the perimeter and was situated in a spot where hostilities hadn't really escalated at that point.

Of course safety was a continuing concern for us. I must admit that I made myself unsafe on multiple occasions starting the first morning I woke up in the compound. I got up and the heat sickness hadn't hit me yet. You still feel great. You don't know that three hours from now, you might be on your deathbed. So I got up, and decided to go running along the Tigris River, which was right behind us—the historical Tigris. Oh, my God! How often do you get a chance to do this? I put on my PT gear and went running along the river. I was running along a dirt road, not paying much attention to anything. I was still awed that I was there and was trying to put it all together. Suddenly I heard somebody yell, "Get down, get down!" What? Then I looked down and saw dirt puffs and it dawned on me that they were shooting at me from across the river. I was making myself a target here because I didn't have enough sense to know better. There was no indoctrination when we got in country about such things. This was quickly corrected.

★ ★ ★

Weber kept a diary of her experiences while in Baghdad and she sent numerous e-mails back home that detailed her activities. These became known as the "Baghdad Diaries," and a number of these messages are currently on exhibit at The Women's Memorial. They are included below to give the reader a perspective of a Soldier's life, and her observations in a far-off war zone.

Baghdad Diaries
E-Mails Home

```
From: Weber, Rosemarie
Sent: Monday, July 28, 2003 10:45 AM
Subject: Items in the news . . .
```

```
Some of you may have been watching CNN following the
deaths of Saddam's sons, Uday and Qusay, earlier in
the week. A CNN commentator in Baghdad stated, "it
is customary that when celebrating, the Iraqis will
```

```
fire weapons into the air, I have seen none of that
celebratory fire occurring." Is CNN in the same city
the rest of us are? Let me tell you about the night
after the deaths of the Brothers Grimm . . .
```

I live in the first row of trailers directly behind the palace, but within the compound. Directly behind the trailers is the CPA property warehouse, behind that a road that runs along the Tigris and then of course, the river itself. All told, we are about five hundred yards from the river, perhaps seven hundred from the part of Baghdad that is directly across the river behind us. At about 1030 on that Wednesday, the 23rd, my roommate and I were just going to sleep when we heard gunfire; nothing so very unusual about that so we acknowledged it and then promptly ignored it. We ignored it that is until it became rapid and sustained. We took real notice when we heard the U.S. troops return fire in equally rapid and sustained bursts. "When out on the river there arose such a clatter, we sprang from our beds to see what was the matter, away to the window we flew like a flash, tore open the shutters and threw up the sash; then we got our guns!" The sky was alight with red tracer fire. As did most others in the compound, we thought for sure the Iraqis were attempting to break through the perimeter. We went outside, gunfire and tracer rounds arced through the sky on all sides of the compound. It was close, very, very close. About that time the call came to evacuate the trailers. No explanation was given, just evacuate to the palace.

My roommate and I opted to stay away from the masses that were headed into the palace, figuring our chances were better if the Iraqis anticipated that and were waiting to mow everyone down. We went to the pool. . . . It put us in an enclosed area, easier to defend and protected from stray fire and in a smaller more manageable group. Now not everyone got the call or heard the fire, based on what they were doing at the time. A friend two trailers down from mine was reading with the headphones on. He thought he heard an external noise, looked up, saw a nasty hole in the ceiling, three dents on the walls, and then looked down to see a round on the bed next to him!

We didn't realize until later it was celebratory fire, never made the connection between the gunplay and the deaths of Uday and Qusay. It made sense the next morning, but truth be told, there was hostile fire intermixed with the other and the Soldiers on the perimeter did have to return fire in a decidedly non celebratory fashion. . . . Two of our perimeter Soldiers were seriously injured by falling rounds. So, I am unsure just where that CNN Baghdad correspondent was, perhaps he had his headphones on, or maybe he's just oblivious, but he certainly wasn't around here!"

From: Weber, Rosemarie
Date: June 2003
Subject: Contradictions

Life here is a series of contradictions. For example, this past whatever day it was, 27th I think, the Iraqi National Symphony played for the first time in over a year. The performance was by invitation only and then each unit got x number of tickets also. . . . The performance was held at the convention center across the street from the palace; it's got some war damage, but is functional. So, we get as dressed up as one can get in clothes that came out of a seabag (duffle bag for you Air Force types) and off we go to the convention center.

We park in a lot strewn with rubble and other war debris and go into a concert hall that is in pretty good shape. The music stands and chairs are all set up on stage, everything looks pretty normal except the chairs are white plastic lawn chairs and the audience is a rather eclectic mix of Iraqis in Western and traditional garb, U.S. and coalition members in every style of dress from D.C. casual to full battle dress, with helmets, body armor and weapons . . . and of the folks that are in civilian clothes, many of those have weapons strapped on. There's something not quite right about a gal in a simple black cocktail dress with an M-4 strapped to her back (no, it wasn't me)!

The performance was great; of note was the fact that they played the traditional Iraqi National Anthem at the end . . . for the first time since 1958 when the Baath party decided it was a no-go. The Iraqis in the audience went nuts, some just broke down in tears, others were clapping, it was a very moving and special thing to witness/be a part of. . . .

I spend most of my time building offices, moving furniture and doing "hired gun" missions. These duties include driving in the convoy that goes to the airport (got shot at the other day when my vehicle got stuck in a tank track,) and going on site recons to places like ammo dumps, weapons factories, barracks and other Ministry of Defense buildings. We often encounter resistance on these trips as squatters don't want to be displaced and rogue members of the Republican Guard are often on site or in the area. Occasionally there are shots fired, but no injuries to date, them or us. There was an explosion on the road two weeks ago that killed a few Iraqis, one a small child of about seven who was standing by the side of the road. We were far enough behind to avoid any danger of shrapnel or anything, but close enough to see, get out, and be unable to do anything for anybody. The two or three from the truck died instantly, we couldn't even accurately say if there were two or three. It was a nasty mess. The most tragic part of it was wondering how anyone would locate that kid's family, did they even know he was gone? How do you find the family of an unidentified kid who may or may not even have a permanent residence?

Water is back on (have you ever been in a port-a-potty when it's 125 degrees?), and the air is finally on in some parts of the palace, not, of course, our part. I now have my own desk and computer and the ice machine works, so twice a day we get ice and actually drink something, anything, cold. My best to all,

```
From: Weber, Rosemarie
Date: June 2003
Subject: Thoughts/Observations
```

I was walking about the Palace a few evenings ago and overheard a conversation that I thought was worthy of sharing.

It is so hot inside this marble stair master that I tend to walk much slower than I do in the Pentagon, so I actually heard a good bit of the discussion I am about to relay. The hall is long; the doors that line it are usually open in an effort to encourage any slight breeze. As I came upon a small room I heard a group of about five to six male voices lamenting the conditions here. Life here is pretty good compared to some deployments so I figured the boys were most likely young with little experience by way of deployments.

The most popular gripes were the lack of air conditioning, the lack of laundry accountability, the repetitive nature of the meals in the chow hall and the lack of women. My initial reaction was to be slightly offended; I then thought I would poke my head in and say something like "hey, I resent/resemble that remark!" Then I pulled up short and gave the remark a moment to settle and I decided it was a great comment about women in combat support roles.

These young men actually did not consider the gals in their unit/ uniformed female members in the palace to be women, they were simply fellow Soldiers. And, behaviorally speaking, that is exactly what I have observed in the actions of everyone in uniform here. The heads are coed, the showers are almost coed, male/female hours are posted, but they tend to bleed into each other, when you have to shower, you have to shower. The big gypsy camps around the palace where people live are coed and not unit-specific; I think that says a lot.

It was never the men and women who would have to be together that said it wouldn't work; it was the politicians and the public. I think we have proven again that our young men and women in uniform do put the mission first. It's when folks are "in the rear" that trouble starts, mostly because we don't keep our young troops busy enough in garrison. Anyway, just thought I would share my thoughts. For the record, however, I still disagree with women on subs, I mean, jeez, have you ever been on a sub? GROSS!

```
From: Weber, Rosemarie
Date: July 2003
Subject: Daily Life in the Palace
```

And the good news is we now have air in our part of the palace!!! Wonder of wonders, miracle of miracles . . . it's like we've been reborn, energy levels are up, papers are coherent, we have stopped having physical altercations in the hall to make all our decisions and most of us can stay awake past 1400. The bad news is now that it's not 130 degrees and we are all not sweating way beyond profusely, we all have to go to the bathroom during the day again. You guessed it, no water in our part of the palace so a seemingly simple task becomes an ordeal. To go to the air conditioned, coed head/latrine/bathroom, we have to go down two flights of a giant marble staircase commonly referred to as the stair master or ass master, traverse a maze of hallways to the south end of the palace, go out the back door and down the back alley. So, while tempers are smoothing out, we are still a bit cranky. Thankfully, the USMC has taught me some self-discipline and I can wait till meal hours when I have to run the obstacle course anyway to go to chow . . . or maybe I'm just afraid of the stair master!!

We have contracted laundry service and dry cleaning. The laundry is Bosnian-run and they do a fair job except that clothes are often lost, well, not lost, they just end up in someone else's bag. As there is no way to trace back and find out where your stuff ended up you just have to wait until you spot someone wearing your clothes and trade back. It's fairly common practice as you end up having to wear the other guy's clothes because all yours are in yet another bag somewhere. Everyone laughed when I packed 179 pairs of Skivvies drawers . . . well, they're not laughing here. They all have Skivvies envy and when they are down to zero pairs they come crying to the Top looking for handouts . . . they all owe me. Power is good!!

```
From: Weber, Rosemarie
Sent: August 2003
Subject: A Day at the Market
```

The tempo of operations has now picked up to the point where I actually have some administrative duties. Along with my Bunkie, I have built our office spaces, to include walls, furnishings, plumbing, and electricity. New arrivals appear daily and so we have begun to attack our actual mission, which is to build a Ministry of Defense for the Iraqis to emulate. Most of our support functions here are con-tracted out [to civilian companies]. They do everything from feed us, to wash our Skivvies to building our walls to providing our billeting. They also subcontract the hiring of local Iraqis for various jobs such as cleaning and translating.

Last week I went down to supply and checked out a person! Unique experience if ever there was one. We needed a receptionist that had dual language capability, English and Arabic, so I figure it's some huge ordeal that will take weeks. So I go to check it out and they have me fill out a hand receipt and voila, I checked out a receptionist. She is twenty-five and has been educated at a university, she speaks very good English, is very sweet, and listens to bad disco music. At any rate, she took me and one of the other gals out to the market today.

The place is a maze of winding alleys; levels and direction change without warning, people and pathetic donkeys are everywhere. Up, down, north, south, dodge a cart, bump into an old lady . . . in a matter of minutes you have no idea where you came in or how to get out.

As you head down an alley into the heart of the market you are overwhelmed! Complete sensory overload. It is a market of metalsmiths, silversmiths, textiles, food, produce, hardware, and antiquities. You smell propane, meat grilling, dust, and garbage and the sweat of a thousand humans who don't shower regularly as they come together in a small space where no air circulates.

You hear the hammering of craftsmen, the chatter of merchants luring customers into their stalls, the aggressive chatter of customers bartering with shop-keeps, the pounding of carts on uneven dirt roads, the cart pushers hollering at the people to get out of the way, and the crackle of the meat you smell grilling. Everything is viewed through a veil of dust and smoke; silver, brass, copper, tin; textiles in every color of the rainbow (although very few people seem to wear anything but black and shades of tan); old men and old women in traditional garb, young citizens in B-movie versions of Western attire; the hollow haunted faces of the old, who have been in this market for decades scratching out a living; the young expectant faces of their grandchildren who will inherit those same stalls.

You touch everything you see, because you are compelled to. The craftsmanship is fine and the craftsmen are proud. The metal is detailed, the textiles are woven tightly, the carpets are pure silk, and soft against your fingers, and the antiques are ancient. You can taste the dust, the smoke, the wafting aromas of kebabs grilling. The merchants are as excited to have you there as you are to be there. They are proud and eager to please, you are respectful and eager to be pleased; a perfect relationship and a wonderful day. I spent very little money on very many useless trinkets that I will, of course, be passing on to some of you! And while the trinkets will fade from my mind quickly, the experience of purchasing them will be with me forever. My love to all, I do so wish I could share this with you, but alas, these brief e-mails will have to do.

* * *

My service in Iraq meant a lot to me. First of all I was never looked at as being a woman. I was simply a Marine in Iraq at that time. And that was very special, because there were very few Marines in Baghdad when I was there in the very beginning. So I got to be one of the first Marines with the CPA. And at that time, I was only one of two enlisted Marines. But as a woman, looking back on it now I feel that it was an opportunity to prove ourselves right. For years we have been hearing the question, "Can women go into combat?" Oh, absolutely not according to the many naysayers and the moms of America who would never allow that to happen. Women will break under pressure, the men wouldn't respond accordingly. Well, we proved them wrong. We are there! We're doing it alongside the men with very few male–female kind of issues going on. So to all the naysayers, we're doing it and doing it with courage and dedication! It's very important for the American public to know and understand that there's no going back, women are now an integrated part of our country's armed forces.

Spc4 Sayra Salas Sanchez, USA

Sayra Salas Sanchez was a Specialist Promotable E4 with the Third Special Forces group, 74 Charlie. She was deployed three times to Afghanistan (Operation Enduring Freedom). Spc4 Salas's remarks offer a unique insight into the operations of Army personnel who support Special Forces' firebases in Afghanistan, home of Al Qaida.

★   ★   ★

I was born in Lodi, California, the twelfth child in our family of eight sisters and four brothers. My parents immigrated to California from Mexico about forty years ago. They're both retired and are very humble people. I was quite active growing up, and my mom and dad, being pretty old fashioned, were upset when I brought up my thoughts concerning military service. Nobody in my family had ever joined the military. When I expressed a desire to do so, they reminded me that I was a female and as such I definitely could not join up.

I graduated from Liberty High School in Lodi in 2000. I played soccer and basketball and was somewhat of a tomboy. I was always active and even considered becoming a firefighter as a career. But three months before I graduated I enrolled in

Sayra Salas Sanchez was interviewed by Kate Scott in Arlington, Virginia, on 14 September 2005. The tape and transcript are deposited at The Women's Memorial in Arlington. *Photo courtesy of USA* the Military Entrance Program Station (MEPS) without my parents' consent. Although they didn't believe me when I told them what I had done, it was too late for them to change my mind. I had signed the papers and was committed. After graduating I joined the U.S. Army in July 2000, having just turned eighteen.

Basic training was at Fort Jackson, South Carolina, which a lot of people call "Relaxin' Jackson," because it's coed. I think it all depended on your drill sergeants whether you were really going to relax or not. I had it pretty tough, only because I had some very demanding drill sergeants. But I got over it and in retrospect I came to appreciate the discipline they instilled in me.

There were other Latina women in my group. One was Puerto Rican and the other, I think, was Ecuadorian, or El Salvadorian. For six of us, basic training was a little longer than it was supposed to be. We went into training in August and completed the program in October. We were held over for six months after graduation and remained at Fort Jackson because it took a while to get processed for our Top Secret clearances. After receiving my clearances I was ordered to Fort Gordon, Georgia, where I spent sixteen weeks in AIT.

My Top Secret clearance was granted as a result of my aptitude tests. I scored high on the technical test and, on the spot, they gave me a typing test. With that I was told that my high scores qualified me for three jobs. One involved helicopter maintenance, another was as a tractor specialist, and the third was 74 Charlie, as a telecommunications operator and maintainer. The latter sounded sophisticated and I chose that specialty.

I arrived to my unit at Fort Bragg, the Third Special Forces Group, home of the Airborne and Special Forces troops, and found that everyone was extremely dedicated. I wondered where I would be going and what was ahead of me.

September 11th changed everything. At the time of the attack on the World Trade Center I was on a water jump (I qualified as a Zodiac boat driver. These boats were really super-fast boats that the Special Forces scuba guys used.) We had a group of airborne Soldiers jumping out of Chinooks (twin-turbine, tandem-rotor transport rotor-craft) and we were basically driving the boats out to pick them up. After the first group jumped, the exercise was interrupted by a big bullhorn announcement to bring the boats in! The helicopter proceeded to land the remainder of the people on shore. The boats came in as well and we knew something was going on. The word spread that we were being attacked! After that, it was 24/7 security guard. We all got our weapons, drew vests, magazines of ammo, and we were guarding every part of Fort Bragg. Security was now so tight that the day after 9/11 it took people six hours to get in the gates.

A month later we were instructed to get ready to deploy. We were read the rules of engagement for our destination. We were told we were allowed to shoot people if we felt threatened. We had what's called PDSS, whereby high-ranking personnel conduct advances and scout the area prior to our deployment, then fall back and inform the unit what the situation was and how many people were going to be needed. They brought back pictures (actual clips and videotapes). They told us we'd see little five- and seven-year-olds with AK-47s on their backs. And we were told that if they started shooting, "you know what to do!"

Shortly after that we were on a plane, en route to hostile territory. We departed from an Air Force base in North Carolina near Fort Bragg. It was a long flight, about sixteen hours. We were ordered to lock and load and to stay in a straight line when we deplaned.

Before we left I called my parents and told them that I was deploying. To quell their anxiety somewhat I told them that we were going to Germany. Once in Germany I called them again and because I knew how devastated they were, I told them that we were going to stay in Germany. After taking to the air again we finally reached our destination, Bagram Air Base, Afghanistan. The C5 transport plane we were in was so huge that we had to be told that we had landed. We looked out through tiny peepholes and all we could see was flat land. It was four in the morning and still dark, so we couldn't tell what was going on. I remember that my stomach was full of butterflies and I felt like throwing up.

I think that from the day we landed, and maybe for a week afterward, I didn't get more than two hours sleep per night. We were housed in tan cloth tents that were old and raggedy. They would constantly be flapping with the wind, often causing the poles to fall over. Not all of us had cots, some of us just slept on the ground in sleeping bags, and you could hear mortars and mines going off constantly. I felt like I was in some surreal war movie. It helped that I had deployed with the Special Forces Soldiers, the Army's cream of the crop. I knew that I was in good hands and shouldn't be afraid. I'm already out here; I might as well make the best of it.

On my first deployment there were probably only four females in our group until the main body came in, and there were around thirty by the end of the deployment. During the first months of the deployment it was rough living in Afghanistan, especially if you were a woman. There were no provisions for our personal hygiene, we didn't have toilets, no showers or real water. We had bottled water, which we had to save for purposes other than drinking. So we just did the baby wipe/washcloth thing. For the sake of our health we had to keep as clean as possible at all times, especially our hair. I remember not washing my hair for a week or two, just having it up completely tied in a knot or braided, and how foul smelling it became after a time. I carried baby wipes with me everywhere because two minutes after I tried to clean up, I'd be dirty again; there was dust everywhere.

Once the medics and the main body arrived, we started getting organized, and a lot of tents were put up, after the DoD bomb squad cleared away any bombs or mines. Birth control pills and other female necessities were distributed. Our med guys were really cool. You usually became really close to them. It was like one big family and they made sure that we had everything we needed.

Our camp became home to us for our initial and future deployments. Eventually we began to get pallets of supplies, which included all the electronic computers, displays, communications gear, cables, wiring, and tools we needed to do our job. I was assigned the job of network administrator/cable dog, everything that dealt with communications. We had to start from the ground up. We had to dig holes in the ground and bury the Cat 5 cable and fiber. If not, they would get torn apart and become useless. As we were burying cables we found bones in the dirt. We just threw them out of the way to make space for our cable track. One of our officers asked me why I was throwing away the human bones. In all honesty I thought that they were animal bones, but evidently our J2 Soldiers had found a full pelvic bone of a woman intact. We were devastated and henceforth were careful to avoid desecrating any bones we came across.

Since I was new to my job and only a private first class, it seemed that everyone was watching us closely and in essence training us. We had to get used to such treatment. Burying cables, putting out switches and setting up computers and then continually moving everything to a new area became an ongoing job that never seemed to end.

Our camp was called CJ SOTF. The nearest town, Kabul, was about forty miles away. In Kabul and another city I visited, Kandahar, a maze of primitive dwellings, chaos often reigned and people lived under the most austere conditions. We made a lot of trips to those cities because we had to get new hubs and routers. We were forced to network with local people to find out where we could get these items since some of our resupplies weren't coming in for another month. We needed them because we had to communicate with our Special Forces Soldiers at down-range firebases.

We had to keep our Special Forces' units up to date on everything, working with our radio people who were situated right next door to us and our satellite unit. We would help each other out; if they had an item we needed they would trade off and vice versa. We all worked in shifts, probably eighteen hours a day when we first landed. The work was constant, it never stopped.

During our first deployment, our interaction with the local community didn't go very well. Our compound was set up right in front of a village, and there was a school nearby that wasn't very active. Female children did not go to school, only male students could attend. The villagers were constantly fighting and shooting at each other, which caused us to always be alert and on guard. We had to pull our fair amount of guard duty, which was somewhat overwhelming because there were only two people on duty at one time. The only thing that separated us from the village was a single strand of concertina wire. At times you would see people outside the wire and although you had your weapon, you often found yourself alone while your partner would be pulling roving guard, going around the compound. It was kind of scary especially when a dog would jump at you out of the darkness.

I wrote a lot of letters and took pictures. There were beautiful snow-capped mountains in the distance. We were in a valley where danger always lurked because there were so many buried mines. There were the white rocks, which meant that mines had been cleared, and red rocks, which the EOD people painted red indicating mines that hadn't been cleared. We would drive to Kabul at high speed because we didn't want to get ambushed. At the same time the air would be filled with dust and you couldn't see the rocks. I was sure that every time our driver swerved we would go over a red rock and be blown up; luckily this never happened.

Some things happened while I was over there that almost put me in harm's way. Two of us were on guard duty at the front gate, and MPs were chasing a couple of locals who were running toward us. At the time I wasn't sure what the cause of the chase was but I saw that one of the locals had a really long knife. My partner was sitting down behind me eating his lunch so I had to react. One man was bearing down on me and I quickly picked up my weapon and cocked it. The man just stopped in his tracks because he thought I was going to shoot him. The MPs tackled him and put zip ties on his wrists and took him away. I did find out later that he was an insurgent. Even though I didn't know whether his intention was to get into the compound or to stab us—or both, I felt that I had done something that perhaps prevented bloodshed.

On another occasion I was riding in a helicopter when we were hit by ground fire. I could hear the sound of bullets ricocheting off the aircraft. I had gone on this mission to spend time away from the monotony of our duties in the compound. The pilots asked if we'd like to ride on a medevac flight and we were all for it, but it turned out to be a resupply mission bringing ammo, food, and weapons to the firebases. Firebases consisted of Special Forces teams. The teams have specialties and they basically go out downrange, or in the actual line of fire. They're fighting on the front lines and they depend heavily upon our support. When we got to the firebase we weren't allowed to land because it was deemed a hostile environment, so we ended up dropping pallets from a higher altitude.

On the way there I got to sit in the cockpit, wear a headset and listen to communications between our pilot and those on the ground. I could hear other chatter. The word "targets" got my attention and upon hearing "they're shooting," I'd heard enough. I felt sick when I left the cockpit; I went back to my seat and fell asleep. I thought to myself as we landed, "I'm never going on a resupply mission again. Never. I'll stay grounded and just fix my computers."

Regarding the weather, the desert climate is one of extremes, searing heat during the day and frigid cold at night. There was no in between, except in the early morning just as the sun was rising, which resulted in pleasantly cool weather. The temperature often rose to 115 degrees during the day, which was fine with me since I preferred hot weather.

Communication with my parents was usually very emotional; I almost dreaded calling them. I've always been full of pride and never liked to reveal my soft side, so I tried very hard not to cry although my mom would always be in tears. She'd hear noises in the background, mines and bombs going off, and would ask about the commotion. I'd tell her they were machines or tractors but I don't think she believed me. My end of the conversation would be words to the effect that I was fine and that nothing had happened to me. The fact that the media would blow things out of proportion added to her anxiety.

Although the issue of women in combat has become irrelevant as a result of the insurgency war in Iraq, I'm still somewhat sensitive to both sides of the issue. Even though I was not in the front lines during my deployments, I was there and witnessed some of the problems regarding the debate. When you compare women's abilities to men, there's a big difference. No matter what anyone says, female Soldiers have to be in top physical shape and super strong, lifting weights every day to do what some of the men do. There was no way I could pick up a fifty-pound .50-cal weapon and sling it over my shoulder. Unless you really, really think that you physically can do everything that a man can do, then I'm all for it, go for it! Some women are stronger and tougher than men. So, I think I lean more for women to be in the thick of things if they're capable. If women were allowed and if I could fulfill the requirements to be in Special Forces, I would probably be a candidate. I would love to be a part of such a group because the things they did were just awesome.

During our first deployment some of the locals continually discriminated against us because we were women in uniform, using degrading language when we were around them, often calling us names. It seemed that the first English words they learned were the most foul ones. One of them offered me twenty dollars to be his wife. We were tasked to fill sandbags, which we placed over cables when the ground was too hard. One of the locals became agitated by our work and tried to stop us, pushing us away, trying to tell us that women didn't do such work. Our presence was a controversial issue for them, especially when they had to take orders from us; they refused to deal with that.

Another memorable experience I had was with a little girl to whom I always gave hygiene gifts. She always seemed to know when I was on guard duty, at what time, and to what post I was assigned. First post was the front gate and the third was overlooking the village. When I had third post she would come up and ask for shampoo or Kleenex, whatever she could think of. This was a first because a lot of times we'd offer deodorant and a variety of hygiene items to the local workers and they'd refuse them. So I'd get out the care packages looking for things we didn't use and give them to her. And she was grateful. She threw me, maybe, five silver bracelets that were really nice. She also threw me a ring and I had to crawl under the concertina wire to get it. I motioned to her that she shouldn't feel like she had to repay me, I just wanted to give her these small offerings. I never did know her name; she was always out there with her mom who was about nine months pregnant and barefoot. The local children were skinny and barefoot. It was heartbreaking to watch them.

Speaking of children, one time when we went to Kabul, an incident occurred that made me cry in front of everybody. This lady left her daughter beside me and took off. The little girl held onto my hand like her life depended on it. We had a little boy who interpreted for us and when I asked him where her mom was, he said that she was crazy. I told him to go and find her because we were about to leave. He wanted money to do this so I gave him two dollars to search for her. He came back and said he couldn't find her. Here I was with this adorable two-year-old child clinging to me and my people calling me to go. We were on a busy street, strangers everywhere, people shooting at each other and I didn't want to leave this child alone. I just lost it and I was in tears. I couldn't believe this lady just left her daughter with me. Finally, she came back and grabbed her. She couldn't speak English but told the little boy that I was to take her, that she'd live a better life with me. The experience just made me break down, because it was difficult for me to believe to what extent these people would go to seek a better life for their children.

When I returned home from my initial deployment I learned to appreciate everything we take for granted in America, all the familiar sights I had left behind when I deployed. I didn't get to see my family for a couple of months and when I did my mom broke down in tears. She couldn't believe that I was alive and home. She kept asking if I had to go back and I tried to make her understand that I was in the Army and I couldn't just quit my job. I told her that I was almost done, that it was only four years. Then she found out I had to go a second time, and then a third time.

It was hard leaving our compound after the first deployment. We felt like we accomplished so much while we were out there. When we left everyone was proud of their work, many were awarded medals. We didn't get word about deploying again until a few months later. We had gone once and the army was rotating units to the camp so we weren't completely surprised when we left again. When we returned this time the locals remembered us, some even called me out by name. I looked for the little girl I always talked to but couldn't find her.

When we arrived the second time we found that the living conditions had been much improved. The other units that were there took over and brought in trailers that were showers. The shower conditions the first time around were disgusting. We wore flip-flops but the water was so muddy that dirt reached halfway up our shins. You had to pull a little chain to start the water flowing; the water was of unknown origin and we never asked where it came from. The water was stored in big containers that were uncovered and as the water came down a cascade of potato bugs, roaches, and spiders came with it. However, when we got the trailers, we actually had hard walls, doors that shut, and real showers that we could turn on. What a treat!

Our second deployment focused on maintaining our equipment. It was a lot easier, but we wanted to move to improve working conditions, since we were still running our operations out of a tent. We eventually moved into the main area of the JOCC. A cement floor was laid down, carpeting was put in, bookshelves were installed, and our area began to look like an office. Also, we enjoyed a new air conditioning system, which greatly improved our working environment.

I did notice that the attitude of the locals had changed since our first deployment. They were a little more lenient, open, and understanding. They weren't as mean and didn't seem to hate us as much. The local females wore less restrictive clothing now, not like the first time when they were always in burquas. They were more laid back and at ease when talking to us.

The second deployment went a lot faster than the first one, only because we knew that it would be a short tour. Food-wise, we really got lucky this time. The Special Forces compound had some really good cooks, they were awesome and were mainly responsible for the high morale we enjoyed during our deployment. They became the most important people on the compound. Dinner was the high point of the day because they made it fun; they had music playing and would always find different ways to cook the food. They began networking with some people from Jordan and we started getting steaks and seafood (crabs). We soon agreed that we were eating better than we did in the States; surf and turf became common fare on our menu.

It wasn't hard to leave on our third deployment because we knew what to expect. Also, a lot of additional improvements had been made. There was one very disappointing aspect, however, in that the unit that had relieved us trashed the place and we had to spend a whole week cleaning everything including the spaces where we ate.

When we were called up to deploy this third time they begged me to go out and train new Soldiers. They knew I wanted to stay in but didn't want to keep deploying because I wanted to finish school and keep going to college. I was taking on-line classes out there and wanted to come home and attend college. Although I was dead set on finishing college, I decided to make a final deployment.

The third deployment was a breeze. I trained new people and ran a million-dollar operation called SOR. I got to order all kinds of equipment and supplies so that for years to come Soldiers deploying to our compound wouldn't have to deal with switches blowing up, bad cables, and other common problems we faced continually.

When I returned I felt that I had done my job and that my time was done. No more Afghanistan, no more all the other places I had gone to, no more traveling. I don't think I'd ever go back since I'm out of the Army and married now. But if I weren't married and looking forward to having a family, I'd consider going out there as a contractor. We often worked with contractors and considering that they made about $90,000 a year compared with our annual military salary of $35,000, it would be appealing.

I stayed in Virginia attending Northern Virginia Community College majoring in information technology, and am in the process of transferring to George Mason University. Currently I'm working as a network tech at the Pentagon.

As I look back over my Army duty, I am proud to have served. The experience made me a stronger and more disciplined person and I learned a sophisticated trade that will be of value when I enter the civilian work force. What I'll miss most are the people I served with. As volunteers serving our country during a dangerous war they continue to give their all, especially those in the Special Forces. They truly are an awesome group of Soldiers: America's best!

Maj. Mary Biglow Krueger (MD), USA

Maj. Mary Biglow Krueger was one of the few American Soldiers who, after receiving her orders, made her own way to Afghanistan because her unit had already deployed. On 23 March 2003, she left Fort Belvoir, Virginia, and flew to Fort Benning, Georgia, and reported to the CRC; it was where Soldiers departed from to go overseas. She deployed as a single Soldier because her outfit had been in Afghanistan since the previous November. Her unique journey and experiences are described in the following excerpts from her interview of 22 October 2003.

★ ★ ★

My parents, Martha Poindexter and James Biglow, born 1940 and 1941 respectively, were both from Richmond, Virginia. Although I was born in Florida, I definitely have had the southern-Richmond-type influence in my life, evidenced by my name, Mary Virginia. Neither my parents nor grandparents were ever in the military. My father was exempt from the draft since he had scarlet fever as a child and was completing his graduate education during this time.

We moved to Massachusetts when I was about eight years old and lived in a little town called Westminster, which had a population of about five thousand.

Mary Biglow Krueger was interviewed by Kate Scott in Arlington, Virginia, on 22 October 2003. The tape and transcript are deposited at The Women's Memorial in Arlington. *Photo courtesy of the Krueger Collection*

While living there I went to Oakmont Regional High School. My dad was in technology at the time and there were a lot of development projects going on in the Northeast. My parents gave me a horse when I was very young with the stipulation that if I took care of it all by myself, I could keep it. Needless to say this was a very big thing and I abided by the rules and was able to keep the horse, which we named Capricorn. I spent many days in the saddle just riding around the countryside. Little did I know this was preparing me to ride around the barren lands of Southwest Asia twenty-five years later.

I graduated from Oakmont in 1987 and went to Houghton College in Houghton, New York, where I majored in biology, and minored in psychology. The only class in which I got a 4.0 grade in college was abnormal psychology. Houghton was a Christian liberal arts school and it had very strong biology and equestrian programs. At that time, I had a new yearling horse named Fantasy, that I was training, so my horse, my dog, my cat, and I all went to college at Houghton.

While in high school I was initially interested in becoming a vet. I interned for one year in my junior year and realized that I loved animals but hadn't yet found my calling. I was talking to the animals way too much. So, I turned to the study of human medicine and focused on premed in college.

The day I graduated from college my father said he shed "tears of joy" because I was now financially independent. This was true but I was also financially insolvent. I had spent my savings to supplement assistance by my parents to pay for college. I had no income at all. That was the first reason I got interested in the Army because a military scholarship would help me pay for medical school, plus, I always loved to travel. And, to be honest, I thought, "Gosh. Someone will keep me accountable so I don't weigh too much or get too inactive!" That was actually a perk. When I first joined the army I couldn't do one push-up and now I run marathons so that has met my intended goals. In any case, I sought out the Health Professional Scholarship Program; no one in my family had previously pursued health care as a profession.

I started medical school in September 1991 and the day that I saw how much the loans would cost was the day I applied for a military scholarship. It took until April to get through the scholarship process and I was granted a three-year scholarship that spring. My parents were glad that I was acting responsibly by paying for my medical school though I knew my choice to join the Army was a surprise to them. I was not going to go into debt when there were other options. We more or less split my college expenses. They were supportive of my choice and I don't remember them ever saying anything negative about it.

After my freshman year at medical school in Philadelphia, I went through the army Officers' Basic Course in the summer of 1992. I spent six weeks at Fort

Sam Houston, Texas. It was at Fort Houston that I was initially indoctrinated into the military. It was the first time I wore a uniform, an adventure in itself. I had to go to a clothing sales store to buy shoes and the only ones they had available were pumps with two-and-a-half-inch spike heels. Being five feet eight inches, I had never worn such heels. Who would guess this would be part of the army uniform?

So there I was teetering around in these horribly high heels and my feet were just killing me. Looking back now, I have to laugh at how I must have looked. I also remember sitting around in the classrooms for hours hearing about battalions and brigades. And, to be honest, I don't think I retained much of that. I did know how to wear my uniform correctly by the end of the course. And I did get to know and appreciate the other people who were with me because we were health care professionals, physicians, nurses, psychiatrists, psychologists, and dentists, and we had a great time. There was a strong sense of camaraderie; I still have friends today from that time who have remained good friends.

Regarding my health care profession scholarship, the first two years of my medical education consisted of sit-down clinical lectures in a classroom, which covered chemistry, science, physiology, and the like. The second two years I completed a series of rotations. Each year scholarship recipients can choose one rotation (which is a full-month block) at an Army assignment. That serves two purposes: One, it covers the student's forty-five days of reserve time for the year and, two, it gives the student some face time with programs that they will be applying to for a residency training slot. Once a student is accepted as a resident, they would be able to train additionally in a specialty of their choice.

For me, my specialty training was and continues to be family medicine. I went on three assignments at Army medical treatment facilities. I first went to Fort Lee, Virginia, reporting in December, and it was awesome. I did a surgery rotation there and really enjoyed the atmosphere, especially the camaraderie. I noticed that there was more closely knit teamwork at Fort Lee than at some of the civilian programs I had attended.

Next I went to Tripler Army Hospital in Hawaii and did obstetrics there because I wanted to do OB. I fully enjoyed my time there but didn't want to give up the chance to treat children, grandmothers and grandfathers, the whole family. That's one reason I ended up in family medicine. I liked everything in family medicine, and had this confirmed during my time at Madigan Army Medical Center.

My last assignment was at Madigan Hospital at Fort Lewis, Washington, just south of Tacoma, where I was selected for residency training and subsequently completed my family medicine residency. I ended up staying at Madigan for seven years and was selected chief resident by my peers, a position whereby you take on some of the faculty teaching and administrative responsibilities. After completion of my three years of residency training I was chosen to stay on as staff.

I think one of the reasons was because I was a woman and there were no other female faculty members on staff. I met my future husband, Keith Krueger, while at Madigan; we got married and had two children.

I was subsequently selected for the faculty development fellowship, which included a master's degree in public health and development training at Fort Lewis and the University of Washington at Seattle. After I completed my master's degree I was considered by three programs to become their residency program director, namely Tripler in Hawaii, Fort Belvoir in Virginia, and Fort Hood in Texas. We eventually selected Fort Belvoir for various reasons even though they didn't need a residency director right away. I reported to Fort Belvoir in September 2002 and took on the role of Assistant Residency Director. It was a significant change going from Madigan, a large medical center to DeWitt, a small community hospital on Fort Belvoir. I arrived off-cycle because I was completing my master's.

Fort Belvoir was a somewhat different environment than I had been in before. Again, Madigan was my only experience. There I was the old lady. I had been there as long as anybody; in fact, I was the dinosaur. The common factor between Madigan and DeWitt was the family medicine residents who welcomed me warmly.

Then, I headed to the Advanced Course at Fort Sam Houston, weeks after arriving at Fort Belvoir, so I never really settled in. My husband and children stayed in Virginia while I was at Fort Houston. Keith was working at the Defense Mapping Agency, which was on the Belvoir post.

The Officers' Advanced Course at Fort Sam was when I first realized that I was entering a life that would require separation from my husband and children. I knew that my kids were in a loving home and a safe place, and so, while I missed them, I threw myself full force into the Advanced Course workload, which was considerable, but very applicable to the chapter of my life which was about to unfold.

The mission of the Advanced Course is to bring an officer to the next level, i.e., to gain knowledge that the individual will need to have as a field grade officer. The attendees are all majors and captains. There were about 140 people in the course, and we were divided into groups of twelve. The people were a mix of nurses, veterinarians, physician's assistants, dentists, and medical services personnel. Although no one had assignments as yet, we were being prepared for the contingency of duty overseas. My small group hit it off from the start and formed an effective working and support unit.

It was what one might call continuing military education, the same system we have established in our national education system. The military has its own system and one completes educational programs to advance in their careers. This often presents a dilemma for young physicians who are instructed to complete those courses early in their careers by their career branch managers. Usually, commands do not like giving people up to go attend such advanced programs because it takes them out of a utility tour seeing patients. But, at the same time, if you don't do them, you will be put behind the ball in terms of military development. For me, it was a decision between required military education and the clinical demands of a new duty station. After discussion with the leadership at Belvoir, I was allowed to proceed to the Advanced Course. I would soon discover how fortuitous that decision was.

While I was at Fort Sam Houston, my husband called me and said, "Guess who is going to Afghanistan?"

I said, "Who? Is it Stephanie? Is it Kyle?"

He said, "No. No. No."

I said, "Is it you?"

He said, "No. It's you!"

I said, "Oh really?"

He said he heard it through the grapevine. I had a friend who worked at the hospital at Belvoir and she said it was announced at this big meeting that Mary was going to Afghanistan. I waited for about a week. I knew that they had all my contact information at the command. Yet nobody contacted me and I got to the point where I really had to find out. So I called the command and they confirmed the fact that I was on the list to go to Afghanistan and were going to contact me. I told them I didn't mind going at all, but would have really appreciated hearing it from them rather than have my husband hear it secondhand. Two weeks later I ran into my Belvoir department head as I was coming down the stairs at the Advanced Course. We exchanged greetings and he said he was there teaching a course, failing to mention anything about my forthcoming deployment. This was a strong lesson to me on how I would handle a similar situation when I was placed into a leadership position.

This situation, I believe, reflected more upon the climate at the time rather than the fact I was a woman. I certainly wouldn't want to believe that it was an intentional slight or form of discrimination. Up until that point, I had been very fortunate during my military career having had strong leadership and having experienced little to no discrimination. I think the biggest form of discrimination, in my opinion, that I have observed in the military is people not wanting to expose women to difficult or dangerous opportunities. Let me explain. For example, my friend who is in another military service is often told, "You know you are really working too hard. You should go home and be with your children." And she gets really offended by that. She thinks, "Do people say that to the men?" Are people well intentioned when they say that? Yeah, they are. But at the same time they protect you from being overly successful.

I saw this again in Afghanistan when female Soldiers were not allowed to go off base, although men were. The explanation given was, "What would I tell your parents if you were hurt?" If that's the logic, then what about the parents of male Soldiers? It didn't make sense.

I got excited about my forthcoming deployment to Afghanistan. It presented some challenges for me personally because people would question how I could look forward to this when I would be leaving my home and family. They would approach me and ask me if I was afraid. I don't remember actually being fearful except for some harrowing moments on missions in Afghanistan. But in time those feelings passed. What I do remember is what I told the people who asked these questions back then: "You know, my children are safe here and I know they are in a loving home, so I feel like this is something that I can actually do to help deny haven for terrorists who attack our country. I can't think of anything I could do to keep my children safer; the thought of people coming to my country and attacking my kids and my family and where they live, that frightens me. This is something I can do to help prevent that from happening. Or at least it is something palpable that I think I can do."

My realization that I was a Soldier and not a civilian any more definitely happened in Afghanistan. We were going on a convoy down to Kabul to take some patients and the first sergeant announced at a briefing, "Major Krueger is our convoy commander."

"Really?" I said to him later when we were in the Humvee, and he answered, "Yep. You are convoy commander."

"Well, sergeant, I've never done that before, but if you're a good teacher, I will be a fast learner."

It was then that I realized that even though I didn't know how to do all of the little specific tasks, I did have the military experience to find out how to do them and the experienced personnel to assist in filling in the gaps.

The first sergeant had put faith in the leadership represented by my rank and had the experience to know he could help with the details. It is at times like that I realized that people in the hospital respect your rank. And the rank is something I think you have to respect even more than other people respect it, because when you wear your rank you know what it means to other people and you conduct yourself accordingly. I get frustrated with other people in the military who sometimes seem to think that our only job is to take care of folks here. I do think that is one of our jobs. However, we can't forget that our first role is as military physicians, not as physicians who happen to be in the military.

Meeting some of the Soldiers overseas and seeing how they care for one another has made me even more convinced about how important that is. In particular I remember one group of guys who had been ambushed and attacked; two of their members had died and one had been shot in the leg. To watch the guy who was shot in the leg pull himself over to his buddy's bed after his surgery and help him suction out the wounds on his face. I mean, it was just heart-wrenching and humbling at the same time. That is when you realize the level of dedication that these men have. When people ask me if I was scared, I answer, "I have no right to be scared! If you could only see those eighteen- and nineteen-year-olds who are going out to the front lines! They are the ones that I am here to support. The only reason they go forward is because they believe that the best medical support and care is right behind them. That is what we need to be committed to. Those are the sort of things that have been really fomented for me and that I feel so strongly about."

Some people say being sent away is a negative. I think in proportion it doesn't have to be, and can be a great growth experience. I really enjoyed my experience in Afghanistan. I have to be careful about how loud I say that. People think I must be crazy for saying that; however, I have to disagree with them. In the military, particularly being a woman in the military, what I especially enjoy is the cama-raderie of the women with whom I worked in the field. Having other female Sol-diers to share a tent and figure out ways to fix and get around things without having brute strength was just very cool. Did we dye our hair in the field? Heck, yeah we did! Did we paint our nails? Yeah we did the whole pedicure thing! So, it doesn't mean you can't be a female. In fact, I think when you are with a group of women you actually hang on to that. You hang on to that one dimension that is uniquely female.

Are we equal to men? We are not the same, but we are equivalent, I guess. Each gender has its own strengths and weaknesses. That is what I would say is most important to recognize. I never try to be a male Soldier because I am not! And I would stink at it. I am proud of being a female Soldier, because there are unique things I bring to the table. When I hear things like, "You could get hurt," I answer, "Well, men could get hurt too or are you saying that men's lives are not as valuable?" Men's lives are just as valuable as women's lives. Men are fathers, brothers, sons, and husbands.

The subject used to come up about being attacked as a woman while I was on deployment. The people of Afghanistan looked at me as an American woman. That is not the same as an Afghan woman. I looked the men in the eye when I talked to them. They respected that and did business with me, just as they did with male leaders. One evening I did a horseback patrol through a northern town and I waved to the people on the street. At first, I may as well have been Lady Godiva sitting on that horse. They were just staring at me with their jaws open. I had my subdued body armor on and my DCUs (desert camouflage uniform) and my sidearm. When I looked them in the eye and smiled at them and waved, the tension broke, they smiled, and some of them even laughed out loud and smiled back. A few of the men got up the courage to practice their English and asked me if I needed a husband. It was then my turn to laugh.

To see how Afghan women are treated and how they view themselves made me sad. For example, when I would ask them how old they were, the answer they would give me was, "I am a Kucchi woman." Kucchi is one of the nomad tribes and it actually means "wanderer" in Pashtun (Pashtun is one of the two main languages spoken in Afghanistan). Her complete answer was "I am a Kucchi woman. God only knows," and would put her hands up. Every woman said this to me; it

Courtesy of the Krueger Collection

Courtesy of the Krueger Collection

was a "pat" response. "I am a Kucchi woman. I am born. I wander the earth like a cow, I suffer and then I die. What does it matter how old I am?" It made me sad that they thought this is what they are actually worth.

What these responses made me do, whenever I was out and about, was to concentrate on looking them straight in the eye, right through the burqua screen and address them as a human. I would smile and wave at the women and little girls to show them that there was an alternative to being property, to just existing. Now, is my way right and theirs wrong? I can't say that. From an American perspective, sure. But, one of my interpreters explained to me the Afghan perspective, "Look at them. We cover our women because we honor them. And they don't have to worry about being hooted and hollered at." So there are different ways to look at it. When I heard my interpreter's statement, it caused me to stop and reflect on how much our cultural assumptions color how we judge the messages of customs and norms.

The most common health problems facing Afghani women surround pregnancy and birth, i.e, maternity-related death. Actually, the average Afghani woman has six children. The average child has a 20 percent chance of dying before the age of twelve. The highest ever reported maternal mortality rates have been reported in the Badakshan province of Afghanistan, the highest ever reported in the history of the world. The two most common causes of death in women are hemorrhage and obstructed labor. They will either bleed out or the baby gets stuck. These women are very little because they are malnourished. When they get pregnant and have babies, they are not big enough to deliver them sometimes. Other health problems are anemia and goiter irregularities.

In many places we visited, there were no medical facilities for women beyond our Army clinics. For some time, I was the first doctor they had ever seen. For that reason they were very pushy with me; they certainly were not shy. They were trying to make the most of their opportunity to access medical care for themselves and their children. That was one thing I had to remind myself about. By the end of the day, when you're seeing several hundred patients, it can get frustrating because you're trying to care for people while also moving them along. In their minds they were thinking, "This is the first time I've seen a doctor and I'm going to make sure she checks out everything!" One time they actually mobbed our tent. There were about fifty Afghani police with us and they couldn't keep the women back. They were crawling through the tent, ripping it aside. I mean it was pretty intense! Anyone who thinks an Afghani woman is meek should think again. They are vibrant and proud. I thoroughly enjoyed the opportunity to spend time with these wonderful women.

How I initially got to Afghanistan is a story well worth telling. I left Belvoir on 23 March 2003, and flew down to Fort Benning, Georgia, where they have the CRC. Basically, it is where people as individuals are processed for deployment overseas. Here is what happened. I was PROFISed to the 48th Combat Support Hospital out of Fort Meade, Maryland. It had already been on the ground in Bagram, Afghanistan, since November of the prior year. I hadn't gone in the first wave, because I was just coming back from the Officer's Advanced Course at that time. I was supposed to replace another woman who was to leave Afghanistan at three months. However, she decided to stay longer because her fiancé was there. And, so she stayed for four months.

I was actually only supposed to stay there for a two-month block. I was going as an individual, so I went through the CRC. After five days at CRC, they gave me a plane ticket back to BWI Airport, telling me that my unit was at Fort Meade, Maryland. Even though I informed them that the hospital had already deployed they were bent on sending me to Baltimore.

The outcome was that I decided to find my own way to Afghanistan. I went to BWI, which had a Military Air Transport terminal there and showed them my orders and they got me on a hop to Frankfurt, Germany. Although there was nothing going to Afghanistan for a few weeks I managed to get a seat on an aircraft that had landed to refuel. The C-17 was en route to Kabul not too far from my destination, Bagram. After I arrived in Kabul, some American civil affairs people provided me with transportation to Bagram. It was a unique journey but I made it and was ready for what lay ahead!

*1st Lt. Rebecca Moore,
USMC*

As of this writing, 1st Lt. Rebecca Moore, USMC, has been stationed at Camp Blue Diamond, Ar Ramadi, Iraq. She considers Rockville, Maryland, her hometown, although she grew up in various places because her father was in the Navy. She graduated from the University of Pittsburgh in 2003 and was commissioned a 2nd Lt. in the Marine Corps. She was promoted to 1st Lt. in May 2005. She has two brothers, one of whom is currently serving in Baghdad as a member of a National Guard unit.

＊　＊　＊

My name is 1st Lt. Rebecca Moore. I'm twenty-four years old and an adjutant in the United States Marine Corps, serving with Headquarters Battalion, 2nd Marine Division, currently located at Camp Blue Diamond in Ar Ramadi, Iraq, which is in western Iraq. It's about seventy miles west of Baghdad. We see a good amount of action here, but so far I've had a very good experience.

Camp Blue Diamond is a forward operating base that has about 1,600 people on it. That includes several different commands. Almost all of them are Marine commands, but there are some Army and Navy personnel here as well. There's also a support group of around 250 civilians who work at anything from serving food in the chow hall to taking care of our electricity and our plumbing.

Rebecca Moore was interviewed by Kate Scott in Arlington, Virginia, on 8 December 2005. The tape and transcript are deposited at The Women's Memorial in Arlington. *Photo courtesy of the Moore Collection*

Our mission is basically to support the commanding general of the division with all of the functions that he needs to be able to shoot, move, and communicate, in order to guide the 2nd Marine Division that operates throughout the Al Anbar province of Iraq.

The camp pretty much just exists to house the headquarters of the 2nd Marine Division, which is actually in the process of transitioning to another location. Our division has been here for the last year, and before that it housed the 1st Marine Division, and before that several different Army commands. The base has been in existence since the spring of 2003.

The base actually used to be the grounds and the palace of a summer home that belonged to the Hussein family, and Uday (Saddam's brother) primarily used it. There are two large palaces on the western end of the camp, and then the rest of the camp has some smaller outbuildings that would be used to house guests and family members. There are also more buildings that were used to support the family. There's a garage for vehicle maintenance, and electrical generators to produce electricity. A part of the camp on the eastern end was at one time used as hunting grounds. They used to release animals out into this hunting area for dignitaries and visiting guests to hunt and shoot game. It's a pretty small area when it comes to hunting, probably only five or six acres.

As the adjutant for my battalion, regarding my daily duties, I am a Marine staff officer whose responsibility is to oversee the administrative functions of the command. I have a shop that accommodates six Marines (clerks), and then I have one chief (my senior staff noncommissioned officer). We cater to the administrative needs of the battalion, which numbers about two thousand now. We process awards, pay, promotions, fitness reports, casualty data, and provide postal services. We also do some processing of security clearances.

I wear "cammies" to work every day. They're digital MARPAT cammies. They're the ones that look like digital pixels, and they're in desert colors, so they're pretty much tan looking. I wear the same thing every day, which gets a little bit boring, but at least I don't have to pick out what to wear.

I usually work from about 7:00 AM 'til 9:00 PM, so I probably work about fourteen hours a day. Sometimes a little longer, sometimes a little less; it depends how busy it is. But I'm on duty pretty much all the time. So if something happens in the middle of the night, they come wake me up, and I come down to my office, and I do whatever it is I have to do.

As far as daily work, we just do whatever it is the Marines or the battalion need us to do. Whether it's fixing pay problems, or printing off promotion warrants or awards—I've been processing a lot of awards, because the Marines have been doing really great things, and they're being recognized for it. Especially now, as we come towards the end of our deployment, we've been doing a lot of awards.

1st Lt. Moore is shown presenting awards to two of her Marines at Camp Blue Diamond, Al Ramadi, Iraq. *Courtesy of Moore Collection*

By the nature of my job, I have to be in the office. I have been on a couple of convoys. When we came out here, we convoyed in, and it was at night, and it was about a three-hour drive. The weather was pretty cold. That was in March. You can't see too much when it's dark out; there's just a lot of desert out there. Then I went on a convoy to another base in April or May; I actually went to visit my fiancé for an hour or two. Just to say hello. Also, I did a little walk-around tour of that base to see how it was functioning there as well. So that was my excuse for going. But I don't really go outside of the wire too much. I definitely don't go on any patrols, so I pretty much stay in my office and on base all the time.

Regarding convoy travel, it can be pretty dangerous. The reason for that is because we're in hostile territory all the time. The only places that are truly secure are the forward-operating bases out here, and even those get attacked. One of the primary enemy TTPs is to use IEDs. They are made up of different types of explosives that get triggered either by a remote device or a triggerman who actually pushes the button and fires the weapons. They specifically target our convoys, and they watch us all the time. They try to figure out how we operate and what our procedures are, and they target specific vehicles, depending on who they think they are carrying.

So it can be pretty dangerous. But luckily the Marines out here who operate the vehicles know what to look for. We have drills and we all know what to do and how to react when we run into one. A lot of times they'll spot them before it ever becomes a problem, and then they just call in a specialized team to come and detonate the device in place, so nobody gets hurt. But other times it will hit a vehicle. Marines and Sailors and Soldiers probably die or get hurt just about every day from IEDs. I don't mean to speculate that someone dies every single day, but there have certainly been a lot of casualties.

I've had a few frightening experiences. On one occasion my life wasn't in danger at all, but I didn't know it at the time. I had been in Iraq for several months, and I was eating in the chow hall. I was sitting there with my staff sergeant and some other Marines, and we were just talking. All of a sudden we heard this really, really, really loud noise. It sounded like an airplane at first, but rocket motors also sound like airplanes, depending on how close they are, and how far away an airplane could be. We all looked at each other, and then everybody just hit the deck. Not that the plastic tables in the chow hall were going to save us from anything, but we just did it on instinct. This was all in two or three seconds, and I remember thinking, oh, my gosh, somebody must be really in trouble if they're calling for close air support. Because that's what it sounds like when the planes come in real close to drop munitions. Then it got closer. I was like, oh, my God, is this a rocket about to hit the exact building I'm sitting in right now? It turned out that it was an airplane, like I thought originally, but it's kind of a chain reaction, that everybody hit the deck. We were all just like, oh, my gosh, we're all about to die.

The plane was coming from the city—the downtown area of our city and there's a river between us and it. There had been a demonstration in the downtown area, and we were doing what we call a show of force, which is one method to break up large crowds which can oftentimes be dangerous because you can't see what's going on inside of the crowds and if somebody's about to blow themselves up. So they just called in for an airplane to come in very close and startle the crowd and get them all to go home. Which worked, but they didn't tell us about it. So it was a scary moment, but it ended up that it really wasn't that we were in danger at all, because it was a friendly aircraft.

Another time I had a good scare was when I was traveling in a helicopter from my base to Baghdad. It was late at night and completely dark, and all of a sudden the helo banked really hard to the right. That kind of made me jump and at the same time three or four small arms fire rounds flew past the window going straight up into the air. The rounds must have been tracer rounds, because I could see them so clearly in the dark. We didn't fire back because there was no way to identify exactly where the rounds came from.

We get indirect fire on a pretty regular basis. It kind of tapers off. It comes and goes in waves. It doesn't really startle me. Even the very first time it happened, I just thought that it was really loud. It's just a big explosion. Even then, it kind of makes you jump for a second, but then you realize what it was and that nobody's hurt. Then you just have to wait and see what happened.

When we first got here, we would probably get indirect fire two or three times every two weeks, so maybe four or six times a month, or less. But then it kind of tapered off. It's really hard to tell what they're doing out there. They shoot when they can, where they can, and they just hope that they kill one of us. They don't have the same kind of discipline and organization that we have. It's not that they're not a smart enemy. They certainly keep us on the alert, trying to see what our next move is going to be, but they just don't have the same kind of leadership and equipment and capabilities that the American military has.

We certainly don't like the enemy, and when they randomly fire at us we joke about it, thinking oh, gosh, they're attacking us again, and now we can't go outside and run. Or now we can't go down to the gym, because there are rounds coming in. But it's hard to have an emotion like hate or anything towards them because they don't have a face. I know what they're doing, but I've never necessarily seen anybody doing it.

I think the biggest emotion I have towards it is, what are you guys thinking? How do you possibly think that you're ever going to beat us? That may sound cocky or arrogant, but it's ridiculous to think of the size of their force, and the kind of equipment and training they have compared to us, and it's like what do you think you're accomplishing? You have to try to get inside their mind, and I think that they think they are revolutionaries who are trying to save their country and their religion. That's not the case, in my opinion, but I don't know what they're thinking, and that's the only thing I can come up with.

It's really amazing to see how the local populace, the people who are just regular Iraqi citizens and who aren't involved in the insurgency, see them. I don't watch the news so much out here, but I know a lot of the times the media portrays that we're losing, or we're getting our butts kicked, and the Iraqi people don't like us, and that is not true at all. There are Iraqis who give us tips all the time of impending attacks, or where we can go to find weapons caches, or where we can go to find bad guys who attacked us or who killed our Marines. They want to help; it's their neighborhood, and it's their children who are getting hurt.

I haven't had any encounters with Iraqi women. For about the first eight months we were here, we used to send females to augment the regimental combat teams in Fallujah, which is a city that's about an hour east of here. Basically, because of the Muslim ideas about women, the male Marines and Soldiers can't search women, because they can't touch them. So they used our female Marines to search the women as they would come in and out of the cities, to find out if they were trying to bring any kind of contraband into the city. In this regard there was a costly incident for Marine women in June of last year (2005).

That's actually how one of my Marines died. She was a searcher out there. Basically what happened is: we would send female Marines out there for a month at a time, and some of them would extend if they wanted to stay there and continue serving that mission. They basically worked shifts, working at the ECPs, to the city. They stood guard right there beside the men. If a woman was trying to come into the city, and she needed to be searched, one of the females would search her instead of one of the males.

I never went out there, but I had two female Marines out there with the troops. One of them was killed, and the other just left to go back to the States a couple days ago. She said it was pretty hard work; it was long hours in the hot sun, and you don't really get to do anything besides just work all day and then sleep all night. But she enjoyed it, and I think it was a very rewarding experience for them. I think that it would be. I would love to be able to work with the Iraqi people, especially the women and children, but it's just not what my job entailed.

The Marine I lost was Cpl. Holly Charette. When she was killed, she was a lance corporal, and she was posthumously promoted to the rank of corporal. As I said, she was serving in Fallujah as a female searcher at one of the ECPs. She had been there awhile and was slated to come home in about four or five days. What happened was that they were transporting some of the females back from the ECP to the barracks where they lived, and it was at nighttime, probably around seven or eight o'clock at night. They were in a truck, in a convoy, going from the ECP to the barracks, and as they were driving down one of the streets, a car approached the convoy. We have different procedures to make sure that civilian traffic stays out of our convoys. It involves flashing lights at them so they know to stop, or using hand and arm signals to get them to stay away, and if they don't heed those, you can shoot at the vehicle—a warning shot—and if they don't correctly respond, then you shoot to kill, because in that case they have displayed hostile intent, and it could very easily be a suicide vehicle-borne IED.

What happened was that the vehicle approached the convoy, and the Marines did what they were supposed to do. They got the vehicle to stop, and it stopped and pulled off to the median, but then, after it stopped, and the convoy kept going, it pulled back in towards the convoy, and ran directly into the truck that Corporal Charette was traveling in, and it blew up. It flipped the truck on the side, which is pretty amazing because those trucks weigh several tons and have armor all over them.

In conjunction with this attack, it's what we would call a complex attack because there was also small-arms fire, which is rifle fire or pistol fire, but generally they use AK-47 automatic rifles. So it was a pretty bad attack, and I'm not sure what the exact count of casualties was, but just from our battalion, we had two Marines die; six or seven were pretty badly burned. They ended up having to go home and

Cpl. Holly Charette, USMC. *Courtesy of Moore Collection*

be treated at the Brooke Medical Burn Center in San Antonio, Texas, where some of them stayed for months. I think all of them are released now. But in addition to the physical scars, they certainly have emotional scars, too.

One of the Marines who was badly burned, Cpl. Teresa Fernandez, is a good Marine. She actually tried to pull my Marine from the burning vehicle, and that's why she got burned, on her hands, arms, and face. Anyway, what ended up happening was that Corporal Charette got badly burned and suffered wounds to her thigh and neck. I think they said the wounds were caused by shrapnel.

She was taken to one of the local aid stations at one of our medical clinics. They tried to operate on her, but she basically ended up dying on the operating table. I found out about the attack when I returned to work after teaching an SAT prep class to about ten Marines.

I was coming back from class, and when I walked in, my chief came to me immediately and he said, "Ma'am, you need to go talk to the XO," and I thought, oh, gosh, I wonder what happened.

I walked in and I said, "Hey, sir, what's going on?"

He said, "We just had a mass casualty situation in Fallujah, an IED hit one of the convoys with the females, and Lance Corporal Charette was in one of the trucks."

I said okay, this is where I start praying very hard. So I did. Two of my Marines were in the shop, and they knew what had happened. So I just waited for further word, started getting together whatever casualty reports that we needed to get together, and then about fifteen or twenty minutes later, the executive officer called me back into his office, and he said, "You want to sit down for this." So I did, and he said, "They took Lance Corporal Charette into the operating room, and they tried to save her, but she died." And so then I took a deep breath, and had to carry on.

I didn't tell the Marines that night, because it's very important that we keep confidentiality so that the next of kin can be notified before it ever gets leaked to the press or anybody else finds out and then contacts the family back home, because the family needs to hear it from the casualty assistance call officer, not from somebody else. But what ended up happening is that I did go and tell my other female Marine, who was very good friends with Lance Corporal Charette. I took her into an office, and I said, this is going to be a tough blow, but this is what just happened. She was very upset, which is totally understandable, but she was also very, very strong about it. She got the initial shock and crying out of her system, and I even told her, if you don't want to come into work right away tomorrow, that's fine. Take your time; get a good night's sleep. Just come in when you're ready. She said, "No, ma'am. I have to be there. I have to sort the mail."

It just wrenched my heart, because Corporal Charette was our mail clerk, and Corporal Dixon, the other Marine, was only sorting the mail because Charette wasn't there. So to think that she wanted to come in to get the mission accomplished even though Lance Corporal Charette had died so suddenly, it just really touched me as a leader that my Marines were so strong, and I was very proud of them for being able to handle it so graciously.

I'll never forget Corporal Charette. Her first name was Holly, but I of course always just called her Lance Corporal Charette. I know I keep going back and forth between her ranks because when I knew her she was a lance corporal, and then she was promoted later on. I never knew her as Corporal Charette.

But in any event, she was a very, very vibrant and bubbly, very personable type of woman. She was cute and had a big smile, and she got to touch a lot of the Marines' and Sailors' lives in our battalion since she did the mail. She sorted the mail and she handed it out to them, and especially out here mail is such a big deal because it's your care packages from home and your letters from your friends and everything. So she was that Marine that everybody knew, she was always smiling, and she was always kind of a breath of fresh air in our shop because she didn't take anything too seriously. She always had a good sense of humor, and she was a very good Marine; she was an excellent mail clerk, too, because she was very dedicated to her job, and she would inspect our mailroom on a regular basis to make sure everything was in accordance with the orders that we have to follow. She made sure that all the mail got out as soon as possible, and if mail had to be rerouted or resent somewhere, she did it. She was extremely dedicated.

Charette was from Rhode Island. Her mother and she were very, very close. I wrote a letter to both of her parents after she died. The mother never replied directly to me, but through the casualty assistance call officer, she stated that she wanted to know when we would be coming home, so she could come to North Carolina and meet all of us. Which is going to be difficult. But it will be great to be able to see her and meet her. I'm sure it's very important for her in the grieving process.

Coping with Charette's loss was difficult. At that time I had four other roommates, and we were all lieutenants and all female, and we just kind of stuck together through everything, through this kind of thing, and through the good times and the bad. They really helped me a lot to be able to grieve properly, but also to be able to carry on with what I had to do. My other Marines were also really good about it. It amazed me because coming out here, you know it's possible, but you certainly never think it's going to happen, that one of your Marines is actually going to get killed. Especially for me, because I do administration. We work in an office; we're not the ones who go out on patrol and get shot at every day. So it was a big surprise, a terrible surprise.

The morning after it happened, I got all my Marines together, sat them down and told them what happened. "It's totally normal for you to feel sad and angry and disappointed, every kind of emotion you could possibly feel. But the important thing is that we as a section stick together and we show everyone else that we can be strong. It's not about hiding your tears or pretending that you're not upset, but it is about making sure you can still continue to carry on this mission and do your job." And that's exactly what they did. They grieved in private, and they grieved together, and they grieved through us talking as a section and remembering Lance Corporal Charette, at the memorial service that was held. But when it all came down to it, they put on their game face for work, and people were totally amazed. People said to me, I can't believe that your Marines are so put together and so open about it. Like I said, it's not that they weren't upset, but they just didn't want everyone else to get all down in the dumps and glum about it happening. They had to put on the strong face and that's exactly what they did.

Since we had two of the Marines die at the same time, we had a joint service for them. We had it at our chapel; there were two of them, one in the morning and one in the afternoon, and it was just amazing the number of people that were there. It was just totally packed to the hilt, standing-room-only type of thing. They had pictures up of the Marines, several different pictures. They did the little set-up that you see in the pictures with the rifle turned upside down with the helmet on top and the dog tags draping over it, which touches your heart when you see it. When I was inventorying her personal effects, I took one of her pairs of dog tags, so it could be her dog tags on the rifle and not just a fake set. I put her dog tags on it with her crucifix attached to it, and then I took them and mailed them back to her family later on.

The chaplain got up and said a few words, and we sang some songs, like "Eternal Father," and I got up and I gave a little speech about remembering her life and how she left such a positive effect on everyone, especially with delivering the mail. It was definitely tough. You can tell even right now I'm still getting a little bit choked up thinking about it. Having to do it three days after it happened was difficult but I made it through it.

One of the things about the whole experience that stands out to me is that I think a lot of people see Marines as a very stoic and unemotional bunch, that they are just Soldiers and their only purpose is to be warriors. There's no emotion and there's no sadness and there's no tears, and that's not true. We're human beings just the same as anybody else. Do we have to be professional and carry on with the mission, yes, but emotions like that are totally natural, and I think everybody does understand that. There were some of our toughest Marines at the service who got a little misty-eyed. Together with my other Marines, we pulled together and got through it, and we're more experienced people for it. We'll always carry Holly in our hearts.

People who say that women shouldn't be in combat and get caught up on that kind of thinking are generally people who don't really know a lot about what's going on over here. Even for people who read the newspapers and try to formulate their own opinion, they don't know what it's really like. They can't know unless they've been over here. It just blows my mind that people who have never even served in the military, been deployed, or been in combat, can try to formulate opinions and make decisions based on what they think is right. Me, personally, I wouldn't be averse to going out and going on patrols. If I had the opportunity, I would probably jump at it.

But it's certainly a very difficult experience, on your body and on your mind. Some days, especially during the summer when it was so hot, I was glad I didn't have to be outside all day, going out and fighting the good fight. But if I had the opportunity, I would probably have taken it, and at least had that experience.

Christmas season this past year was different, because obviously there wasn't the being together with your family, and getting dressed up and going to church, and putting up the decorations, and hanging out with everybody and having the fire lit, and everything. But we made the best of it, and I think we had a pretty good time. People mailed all kinds of decorations out here. We had everything up. I had all kinds of garlands up, and ornaments hanging—we actually even got real Christmas trees. I don't know where they came from, but they just showed up. We put one up in our conference room, which is one of our common areas.

My mom sent us out some Christmas ornaments, so we decorated it. We even had Christmas lights. But there wasn't waking up on Christmas morning and opening presents. I think we made the most of it.

Being out here for so long with the same people, you live with them, you work with them, you eat with them, you see them every day, and so they kind of become your family, as clichéd as that sounds. We exchanged gifts, and I made stockings for all of my Marines and filled them up with candy and key chains that I made. It wasn't your quote unquote normal Christmas, but it was definitely a very memorable Christmas. It's in a good place in my heart that I'll like to remember it and recall it later on down the line.

During my deployment, I've made some really, really strong friends out here, with the other women that I served with, and it's really kind of amazing that we all got put together in the same place at the same time because we're all so much alike. We go to each other with everything. We laugh about the funny things that happen, and we complain about the jerks that are out there, and we eat together and we all share the same room. So that's been really positive. We've had some great times, in terms of that. I think, for me, coming out here with my Marines and really being a leader has been a huge positive experience for me, especially in my line of work, because I'm in administration and I'm a staff officer, I don't have my own platoon like a lot of lieutenants start out with, i.e., a platoon of like forty people. The most Marines I've ever had is thirteen. But we've all grown. It's just amazing to look back at how young some of my Marines seemed when we got here, and now how much they've grown just from being out here, just from being around the violence and having to deal with the casualties, and talking to their friends about what happens out there, and being away from home, and not having all the comforts and having to adapt to what you have out here. They really impressed me, and I like to think that I had a little bit to do with their growth. That's been a very positive experience.

I think my deployment is definitely the highlight of my career, so far, because as Marines we're constantly training to go out and fight, to another area of the world, and bring peace, or democracy, or whatever the mission is, to people who don't have it. So it's kind of like you're always gearing up for the big show, and then wow here we are; it's the big show. I think that when I look back on it twenty years from now, I'm sure I'll remember the friendships that I made and the fun times we had, and though it's not a positive thing, I'll always think about Lance Corporal Charette.

The first meal I want to have when I get back will be Taco Bell for starters. Then maybe I'll get a good steak or something after that. The food out here is actually pretty good, but it's very repetitive. They just repeat the same menus over and over again. It's like, oh, my gosh, if I have to eat spaghetti and meatballs one more time.

Being a part of a Marine Corps team in the global war on terror is just one of the best things I can ever imagine doing with my life, because I truly, truly believe in what we're doing over here, and feel like, as Americans, it's our obligation. We're a wealthy and powerful country, and it's our obligation to help people who don't have what we have, to be able to have better lives. That's what we're doing over here. We're bringing peace to this region, and we're building schools, and giving the kids soccer balls, and restoring the infrastructure of their cities that were substandard to begin with, and even worse because of the war. They just don't even know what to do with their freedom, some of them, and it's really great, I think, that the United States has stepped up to take this on and really make a difference in the world.

And to be able to say I was a part of it, I mean I don't feel like my existence here is really as huge as I guess some people might think that it is. A lot of people back home want to call us all heroes and I don't feel that way at all, but I feel proud, especially as a woman, to be able to say I deployed to Iraq, and fought in the global war on terror. Even though maybe I never pulled a trigger, I enabled people to be able to protect the lives of the Iraqis and help them to have better lives. It's something I'm always going to be able to say, "I was a Marine and I went to Iraq." I just think that's so cool. And I'm proud to be doing it. I am very, very grateful to be here and to be a part of this, and I'm just very happy that I've had the opportunity and that I made it this far.

With all the training we go through, I think there are definitely times when you feel like, whoa, what did I sign up for? But I made it through that, and now here I am, and this is exactly what I want to be doing. I love my job, I love the people that I'm able to work with, and I love to think that I'm maybe making a difference in someone's life.

Maj. Marie T. Rossi-Cayton, USA

On 2 August 1990 Iraq invaded its southern neighbor, oil-rich Kuwait. More than 100,000 Iraqi soldiers overran the small nation in six days. Iraq President Saddam Hussein justified his action by accusing Kuwait of deliberately harming his nation by encroaching on its territory, stealing its oil, and destroying its economy. Censured by the United Nations Security Council, a trade embargo was imposed on Iraq and occupied Kuwait.

When Iraqi troops began to mass on the Saudi Arabian border, the Saudi government requested that President Bush deploy American forces to safeguard its border, fearing that Iraq might invade their country. Bush agreed and, with the pledge of support from other countries, a multinational force was positioned in Saudi Arabia by the end of 1990 to counter a potential attack by Iraq. This defensive deployment became known as Desert Shield.

The United Nations Security Council gave Iraq until 15 January 1991 to unconditionally withdraw from Kuwait. Although America and Iraq representatives met several times to discuss the growing crisis, Iraq continued to occupy Kuwait. On 17 January 1991 U.S. attack aircraft bombed targets in Iraq and Kuwait and multinational ground forces crossed the Saudi border to engage the Iraq army. The war ended within four days when a defeated Iraqi army surrendered in mass numbers as other troops fled Kuwait.

Photo courtesy of The Women's Memorial

U.S. forces in the war numbered approximately 700,000, of which 33,300 were women. The women participated in a vast array of support roles including the flying of unarmed helicopters, transport aircraft, and AWACS planes.

Among the American military personnel captured during the war were two servicewomen, Maj. Rhonda Cornum, an army flight surgeon, and Spc4 Melissa Rathbun-Nealy. Both were later released. Thirteen military women were killed during Desert Shield and Desert Storm.

The last of those who lost their lives in Desert Storm was Maj. Marie T. Rossi-Cayton, an army helicopter pilot who was awarded the Bronze Star, Purple Heart, and Air Medal posthumously. She was buried with full military honors at Arlington National Cemetery on 11 March 1991, the only female Gulf War casualty to be so honored at that time.[1]

★ ★ ★

Marie T. Rossi-Cayton was born on 3 January 1959 in Oradell, New Jersey, the third of four children. Her father, Paul Rossi, was a decorated Marine during World War II and worked as treasurer of a book-binding company. Her mother, Gertrude, worked as a secretary on Wall Street.

Rossi showed natural leadership abilities as a young girl, and was active in the Girl Scouts and 4-H, as well as working as a lifeguard and joining the swim club in high school. After graduating from River Dell Regional High School in 1976, Rossi enrolled at Dickinson College in Carlisle, Pennsylvania, where she entered the ROTC program while pursuing a psychology degree. Rossi discovered that she liked the military, and considered it as a career.

After graduating in June 1980, Rossi was commissioned a second lieutenant in the U.S. Army on 27 August 1980, and was sent to Fort Bliss, Texas, to attend the ADA Officer's Basic Course, followed by the ADA Command and Control Course in 1981. After training, Rossi was assigned to Alpha Battery, 3rd ADA Training Battalion, 1st ADA Brigade at Fort Bliss with a promotion to first lieutenant, winning the Army Achievement Medal for her performance as executive officer of Delta Battery.

In 1985, Rossi volunteered and was accepted for flight training and was sent to Fort Rucker, Alabama, for the Officer Rotary Wing Aviator program. After graduating in 1986 on the commandant's list as rotary wing pilot, she was sent to the Aviation Officer Advanced Class in 1987. Following the completion of her training, Rossi was sent overseas to South Korea to fly Chinook helicopters assigned to the 213th Combat Aviation Company. While in Korea, she met her future husband, Chief Warrant Officer (CWO3) John Andrew Cayton, who was also a chopper pilot. They married in 1990.

Returning stateside after the completion of her overseas tour in 1989, Rossi was sent to Hunter Army Airfield in Georgia where she took command of Second Platoon, Company A, 1/58th Aviation Regiment. On 11 June 1990, she was promoted to major and commanding officer of Company B, 2/159th Aviation Regiment. During this period, she also attended the Combined Arms and Services Staff School at Fort Leavenworth, Kansas.

Rossi was deployed overseas to Dhahran, Saudi Arabia, for Operation Desert Shield on 19 September 1990. She flew missions delivering troops, supplies, and ammunition and was one of the first officers to fly into enemy territory, in support of the 101st Airborne and the 18th Aviation Brigade, at the start of Operation Desert Storm. She gained national attention when she was interviewed on CNN on 24 February 1991, one day before the ground phase of the war began. Commenting on a remark that she would be one of the first U.S. military to cross over into Iraq once the war started, she stated that, "Personally, as an aviator and a Soldier, this is the moment that anybody trains for, so I feel ready for the challenge." Like any Soldier who had been trained for battle, she was willing to die if necessary, and felt that her death would be no greater tragedy than that of one of her male colleagues.

Several days later, on 1 March 1991, Major Rossi and three of her four-man crew were killed when her helicopter hit an unlit microwave tower in bad weather at night in Northern Saudi Arabia. They were returning from a mission transporting Iraqi POWs. Her lost crewmen included CWO Robert Hughes, SSgt. Mike Green, and Spc4 William C. Brace. Gunner specialist Brian Miller survived but was seriously wounded.

Ironically, Rossi died on the day following the cease-fire. She was buried with full military honors at Arlington National Cemetery on 11 March 1991, the only female Gulf War casualty to be so honored at that time.

Her statue is displayed in the Aviation Hall of Fame at Fort Rucker, but perhaps the memorial closest to the true Marie Rossi-Cayton is the one on her tombstone that marks her resting place at Arlington. Designed by her husband, it is inscribed "May Our Men and Women Stand Strong and Equal!"

In 1993, Rossi was chosen as a symbol of the female veteran, appearing on posters promoting the creation of a memorial honoring Women In Military Service For America. On 18 October 1997, The Women's Memorial was dedicated and opened to the public. It is situated on 4.2 acres of land at the ceremonial entrance to Arlington National Cemetery. The Women's Memorial is the first major U.S. memorial honoring women who have served in our nation's armed forces during all eras and in all services.[2]

ENDNOTES

1. Kassner, Elizabeth. *Desert Storm Journal: A Nurse's Story.* Lincoln Center, MA: The Cottage Press, 1993; Cipkowski, Peter. *Understanding The Crisis in the Persian Gulf.* New York: John Wiley & Sons, Inc., 1992; Lewis, Vickie. *Side-By-Side: A Photographic History of American Women in War.* New York: Stewart, Tabori & Chang, 1999.
2. Francke, Linda, journalist. "Hers: Requiem for a Soldier." *The New York Times* Magazine, 21 April 1991; http://arlingtoncemetery.net/mariethe.htm; Army Aviation Hall of Fame 1992 Induction of Major Marie T. Rossi-Cayton, USA; http://www.quad-a.org/Hall of Fame/personnel/rossi-cayton.htm; "Marie Rossi, Gulf War Casualty." *People* Weekly, Summer 1991, p. 12(4); http://web2.searchbank.com/itw/session/566/546/30864411w3/106!aln_2+0+0; *The 15 Most Intriguing People of the War: Marie Rossi.* Lexis Nexis Academic Universe Database, Spring/Summer 1991, p.12.

Soldiers pose on an Apache helicopter in Baghdad, Iraq. *Courtesy of Maj. Ann Kramarich, USA*

Lt. Carol Watts, USN (center) flies with her hands as she discusses with Lt. Lyndsi Bates (right) her night-time strike against Iraq, after returning on board the aircraft carrier USS *Enterprise* (CVN 65) during Operation Desert Fox. Watts was a F/A-18C Hornet pilot from the Strike Fighter Squadron 37, Naval Air Station Cecil Field, Florida. *Courtesy of PO 3rd Class Tedrick E. Fryman III, USN*

Capt. Jaden Kim, USMC, flying a mission over Baghdad, Iraq. *Courtesy of the Kim Collection*

1st Lt. Jeannie Flynn, USAF, poses behind a model of an F-15E Strike Eagle. Lieutenant Flynn was the first female to enter the Air Force fighter pilot training program. *Courtesy of Airman Holly Castano, USAF*

SSgt. Karen Fulce, USAF, 401st Aircraft Generation Squadron, checks Mark 84 two-thousand-pound bombs as the ordnance is readied for loading aboard 401st Tactical Fighter Wing F-16 Fighting Falcon aircraft. The aircraft conducted the first daylight strike against Iraqi targets during Operation Desert Storm. *Courtesy of SSgt. Lee E. Corkran, USAF*

Capt. Kim Reed Campbell, USA ("Killer Chick"), an A-10 Thunderbolt II pilot deployed with the 332nd Air Expeditionary Wing, surveys the battle damage to her plane. Campbell's A-10 was hit over Baghdad during a close air support mission. *Courtesy of USA*

The first female F-16 Fighting Falcon pilot, 2nd Lt. Kristin L. Bass, USAF, of the 188th fighter wing, gets strapped into her F-16C Fighting Falcon by crew chief TSgt. Kevin J. Jones. *Courtesy of SmSgt. Dennis L. Brambl, USAF*

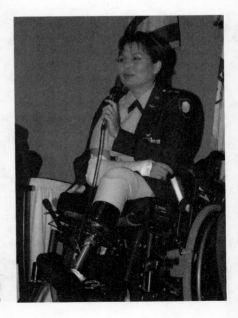

Maj. Ladda Tammy Duckworth, USANG, speaking on the significance of Veterans Day 2005 at The Women's Memorial, Arlington National Cemetery. *Courtesy of Donna H. Parry Collection*

Sgt. Leigh Ann Hester, USA, stands at attention before receiving the Silver Star during an awards ceremony at Camp Liberty, Iraq, on 16 June 2005. Sergeant Hester was assigned as a vehicle commander with the 617th Military Police Company of the Kentucky National Guard and is the first female soldier to receive the Silver Star since World War II. *Courtesy of Spc. Jeremy D. Crisp, USA*

Spc. Melissa Rathbun-Nealy, the first female to be taken as a prisoner of war by Iraqi forces during Operation Desert Storm, holds her mother's hand as she listens to a speech by Secretary of Defense Richard Cheney upon her return to the United States along with other former POWs. *Courtesy of SSgt. Mark Allen, USA*

First Lieutenant Alison, Captains Heather and Waynetta, and Senior Airman Lyndi, all from the 376th Expeditionary Air Refueling Squadron, flew an all-female KC-135 Stratotanker air refueling mission over Afghanistan. *Courtesy of Capt. Elizabeth Ortiz, USAF*

A U.S. Navy Sailor mans a .50-caliber machine gun mount on the Khawr Al Arnaya Oil Terminal during sunset. The terminal, located off the coast of Iraq, is one of two major platforms that export the majority of the country's oil. Coalition forces are training Iraqi personnel in force protection and search-and-seizure operations in an effort to turn over the oil terminals in the area to Iraq. *Courtesy of Photographer's Mate 3rd Class Randall Damm, USN*

From left to right, SSgt. Josie E. Harshe, flight engineer; Capt. Anita T. Mack, navigator; 1st Lt. Siobhan Couturier, pilot; Capt. Carol J. Mitchell, aircraft commander; and loadmasters TSgt. Sigrid M. Carrero-Perez and Senior Airman Ci Ci Alonzo, pause in the cargo bay of their C-130 for a group photo following their historic flight. *Courtesy of USAF*

Former prisoner of war Maj. Rhonda Lee Cornum, a flight surgeon assigned to the 2nd Battalion, 229th Aviation Brigade, sits next to Col. Richard Williams, USA, on a C-141B Starlifter transport aircraft after her release by the Iraqi government during Operation Desert Storm. *Courtesy of SSgt. Dean Wagner, USA*

PART II

★ ★ ★

Vietnam

Unlike other American armed conflicts that had their beginnings in a clearly defined event (such as Pearl Harbor in World War II), the American involvement in Vietnam was incremental; a series of events that eventually resulted in a full-scale commitment of American forces.

Following World War II, the same feelings of nationalism that had motivated resistance to the Japanese occupation in Asia now caused native peoples to seek independence from their prewar colonial masters. In Indochina, the Viet Minh (later, the NLF) agitated for independence from France, a struggle that rapidly degenerated into a guerilla war.

In May of 1950, President Harry S. Truman, concerned by the loss of China to Communist forces, and fearing a domino effect that could lead to Communist domination in the region, authorized a modest amount of military and economic aid to the French in Indochina. With the defeat of the French forces at the Battle of Dien Bien Phu in 1954, and France's abdication as a power in the region, Vietnam was partitioned into two countries: a Communist Vietnam north of the 17th parallel, and the Republic of South Vietnam south of the parallel.

President Dwight D. Eisenhower sent military advisors and the CIA to assist the newly formed government of South Vietnam on 12 February 1959. Later, the newly elected Democratic president, John F. Kennedy, secretly sent four hundred Special Forces advisors to Vietnam in 1961 to train South Vietnam forces in counterinsurgency measures. He also sent two thousand conventional advisors.[1]

Women who served in Vietnam experienced many of the same common combat problems as their brothers-in-arms: they came under enemy fire, endured the stress of being far from the comforts of home, and suffered from social and psychological isolation from their peers stateside. Returning to the United States, they suffered from dislocation, posttraumatic stress disorder, and the effects of Agent Orange. However, women who served in Vietnam also faced additional problems specific to their gender, particularly because women were a minority in the war in Vietnam. Their movements were restricted—both by location and curfew—and they were required to be accompanied by armed guards when leaving the base. They often lived in guarded and fenced-in compounds, although women in Saigon enjoyed greater freedom than those stationed at Long Binh.[2]

Some annoyances were strongly resented by the women, such as the PX carrying nylons, but not tampons, or the shortage of female latrines. Others were potentially life threatening, such as flak vests and helmets that were not configured to the female form, or having to sandbag their barracks against nighttime mortar attacks because the military would not allow the possibility of scantily clad women in the bunkers with the men.

One nurse, Wendy Weller, tells a story that defies belief. Weller arrived in Vietnam in February 1969 and, while staying temporarily in the nurses quarters of the 93rd Evacuation Hospital at Long Binh, she experienced the following: "That night, the hospital came under fire. We were told to lie on the floor in our flak jackets and helmets . . . then I heard small arms fire. Flares lit up the whole area." After the attack, she thanked the Soldier who had stood guard at the entrance armed with an M-16. "Thank you for guarding us," I said. "I really felt safe with you here." She remembered that he got a funny look on his face, and replied "Well, ma'am, I wasn't here to protect you. Actually, we were to shoot the nurses if we got overrun."[3]

It was a contradictory existence. One nurse described it as the unwritten rule that "Men protected women, women comforted men." Another recalled being "valued as professionals yet exploited as women." They were both: adored and harassed, admired and minimized.

Although the largest percentage of the women in Vietnam served in the medical field (doctors, nurses, medical technicians), many women were WACs employed in a wide variety of positions, including air traffic controllers, photographers, air reconnaissance interpreters, and intelligence analysts, as well as those who served more traditional roles in supply, communications, transportation, and administration.

By the early '70s, what the U.S. government had considered "the light at the end of the tunnel" was acknowledged to be an illusion, and plans were initiated for a gradual withdrawal of U.S. forces from Vietnam. Concurrently, the strength of the WAC detachment decreased. In February 1970, 136 women were assigned to the WAC detachment. No WACs were requisitioned to replace WACs rotating out. By the end of December 1970, the WAC detachment numbered seventy-two. By 31 December 1971, only forty-six WACs remained in Vietnam.[4]

When a unit was deactivated in Vietnam, the event was called a stand down. The last commander of the Long Binh WAC detachment, Capt. Constance

C. Seidemann, the first sergeant, 1st Sgt. Mildred E. Duncan, and the twelve women remaining had a stand-down party on 21 September 1972.[5] On that date the WAC detachment at Long Binh was closed, and the remaining WACs were moved to Saigon. By the end of December, two WAC officers and seventeen enlisted women remained in Saigon. By the end of March 1973, all the WACs had left Vietnam.[6]

Vietnam was the longest deployment (1961–73) of American military forces to a hostile environment in the history of the United States. It is estimated that 2.7 million servicemen and servicewomen served in Vietnam (543,400 at its peak in April 1969) with approximately 1.6 million serving in combat and 58,000 killed or missing.[7]

ENDNOTES

1. Chambers, John Whiteclay II. *Oxford Companion to American Military History*. New York: Oxford University Press, 1999, pp. 758–9.
2. Norman, Elizabeth. *Women at War: The Story of 50 Military Nurses Who Served in Vietnam*. Philadelphia: University of Pennsylvania Press, 1990.
3. Powell, Mary Reynolds. *A World of Hurt: Between Innocence and Arrogance in Vietnam*. Chesterfield, OH: Greenleaf Ent., 2000, pp. 143–4.
4. Ibid.
5. Vietnam Women Veterans Inc. website _http://www.terrispencer.com/vwv/history.htm http://www.terrispencer. com/vwv/history.htm.
6. Monthly Rpts, WAC Det, USARV, to WAC Staff Adviser, Mar 70, Jan 71, Jan 72, ODWAC Ref File, Vietnam, CMH; Morden, Col. Bettie J. *The Women's Army Corps during the Vietnam War: Special Series by Office of the Chief of Military History*. Washington, D.C.: Government Printing Office, 1990.
7. Staff Adviser, USARPAC, Historical Rpts, 1972 and 1973, ODWAC Ref File, USARPAC, CMH. The last two WAC officers to leave Vietnam (Mar 73) were Maj. Georgia A. Wise and Capt. Nancy N. Keough.

Lt. Col. Anne Marie
Doering, USA

The first U.S. WAC officer to serve in Vietnam was Maj. Anne Marie Doering (1962–63), who was assigned to the MAAG in Saigon as a plans officer in the G-2 intelligence section.[1] She was uniquely qualified for the position.

Born and raised in the port city of Haiphong, French Indochina (North Vietnam) to a French engineer and his German wife, Gertrude, Doering was fluent in French, German, Chinese, Japanese, English, and several dialects of Vietnamese. In addition, she was a decorated veteran of World War II.

After Doering's father died, when Doering was six, her mother married Earl Solomon, an American working for Standard Oil. She was educated in Catholic schools in French and Chinese until the age of fourteen, when she traveled to Dayton, Texas, to live with Solomon's sister. There, in a large extended family, she learned English well enough to graduate salutatorian at the local high school. Doering graduated from Southwestern University in Georgetown, Texas, in 1931. Following graduation, she moved to New York City, where she worked in the National Library and studied with the Metropolitan Opera (she sang alto). Doering was in New York when the Japanese attacked Pearl Harbor.

On 14 May 1942, the bill to establish a Women's Army Auxiliary Corps became law and Oveta Culp Hobby, wife of the former governor of Texas, was

Bob and Anne Jamison were informally interviewed by Scott Baron in November 2005. *Photo courtesy of USA* named director. Doering was one of the first to volunteer for the New Women's Corps. Her niece, Anne, recalled, "Her blood ran red, white, and blue. Once when I was twenty, I considered buying a car that wasn't American made. In military style she gave me her opinion. Yikes!"

Doering was selected for officers training at Fort Des Moines, Iowa, after which she was sent to the Pacific Theater of Operations. Her first assignment was to the Philippines, assigned to General MacArthur's headquarters in Manila, where she supervised telephone operations. She recalled the general's first words to her: "about time somebody got here that spoke English."

From the Philippines, Doering was sent to Hollandia, New Guinea. She remembered it as "miserable." It rained all day, every day, so it was impossible to keep things dry. In addition, she recalled frequently coming under enemy artillery and small-arms fire.

It was in New Guinea that Doering was awarded the Bronze Star with a "V" for valor. "If you asked her why (she was awarded the medal) she would laugh and wave you away. If you persisted, she would say she only sat on a guy who was starving. What happened was that somebody came to Anne Marie—an officer— and said they witnessed a Japanese soldier in their camp. She and another WAC officer found that an unarmed Japanese soldier had broken into the mess hall. They fought him, subdued him, and called for assistance. So, yeah, Anne Marie, in all her 100 pounds, sat on a starving guy and was awarded a Bronze Star. But the sobering fact was that Anne Marie was close enough to big trouble not only to get shot at but close enough to encounter enemy personnel."[2]

Following VJ Day, Doering did duty in occupied Japan, again assigned to MacArthur's headquarters in Tokyo. She left the Army a captain, but reentered at the start of the Vietnam War, taking command of the WAC detachment at Fort Hood, Texas, under the command of Gen. Bruce Clark. Later, she went to Orleans, France, where her knowledge of French and German assisted her in her duties as billeting officer. From France, she was sent to Saigon, the first American WAC in country, serving from 1962–63. It was her second war.

After returning from Vietnam in 1963, she retired from the Army as a lieutenant colonel, and spent her last years at the Air Force Retirement Village in San Antonio, Texas. She stated at her retirement that she was "an American by choice," but that serving her country was "the proudest period of (her) life."

ENDNOTES

1. Morden, Col. Bettie J. *The Women's Army Corps during the Vietnam War: Special Series by Office of the Chief of Military History.* Washington, D.C.: Government Printing Office, 1990.
2. Bob and Anne Jamison, informal interviews by Scott Baron, November 2005.

*Lt. (jg) Ann Darby
Reynolds, USN*

In March 1964, when Lt. (jg) Ann Darby Reynolds, NNC, arrived in Saigon, Vietnam it was not considered a hardship post, nor was it yet perceived as especially dangerous. American advisors had been in country since 12 February 1955 when President Eisenhower sent the first advisors to assist in training the infant South Vietnamese Army. But the situation in Vietnam was in transition in 1964.

Reynolds had received orders to Vietnam just prior to the previous Christmas, while home on leave.[1]

"I didn't know where Saigon was," Reynolds recalled. "We got the encyclopedia out and looked it up. My family said 'Oh, that's where they are burning all the Buddhists.'"

Reynolds was sent to the West Coast, and departed by air from Travis Air Force Base in California. "There were two other females on the plane going over there. I was very nervous. Most of the folks were Army and there were very few Navy. They were carrying their rifles and their bags. That was my first exposure."

She traveled to Vietnam via Hawaii and Guam, and arrived at Tan Son Nhut Air Base, Saigon, in March 1964, still wearing her dress blues in the tropical heat.

Ann Darby Reynolds was interviewed by Kate Scott in Arlington, Virginia, on 19 August 2004. The tape and transcript are deposited at The Women's Memorial in Arlington. Lt. (jg) Ann Darby Reynolds, USN, shown receiving Purple Heart medal for injuries received in the Christmas Eve bombing of Brink Bachelor Officers Quarters, Republic of Vietnam. *Photo courtesy of NHC*

"(Saigon) had a very distinct odor. I can't really describe it. Something rotten. With the humidity, there was just this very pungent odor. We all got out and dispersed, and I was met by my Chief Nurse."

Because of conflicts between Catholics and Buddhists, the city was under martial law and battle-dressed ARVN troops patrolled the streets. Tanks and armored vehicles sat parked at major intersections.[2] It was a world away from the one in which Reynolds had grown up.

Ann Darby Reynolds was born in Dover, New Hampshire, on 12 September 1939, the older of two daughters of Frank and Annie Hawkins Reynolds. Her father, a Navy Seabee during World War II, worked at the Naval shipyard at Portsmouth, New Hampshire, and her mother stayed at home. The holidays were filled with family.

Inspired by an aunt who was a nurse, Reynolds entered the nursing program at St. Anselm College in Manchester, New Hampshire, shortly after graduating from Dover High School in June 1957. Four years later, in June 1961, she passed her state boards and graduated.

"I was in a very small nursing class. The recruiters from all the branches of the service came to talk to us. They all interested me, but I fell in love with the Navy uniform. But, I also chose the Navy because they were stationed along the coast and had large hospitals."

After completing the physicals and interviews in Boston, she gained practical experience working as a nurse at the Wentworth Hospital in Dover while she waited to be called up. In January 1962 Reynolds was sent to the Women's Officer Indoctrination Program at Newport, Rhode Island, after which the newly commissioned Ensign Reynolds reported to her first duty station, Pensacola Naval Air Station, Florida, in March 1962.

Reynolds remained at Pensacola for almost two years, except for brief service at Camp Lejuene during a flu epidemic, and attendance at a Mass Casualty Management Course at the Army Field Services School, Fort Sam Houston, Texas, before her transfer to Vietnam.

After arriving in Vietnam, Reynolds attended two or three days of orientation, which included classes on personal safety (travel in pairs, avoid bicycle taxis because of their vulnerability to hand grenades); security (demonstration protocols, off-limit areas); and some basic Vietnamese phrases, Reynolds reported for duty at the Naval Station Hospital, Headquarters, Support Activity–Saigon. "It was an old apartment building that had been converted to a hospital. We had the elevator which was right in the middle of it . . . it never really worked most of the time." Reynolds was assigned quarters at the Brink, a junior officer BOQ.

Fighting had escalated in all sectors around Saigon by Easter 1964. On 2 May, the cargo ship USNS *Card* was blown up while moored in Saigon Harbor. With the start of the build-up in the number of American troops in July 1964, the number of demonstrations and attacks on Americans only increased.[3]

"We had mostly Army patients. They would bring them right in from the field. In the beginning of my tour, it was not that hectic. But, I would say that as time went on, the fighting escalated and we got more patients. We would get them for a day or two and then we would medevac them and take them out. At that time, we were one of only two hospitals. They had the Army 8th Field Hospital which was up at Nha Trang. We were the Naval Station Hospital in Saigon."[4]

Christmas 1964 was an exciting time for the nurses. Bob Hope was visiting Saigon, and security was tight. On Christmas Eve, Reynolds was in her billet, at the French doors, watching to make sure her maid safely exited the compound, when there was an explosion.

"I had my face pressed right up against the glass . . . I was right close to it. The explosion went off. The door blew in on me and the glass shattered on my face. It shattered right on my face and onto my body. The only thing that saved my life was the fact that I was so close to the door that the glass did not have time to penetrate."

A Viet Cong terrorist had driven a jeep loaded with two hundred pounds of plastique into the underground parking area and detonated it. Two officers in the apartment next door were killed, and another fifty-eight were wounded.[5] Although injured themselves, Reynolds and three other Navy nurses quartered at the Brink rushed to the hospital to perform triage and work on the wounded throughout the night. Bob Hope and Jerry Colonna came over to visit with the wounded. A day or two later, officials announced that everyone injured at the BOQ would be awarded the Purple Heart.

"They had a debate. They didn't know what to do with (us) because they did not want word going out that the females had been injured. They wanted to keep it quiet."

On 8 January 1965, three lieutenants—Barbara Wooster, Ruth Mason, and Frances Crumpton (hospitalized)—and Lieutenant Reynolds were awarded the Purple Heart Medal. They were the first American women to receive the award for service in Vietnam.[6]

"My tour was almost up, and I was ready to think about getting out. I was really having mixed feelings about the military. They were going to give us the (medals) in our summer blues. I said 'No. We are all nurses and we are going to get this award in our nurse's uniforms.'"

Reynolds remained in the Navy, returning from Vietnam in February 1965 and reporting to the Naval Hospital at Portsmouth in April. A number of state-side postings followed, including recruiting for nurses in Boston and earning her master's in nursing at California State University–Fresno. She retired from the

Navy on 30 September 1988 with the rank of captain after twenty-six years of service, and returned to Dover, where she currently lives.

ENDNOTES

1. Ann D. Reynolds, interview by Kate Scott, 19 August 2004, transcript, The Women's Memorial Arlington, Va.
2. Hovis, Bobbi. *Station Hospital Saigon: A Navy Nurse in Vietnam, 1963–1964.* Annapolis, Md.: Naval Institute Press, 1992, pp. 17–21.
3. Ibid.
4. Ann D. Reynolds, interview by Kate Scott.
5. Horne, Al. N. H. "Navy Nurse Tells of Viet Raid," *Boston Record American,* 9 January 1965.
6. Ibid.

Spc5 Sheron Lee Green, USA

As a child, Sheron Lee Green wanted to be a missionary. In 1966, Green left a good position as a legal secretary and enlisted in the U.S. Army for many of the same reasons young men of her generation were enlisting. Like many children of the '60s, she said, "I was looking to redefine myself." And like countless generations before her, she was looking to "do something personal and noble, make a difference."[1]

Born in Seattle, Washington, on 10 March 1942, Green was the oldest of three children of Rexford and Dorothea Green. After her parents divorced, she moved to California with her mother and siblings and graduated from Norte Del Rio High School near Sacramento in June 1960. After several successful years as a legal reporter, she decided to change her life, and enlisted in the U.S. Army at Oakland, California, on 4 May 1966.

Green was sent to Fort McClellan, Alabama, on 23 May, for ten weeks of basic training, which at the time was gender-segregated. She remembered it as "very regimented" and "the same training as men received." The women recruits carried weapons on field exercises, but received no small-arms training and never fired on the range. "They were basically props," she recalled. She also had one other additional obstacle; "The prettier you were, the more you were picked on by cadre."

Sheron Lee Green was interviewed by Scott Baron on 13 November 2005. The tape and transcript are deposited at The Women's Memorial in Arlington. *Photo courtesy of Sheron Green Collection*

After basic training, she was promoted to Private E-2 on 23 September and E-3 on 15 December 1966, and remained at Fort McClellan assigned to HHC of the WAC training center where she served as a legal clerk. On 27 October 1967, she reported to the Naval Justice School, Newport, Rhode Island, for a ten-week Military Justice Course. Qualified as a court reporter, she returned to Fort McClellan where she was assigned to the Staff Judge Advocate.

In April 1967, she was ordered to D.C.; there she interviewed for a stenographer's position with the DoD. She was selected, and assigned to the office of the Secretary of Defense, Robert McNamara.

Promoted to E-4 on 8 May 1967 and granted a "secret" security clearance, Green worked for the JCOC tasked with investigating and clearing celebrities and prominent civilians for tours of NORAD facilities. Her primary duty was acting as a courier of documents. Her next assignment was to Headquarters—OJCS as a stenographer, stationed at Fort Meyers, Virginia, but working at the Pentagon.

On 14 August 1967, Green was reassigned to the WAC Detachment, 4th Army at Fort Sam Houston where she received training in and was covertly tested on her psychological response to stress and isolation. After graduating from the Counter-Insurgency Ambush and Evasion Course, which was an eighteen-hour POM/POR qualification course for Vietnam, Green was asked where she'd like to be assigned next. Green chose Vietnam. "If I was going to put in the time, I was going to make it count. Colonel Hoisington (the WAC Director) was determined not to put WACs in harm's way. That didn't bother me. I needed to do that, to do something worthwhile."[2]

Green went into "casual" status, en route to USAPAC-Vietnam on 11 March. She arrived in Vietnam on 5 April 1968 and was sent to the 1st Aviation Brigade at Long Binh. She was assigned as secretary to Col. Michael Lynch, Chief of Staff-Aviation. Like most women in Vietnam, she worked twelve hours a day, six days a week. Although she dressed in fatigues, she worked in an air-conditioned office processing correspondence and coordinating logistics and intelligence reports on aviation assets. For recreation, she would occasionally grab a pizza at the EM club, but most nights would dine with the sergeant major and the headquarters drivers. "We ate very well," she recalled.

Green was still adjusting to her new life and work in Vietnam when, on 9 June, she was returning by air from a courier mission to Nha Trang, flying in a U6-A Beaver piloted by "a light colonel who just wanted out of the office." They were flying low along the coast south of Phan Rang when they came under small-arms and antiaircraft fire.

"It was the monsoon season, and we were flying low, about 1,800 feet, when we came under fire from antiaircraft guns. I could hear them come up through the fuselage. We were partially protected by seat armor."

Despite the armor, Green sustained shrapnel wounds all along the left side of her body. The pilot was untouched. "When you're shot, you're not aware of it. There was a loud explosion in my head, but I had nothing to relate it to. My head was searing like it was being pressed by a branding iron. I felt a wetness, but I was dazed."

The pilot saw the blood and flew her to the nearest medevac, a small Marine base at Phan Thiet.

"After we landed, a Capt. Murad removed the larger pieces, but they had no X-ray unit, so we returned to Long Binh, where the medical officer ordered X-rays, and they got most of it. I still carry some [shrapnel] in me."

An official report of the incident stated Green "was struck by fragments yesterday when an enemy round penetrated the floor of the aircraft in which she was riding. It went through her parachute and seating, spraying fragments. These imbedded in left shoulder, upper back on left, left side of neck, left cheek, lateral to the left eye, forehead and left temporal scalp."[3]

On 3 July 1968, Green became the first WAC to be awarded the Purple Heart in Vietnam.

On 11 July, Green requested a transfer to Saigon and MACV headquarters, but instead was assigned to USAHAC, located on a walled-in plantation on the outskirts of Saigon, where she served as secretary to Gen. Irzk. For administrative purposes, she was carried on the roster of the 716th Military Police, and was billeted at Tan Son Nhut, on Vo Than Rd.

"Saigon was hot, a lot more dangerous than Long Binh. There was a large cadre of VC in the city. I shared quarters with an Air Force sergeant, Marti McAllister, on the air base at Tan Son Nhut, the most secure place in Saigon. Still, they would grenade or machine-gun the billets."

Like many military women who served in Vietnam, Green volunteered her off-duty hours assisting at an orphanage. She remembers it as a Buddhist orphanage, and recalls that America only supported the Catholic orphanages. "Catholic orphanages were connected with the French and upper class. Vietnamese put their children there so they would be well taken care of; Buddhist orphanages were connected to the common people, and did not get the support of our agencies in Vietnam."

"Four of us would drive out in a jeep. It was about a half hour out in the country, and we'd often ignore curfew to go out there. It was run by two Vietnamese nuns and was home to about 500 mixed race children of American Soldiers. The VC resented any American help and came in one night and killed both the nuns and all the children. It wasn't only a war of North and South. It was also a war of Catholic versus Buddhist."

In Saigon, Green also worked part-time at the U.S. Embassy, where she filled in for Evelyn Canastia, the secretary to the U.S. Ambassador, Ellsworth Bunker.

"Because I was the only U.S. military female in Saigon with the clearance for high-level meetings, I filled in for the ambassador's secretary. It was good duty. I was picked up by an Embassy car in the morning, and I worked out of uniform. I developed friendships with military attaches from Allied countries and South Vietnam. I handled and worked with protocol matters."

Green extended her tour of duty for two months, and departed Vietnam en route to the CONUS on 21 June 1969, flying out of Saigon to Travis AFB in California, with a stopover in Hawaii. She was honorably discharged at Oakland on 3 July. Besides the Purple Heart, her awards included an Army Commendation Medal, a Good Conduct Medal, and other awards for her service in Vietnam.

"I had mixed feelings about coming home. Part of me didn't want to come home. I even extended two months. At first, any loud noise put me on edge. Most people didn't understand. We were expected to 'get on with it.'"

After leaving the Army, and after the end of a short marriage that produced a daughter, Green moved to Apple Valley, California, where she developed a friendship with Roy Rogers, hosted a TV show, and worked in real estate. During a visit to Montana in 1991, she fell in love with the area, moved there in 1993, and has been living there ever since. She has worked to raise awareness on the importance of communities working together to create solutions and has received numerous awards for her work.

ENDNOTES

1. Sheron Green, interview by Scott Baron, 13 November 2005, transcript, The Women's Memorial, Arlington, Va.
2. Ibid.
3. Chronological Record of Medical Care (SF600) dated 10 June 1968, Surgeon, 1st Aviation Brigade, APO SF 96384.

Spc5 Karen Irene Offutt, USA

On 20 January 1970, Spc5 Karen Irene Offutt, a twenty-year-old farm girl from Pine Bluff, Arkansas, was off-duty in her quarters at the Medford BEQ off Vo Tanh Street, Saigon, when she smelled smoke. After alerting the other women on her floor, she observed where the fire was coming from:

"We were on the second floor of an old hotel. Across the alleyway were a series of Vietnamese shanties, made of beer cans and thatch roofs. A bamboo-type awning extended across all the houses. That awning was on fire, and [Vietnamese] were running around trying to salvage their things. I ran down and pulled some women and children out. I was barefoot and burned my feet. I don't remember much. Eventually, the fire department showed up."[1]

Offutt doesn't feel she did anything especially heroic, and remembers with more clarity that she wrote home about the incident, and her mother organized churches and neighbors to collect clothes and send them to Vietnam for the children. Offutt was surprised when she was called to MACV and informed that the Hamlet Chief had written a letter commending her for saving numerous lives, and that she was to be awarded the Soldier's Medal. Then, on 24 January, officials told Offutt that women were not awarded Soldier's Medals; instead, Offutt was

Karen Irene Offutt was interviewed by Scott Baron on 18 November 2005. (Spc5 Karen Irene Offutt, USA, shown receiving a Certificate of Achievement for Heroic Action, Vietnam, 24 January 1970. *Photo courtesy of USA* presented with a Certificate of Achievement for Heroic Action. "I wasn't really upset at not getting it [the Soldier's Medal] because I did what anybody should have done anyway."[2]

Karen Irene Offutt was born in Pine Bluff, Arkansas, on 26 October 1949, the daughter between two sons. Her older brother died at a young age, and her younger brother suffered from poor health. They were extremely poor and moved around a lot, trying to find a good climate for her brother's health. She attended Quartz Hill High School, near Lancaster, California, where she was an outgoing and popular student. She was student body vice president, ran track, and belonged to many clubs. She graduated in June 1967 at the age of seventeen.

She entered the California Hospital School of Nursing in Los Angeles, but quit in her second semester, feeling "academically overwhelmed." She had planned to enlist after nursing school, but one day in June 1968 she passed the recruitment trailer at the employment office and, on an impulse, enlisted.

"I'd always been super patriotic, always had chills from [hearing] the 'Star-Spangled Banner.' My uncle had served in the Army, but not my father, and my brother wouldn't be accepted with asthma, so I guess I wanted to represent the family."

Offutt enlisted in the Army, and chose training as a stenographer with the promise of assignment to Fort Benjamin Harrison, Indiana, after basic training. She reported to Fort McClellan, Alabama, in July 1968. "It was like a women's prison. I'd never been cursed at before. And it was *hot!*"

After completing basic training, Offutt received orders to report for communications training at Fort Benning, Georgia. "I was really surprised because the recruiter had made promises. If you gave your word, that was it."

She went to her sergeant to tell her she'd received the wrong orders. "I was told to write my congressman," she remembered. "I left, but then returned. I don't know who my congressman is," she informed her sergeant.

"Then write the president," she was told.

"So I did! I sent a long letter to President Johnson," recalls Offutt.

A week before her transfer to Fort Benning, she was called to the dayroom. There was a call for her from the Pentagon. They advised her that President Johnson had read her letter, and had directed them to be sure she was sent to Fort Benjamin Harrison. For her remaining time at Fort McClellan, she caught "every crappy detail." "My sergeant asked me, 'Why did you do it?' I said, 'You told me to.' 'Yes,' came the reply, 'but I didn't mean it.' I was scared, because I knew that all eyes were on me, and I had better do well."[3]

Offutt reported to Fort Benjamin Harrison in September 1968 for sixteen weeks of training as a stenographer; she graduated second in her class with the ability to take 140 words per minute dictation. She was selected for duty at the Pentagon.

"I was stationed at Fort Meyers, where the Old Guard is quartered. I would see coffins pass my quarters every day, en route to Arlington, but I never connected them with Vietnam. I was a kid."

By 1968 protests against the war were becoming more common and even young Soldiers insulated on military bases were starting to question American involvement. "I was working in logistics at the Pentagon, and it seemed everyone was protesting and I wanted to find out the truth. There was no way to know until I went. I knew many high-ranking officers, and I bugged them until I got assigned [to Vietnam]."

Offutt flew into Bien Hoa, Vietnam, on 19 July 1969, the only female on the plane. She was surprised to hear cheers as they deplaned, and was warmed by the welcome. Later, she learned that the men were cheering because their arrival meant others were going home. She was supposed to be assigned to Saigon, but instead was placed on a bus and taken to the WAC detachment at Long Binh.

"We were mortared that first night. It was the worst night of my life, and I wondered if I'd make it out."

Making it out of Long Binh proved almost as tricky. The Unit at Long Binh seemed reluctant to send Offutt to her duty station in Saigon. "They had me filling in, doing odd jobs, and I didn't even have fatigues, and felt out of place. I finally called MACV headquarters, and a sergeant major showed up from Saigon. They didn't want to release me and I was afraid he'd leave without me. He must have seen it in my eyes because he yelled at me to get my gear and get in the car. That's how I got to Saigon."

Offutt was quartered at the Bedford BEQ, on the outskirts of Tan Son Nhut, where like most, she worked six-and-a-half days a week, twelve to fifteen hours a day, and volunteered her free time at a Catholic orphanage. Her quarters were fronted by a high chain-link fence, complete with grenade catcher, and guarded by ARVN soldiers; however, she never felt safe.

"I never felt protected. There were rocket attacks, they blew up jeeps, we were shot at by snipers while on the roof on New Year's Eve. I never felt safe . . . we were told they would booby-trap the children!"

Offutt worked first in logistics for generals under Gen. Creighton Abrams, dealing with matters as diverse as air strikes, relations with Vietnamese generals, and day-to-day correspondence. She remembers that life was regimented in Long Binh, but that in Saigon, "you were more on your own."[4]

Following the award of her Certificate of Achievement on 24 January Offutt finished her tour of duty, and returned stateside in June 1970, a few weeks earlier than planned in order to be present for surgery her mother was having. Offutt was temporarily assigned to Fort MacArthur, California, and was honorably discharged as a Spc5 on 16 September 1970.

While at Fort MacArthur, Offutt met a man whom she married after they had dated for three weeks. The marriage ended sixteen years later in divorce, leaving her with three children. Of her marriage, she'll only say "I wasn't thinking when I got back."[5]

Coming home was a difficult transition for Offutt. Outgoing before the war, she became reclusive and more private afterward. "I cried the whole way back. America didn't seem normal when I got back. Everyone seemed worried over inconsequential matters . . . foo-foo crap. . . . Vietnam really affected my life. It's been very difficult afterwards. Holidays are difficult. Anniversary dates of in-country events are difficult. I didn't believe it before; I do now."[6]

Offutt later returned to school and earned her RN in 1984. Offutt also became active in veteran's affairs. She testified in Congressional hearings regarding the effects of Agent Orange, because her three children suffer from cancer, epilepsy, and ADHD, which she traces to her exposure to Agent Orange. Offutt also networked with other Vietnam vets via the Internet, and as skeptical veterans learned her story, they lobbied on her behalf.

On 7 April 2001, at Medard Park, east of Tampa, Florida, Karen Offutt was finally presented the Soldier's Medal she had earned thirty-one years earlier in Vietnam. A guest speaker at The Moving Wall, she was presented the medal in a surprise ceremony by a representative of Congressman Mike Bilirakis (R-Fla). The official citation reads:

(Then) Specialist Five, United States Army for heroism not involving actual conflict with an armed enemy: Specialist Karen I. Offutt, Women's Army Corps, United States Army, assigned to Headquarters Military Assistance Command Vietnam, J47, distinguished herself by heroic action on 24 January 1970 while in an off-duty status.

Observing a fire in Vietnamese dwellings near her quarters, she hurried to the scene to provide assistance. Without regard for her personal safety and in great danger of serious injury or death from smoke, flames, and falling debris, she assisted in rescuing several adults and children from the burning structures. Without protective clothing or shoes she repeatedly entered the buildings to lead children that had reentered their homes to safety. She continued to assist the Vietnamese residents in removing personal property and livestock, although danger increased until fire-fighting equipment and personnel arrived. Specialist Five Offutt's heroic action reflects great credit on herself, the United States Army, and the United States mission in Vietnam.

Time has not softened the memories of her Vietnam experience for Offutt. She continues to suffer from post-traumatic stress disorders. "People keep saying, 'Why don't you forget Vietnam?' I don't think I'll forget Vietnam because it changed my trust in people . . . it isolated and changed me. The babies I took care of, babies with their legs blown off and shrapnel wounds. I felt so helpless and the guilt of having seen what I had . . . I'd like to forget about it, but I think about it every day."[7]

ENDNOTES

1. Karen Offutt, interview by Scott Baron, 18 November 2005, transcript, The Women's Memorial, Arlington, Va.
2. Steinman, Ron. *Women in Vietnam: The Oral History.* New York: TV Books LLC, 2000, p. 254.
3. Karen Offutt, interview by Scott Baron, 18 November 2005, transcript, The Women's Memorial, Arlington, Va.
4. Steinman, Ron. *Women in Vietnam: The Oral History.* New York: TV Books LLC, 2000, p. 260.
5. Karen Offutt, interview by Scott Baron, 18 November 2005, transcript, The Women's Memorial, Arlington, Va.
6. Ibid.
7. Ibid.

PART III

★ ★ ★

Korea

Following the end of World War II, there was a massive demobilization of American military forces, including the women's services. No longer a military necessity, the WACs, WAVES, Women Marines, SPARs, and Air WACs were reduced to skeleton strength.

On 12 June 1948, Congress passed the Women's Armed Forces Integration Act (PL 625) that admitted women into the regular and reserve of the Army, Navy, Marine Corps, and Air Force, and accorded a permanent role for women in the military—with full rank and privileges. Simultaneously, however, it placed a cap on enlistments (2 percent of the active duty force) and promotions, limiting women to the rank of lieutenant colonel or commander. In addition, women were specifically excluded from combat.[1]

During that same period, there was another significant change occurring. The end of World War II brought about another significant change that would affect the military. The alliance of convenience between the United States and the Soviet Union, which had joined forces to defeat the Axis powers of Germany and Italy, ended with the war. With the defeat of national Socialism, both nations were free to return to their more traditional roles of competition and mistrust. The situation was further complicated by the emergence of a second Communist nation on mainland China in early 1949.

The resulting competition for influence and control in the postwar world would become known as the Cold War. The first arena for a military contest between Communism and democracy was in Korea. In the years following World War II, Korea was 450 miles long and 160 miles wide, bordered by the Korean strait, the Sea of Japan, the Yellow Sea, the Soviet Union, and Communist China. At the Cairo Conference in 1943, during World War II, Korea, which had been occupied by the Japanese for thirty-five years, had been promised independence but instead was provisionally divided in half following its liberation in 1945. The

Democratic People's Republic of Korea, a socialist dictatorship, under Kim Il Sung occupied the area north of the 38th parallel and the Republic of Korea, a right-wing republic under Syngman Rhee was south of the 38th parallel.

Both governments claimed to be the legitimate government of all of Korea, and there was a continuing series of border incidents between North and South Korean forces. In 1948, both the Soviet Union and the United States withdrew troops from Korea. By 1950, there were between one hundred fifty thousand and two hundred thousand Soviet-trained troops in the north equipped with Soviet T-34 tanks and Yak fighter planes compared to an ill-equipped army of one hundred thousand in the south (supported by a small group of American military advisors).[2]

On 25 June 1950, North Korea, with the knowledge and support of the Soviet Union, launched a full-scale invasion across the 38th parallel into South Korea. The international response was rapid. On 27 June, President Harry Truman requested and received permission for military intervention in Korea, and ordered U.S. air and naval forces to the area, deploying the 7th Fleet to the Sea of Japan, and placing all American forces under the command of General of the Army Douglas MacArthur. On the same day, the United Nations approved a resolution in support of the Republic of Korea. In addition to the United States, fifteen countries agreed to send combat troops and another five countries[3] agreed to provide medical support. It was the first time a multinational force had been constituted to repel Communist aggression.[4]

ENDNOTES

1. Chambers, John Whiteclay, II. *Oxford Companion to American Military History.* New York: Oxford University Press, 1999.
2. Savada, Andrea Matles, editor. *The Korean War* (1950–1953). The Library of Congress Country Studies–North Korea, Washington: The Library of Congress, Federal Research Division, Call #DS932 N662: US Government Printing Office, 1994.
3. Walker, Jack D. "A Brief Account of the Korean War." Korean War Educator. http://www.koreanwar-educator.org/topics/brief/brief_account_of_the_korean_war.htm
4. *The Korean War in Brief.* Office of Public Affairs, Veterans Administration, June 2000 (Fact Sheet); and Blair, Clay. *The Forgotten War.* New York: Random House, 1988.

Lt. Margaret Fae Perry, USAF

Women in the newly formed U.S. Air Force served in Korea as flight nurses aboard air evacuation flights. An estimated fifty air nurses served during the war, and most came from backgrounds similar to Lt. Margaret Fae Perry, USAF.

Already a nurse in February 1950 when she enlisted in the USAF to further her education and perhaps travel, she arrived for training at Fort Sam Houston in San Antonio, Texas, shortly after the start of the Korean War in June 1950.

After her commission as a second lieutenant, she applied for and was accepted to military flight school. She reported to Montgomery, Alabama, in November for a six-week course of training in air evacuation of wounded personnel, after which she was assigned to the 1453 Squadron at Hickam AFB, Hawaii.

She flew numerous air evacuation flights from Korea to Guam, Japan, Hawaii, and the mainland United States, participating in two major campaigns, the Summer Campaign of 1952, and Third Korean Winter Campaign. She earned an Air Medal as well as campaign and service medals, including the Korean and United Nations Service Medal.

On 22 December 1952, she boarded a C-47 on her last evacuation mission before rotating home for discharge. Due to confusion in takeoff instructions, her plane collided with an F-80C fighter, also cleared for takeoff. The collision resulted in an explosion that killed personnel aboard both aircraft, including Perry and fellow air nurse Virginia May McClure.

The Margaret Fae Perry Scholarship at the West Virginia University School of Nursing was created to honor her memory.[1]

One other USAF nurse, Capt. Vera Brown, died when the evacuation flight she was on crashed in the Kwajalein Islands after taking off from Ashiya AFB, Japan, on 26 September 1950. In addition to Brown, nineteen others died in the crash.

ENDNOTE

1. Stump, Shelly. "Flight Nurse Honored with Scholarship Fund." Morgantown, WVa., West Virginia University Magazine, Vol. 27, Number 1, Spring, 2004.

Col. Margaret Brosmer, USA

Margaret Brosmer stood on deck of the USS James O' Hara, which was carrying her west across the Pacific, and listened to the sound of gunfire. It was a clear morning in early August 1950, and some of the officers were giving the nurses of the 1st MASH unofficial training in the use of the .45 automatic pistol. This served to remind Brosmer that she was en route to a combat zone.[1]

Brosmer's background was similar to that of many of the women who served during the Korean War. Born into a family of modest means in Columbus, Ohio, on 23 August 1922, she was the middle child of five. After graduating from Rosary High School, she attended St. Elizabeth Nursing School in Dayton, Ohio, and enrolled in the Cadet Nurse Corps, which provided free training— paid for by the government—to help alleviate a nationwide nursing shortage.

Brosmer enlisted in the Army Reserve in March 1949 because she wanted to earn a living, use her training, and because she thought it would be fun. She was placed on extended active duty on 9 November 1949, and sent to Fort Sam Houston in Texas for basic training, after which she was assigned to Walter Reed Hospital in D.C. On 20 July 1950, Brosmer was alerted for duty with the FEC and was ordered to report to Fort Lewis, Washington, where she was assigned to the newly formed 1st MASH. The FEC sailed from the port of Olympia aboard the USS *James O'Hara* on 4 August.[2]

Margaret Brosmer was interviewed by Scott Baron on 29 May 2005. *Photo courtesy of Margaret Brosmer*

Although the *O'Hara* was scheduled to land at Wonsan Harbor in Korea, the discovery that the harbor had been armed with more than two thousand mines caused the ship to be diverted to Yokohama, Japan, where they docked on 11 August. Brosmer recalled: "We landed in Yokohama. We were there for just about a month, and worked with the nurses at the [field] hospital. We worked with them . . . while they tried to decide what to do with us. In the meantime, MacArthur was planning the Inchon landing."[3]

Gen. Walton Walker's Eighth Army had withdrawn behind the Naktong River and withstood counterattacks on 5 and 31 August. By 12 September, North Korean forces were exhausted. MacArthur's plan was to land behind the enemy at Inchon and disrupt their operations by trapping the North Koreans between his forces, cutting them off from the north.

In a brilliant maneuver, MacArthur sent the X Corps ashore at Inchon and up the western coast of Korea on 15 September 1950. X Corps consisted of the Army's 7th Infantry Division and the Marine 1st Division, and it moved to cut the enemy's lines of supply and communication to the forces besieging the Naktong Perimeter to the south, forcing North Koreans to withdraw in panicked disorder. While X Corps pressed to recapture Seoul, South Korea's capital city, the Eighth U.S. Army and ROK forces broke out of the Naktong Perimeter and linked up with X Corps near Osan on 26 September.[4]

With the landing at Inchon, the 1st MASH finally had a mission, as the unit was selected to support X Corps and they loaded aboard the USS *Gen. W.A. Mann* for transportation to Korea. They sailed from Japan on 23 September, and arrived at the docks of Inchon on 26 September. "We went into Inchon ten days after the Marines landed. We went in just like they did. We went in on the high tide, and we went over the side of the ship, down rope ladders and into the LCM [landing craft] and into the dock. When we got there, things were pretty much in hand, because that [the landing] was such a surprise, and the Koreans just turned tail and left fast."

Because of the success of the landing, there were very few American casualties, so the majority of the medics time was spent treating North Korean POWs and Korean civilians. By 4 October, the 1st MASH was working with nurses of the 4th Field Hospital in Seoul, which had been liberated on 28 September. Seoul, located at the intersection of most major highways and railroads in South Korea, would remain a target, and change hands several times during the war.[5]

Following up with his success at Inchon, MacArthur planned a second amphibious landing, this time farther north on the eastern coast, at Wonsan. On 7 October, elements of the Eighth Army captured the northern capital of Pyongyang, and the UN passed a resolution changing the aim of the war from saving South Korea to the unification of Korea. That same day, the 1st MASH was ordered back to Inchon, where they joined a convoy of the 7th Medical Regiment conveying wounded south to Pusan.

On 7 October, the 1st MASH departed Inchon for the eight-hundred-mile trip to Pusan. Brosmer recalled: "It was quite a long trip, about ninety-six hours, with nothing but dirt roads. It was dry, and the dust was so bad we took the masks we wore in the operating room and wet them down . . . because we couldn't breathe. On the way down, we had to go down the canyons and there were hills on both sides. . . . We nurses traveled in ambulances. There were thirteen of us. . . . We put six (nurses) in one ambulance, seven in another."[6]

The convoy stayed overnight at An Yan Ni, leaving there the morning of 8 October and proceeding along the Suwon-Taegu Highway south toward Pusan. On the morning of 9–10 October, the convoy was ambushed south of Chungju.

The Chief Nurse, Capt. (later Maj.) Eunice Coleman, USA remembered: "It was three in the morning when we were ambushed. We were riding in an ambulance and had to jump for the ditch. The whole sky seemed to be on fire, lit up by gunfire and burning vehicles. The shooting lasted until daybreak. At 7:00 AM our hospital was already working by the roadside."[7]

Brosmer, in the second ambulance, recalled she slept through a good part of the ambush. "Someone came banging on the back door of the ambulance and said, 'Get out! Get out of there. They're shooting at us. Get out in the ditch.' Well, the thing was over by this time and the girls in the ambulance in front of us were all out in the ditch—cold, wet, and gooey. And here we were, in there . . . asleeping away. They'd been out there most of the night. They were shooting at us pretty good, I guess, but they didn't get to us, because they were shooting at them. We were oblivious to all of this, so we just slept through the whole thing. From that point on, they called us the 'Lucky Thirteen.'"[8]

With eight fatalities and numerous casualties, including several serious head and chest wounds, the convoy continued on to the nearest field hospital, at Taejon. After leaving the wounded at the field hospital, the 1st MASH proceeded to Pusan, arriving on 10 October. They worked in a POW hospital under the control of the 64th Field Hospital for about a week before leaving Pusan and boarding the transport USS *Gen. E. D. Patrick* on 16 October in preparation for traveling north with X Corps for the landing at Iwon on the northeastern coast.

After being allowed to disembark on 25 October to attend a Bob Hope Show in Pusan, they reboarded the ship and sailed from Pusan Harbor on 29 October bound for North Korea. They dropped anchor off Iwon on 30 October. The landing was delayed when it was discovered the harbor was heavily mined, and it wasn't until 4 November that the nurses touched dry land. They traveled by convoy, arriving in Riwon the first night, and continuing on to Pukchong, where they set up the hospital and opened for business. There were plenty of customers.

Wonsan had fallen to the South Korean Army on 11 October, and the Eighth Army captured Pyongyang on the 19 October. The Marines landed at Wonsan on 20 October, and U.S. and ROK forces continued north unopposed.

The Lucky Thirteen. *Courtesy of Margaret Brosmer*

Unbeknownst to the American command, two hundred sixty thousand Chinese troops (CPV), at the request of Soviet Premier Josef Stalin, had crossed the Yalu River on 19 October in support of North Korean forces and were now massed along the front. On 24 October, replenished and resupplied, American forces advanced north. The following day, Communist forces counterattacked, first on the Eighth Army, and two days later on the X Corps in the mountains to the east.[9]

General Walker's Eighth Army rapidly retreated from the Chongchon River south to Pyongyang. Before the month was over, the Eighth Army had fallen back nearly three hundred miles, and had air-evacuated all of its forward hospitals. Pyongyang fell to Communist forces on 5 December. The 8076th didn't leave the city until 4 December, when the nurses were flown to Kimpo. The Eighth Army's retreat exposed the flank of the 1st Marines, which didn't receive orders to withdraw until it was almost too late.[10]

Encircled and trapped, the 1st Marines fought their way out of the Chosin Reservoir along narrow paths slick with ice in temperatures as low as 24 degrees below zero. The Chinese, in control of the high ground, peppered the retreating troops with machine gun and mortar fire, resulting in a high number of casualties.

"The men were ragged, their faces swollen and bleeding from the icy wind. A few were without hats, their ears blue from the cold. Others were barefoot because they couldn't get their frostbitten feet into their shoepacs. Casualties were enormous, but the Marines stayed together in a column and struggled with their equipment, their wounded and their dead, all of whom were carried out."[11]

From early November until 4 December, the 1st MASH was swamped with casualties. "We had three operating tables going constantly and had only two nights without operations. For the rest of the month, we had surgical operations around the clock."[12] Temperatures were so low that medical personnel had to chip ice out of the washbasins in order to scrub raw, red hands.

MASH units were located—by necessity—near the front lines, and were frequently on the move. Lt. Genevieve Connors of the 8055th recalled, "We went where the action was, either forward or backward depending on the front line's location."[13]

With the Communists close in pursuit of the retreating Marines, the hospital was ordered to withdraw to Pusan on 3 December. They left in convoy, and traveled eighty-six miles over icy mountain passes to arrive in Hamhung at 9:00 PM They proceeded to Hungham on 6 December and set up a hospital in an abandoned school.

"We had to leave Pukchong at twenty-minutes' notice," Major Coleman remembered. "It was an all-day ride down the mountain roads covered with frozen snow, edged by a steep precipice. We reached the Hungham perimeter on December 6th and found patients waiting for us. They were men of the 3rd and 7th Divisions, (1st) Marines and many Chinese prisoners of war. We were operating within an hour of our arrival."[14]

The Chinese continued to advance on Hungham, prompting one of the greatest evacuations under fire in military history. On 11 December, the evacuation began, and by 24 December, Christmas Eve, the evacuation was complete. Two hundred thousand U.S. and ROK troops, and Korean civilians were safe. The last of the evacuees left under cover of naval bombardment.[15]

On 15 December, the 1st MASH loaded aboard LCMs and rode out to the USNS *Fred C. Ainsworth,* setting up an onboard hospital, along with the 121st Evacuation Hospital. The *Ainsworth* sailed from Hungham Harbor at 1:40 PM on 24 December, only after the last men were off the beach and aboard ships.

Brosmer witnessed the final hours from the deck of the *Ainsworth:* "The USS *Missouri* was sitting down about a mile from us, shooting those big sixteen-inchers right over our heads. . . . There were two cruisers, the *St. Paul* and the *Minneapolis* sitting right next to us. . . . It was just like the Fourth of July . . . and the Air Force was up there overhead, just bombing the heck out of them, keeping them back. . . . I think they finally got the last man off the beach at 2:00 PM on Christmas Eve. After they got the last man off the beach, the engineers blew up the harbor from one end to the other. What they couldn't get aboard a ship was destroyed when they blew up the harbor. There was nothing left but dust."[16]

Lt. Gen. Matthew Ridgeway, the new Eighth Army Commander (after the death of General Walker in a jeep accident), initiated a series of offensives at the start of 1951; Operation Thunderbolt in January, Operations Round-up and Killer in February, Operation Ripper in March, and Operation Rugged in April.[17]

After landing at Pusan on 26 December, the 1st MASH left in convoy arriving at Chonju the following day, remaining there until after the new year. The unit moved to Andong on 24 January 1951, and then further north to Chechon on 3 February. At one point, the Chinese advanced to within three miles of the hospital.

"While we were in Chechon, patients came in by helicopter and ambulance. There were two planes and four pilots who did nothing but ferry patients from the front back to us. We were always fifteen hundred to two thousand yards from the front line. We could hear the fighting because we were that close. The key was to stay close so that the faster you could get them into surgery and taken care of, the more you could save."[18]

In April, MacArthur was relieved of command, and the nurses of the "Lucky Thirteen" became eligible for rotation out of Korea. Brosmer recalled: "In mid-April they gave us nurses the choice of either staying with our units in Korea or going back to Japan and out of the combat zone. I didn't have any desire to go back to Japan; I wanted to go home. If you stayed in Korea, you got points towards rotation back to the States, but if you returned to Japan, you would have to stay six more months, so I opted to stay in Korea."

Brosmer spent her remaining time in Korea assigned to the 4th Field Hospital in Taegu until leaving Korea and rotating home on 20 May 1951. She sailed from Japan aboard the USNS *Marine Phoenix* and arrived to a hero's welcome and parade on 25 August, one of the first seven nurses to return stateside from Korea. For Brosmer, the Korean War was over.

The character of the war itself was changing. By the summer of 1951, the dynamic advances and retreats that characterized the first year were replaced with a war more static in character, reminiscent of the World War I. The Chinese and North Koreans, suffering from heavy casualties as a result of UN offensives, were amenable to entering into an armistice, and formal truce talks began on 10 July 1951.

Brosmer remained in the Army and served another nineteen years, rising to the rank of lieutenant colonel. She saw service overseas in Germany, Italy, and Puerto Rico, as well as in stateside postings as prestigious as West Point and Walter Reed Medical Center where she helped pioneer open-heart surgery. She retired at Fort Campbell, Kentucky on 31 August 1970 with twenty-one years of service.[19]

Brosmer currently lives in Southern California where she makes public appearances speaking about the Korean War. She is also one of the few female members of the "Chosin Few," an elite organization of veterans of the Chosin Reservoir, who have affectionately dubbed her "Hot Lips," referencing the fictional MASH operating room nurse, Maj. Margaret Houlihan, from the 1968 novel *M*A*S*H* by Richard Hooker.[20] Brosmer considers the movie and TV series "pretty accurate, except for all the hanky-panky."

Having experienced firsthand the result of entering a war unprepared, she remains an advocate of a strong military.

ENDNOTES

1. Margaret Brosmer, interview by Scott Baron, 29 May 2005, transcript, The Women's Memorial, Arlington, Va.
2. Ibid.
3. Strait, Sandy. *What Was it Like in the Korean War.* New York: Royal Fireworks Press, 1999.
4. Summers, Col. Harry G. The Korean War: A Fresh Perspective. *Military History Magazine,* April 1996.
5. Chambers, John Whiteclay, II. *Oxford Companion to American Military History.* New York: Oxford University Press, 1999.
6. Margaret Brosmer, interview by Scott Baron, 29 May 2005, transcript, The Women's Memorial Arlington, VA.
7. O'Connor, Rev. Patrick. "Catholic Nurse Describes Life on Korean Battlefield." The New World (NCWC News Service), 16 February 1951.
8. Margaret Brosmer, interview by Scott Baron, 29 May 2005, transcript, The Women's Memorial Arlington, VA.
9. Author. *Oxford Companion to American Military History.* New York: Oxford University Press, 1999.
10. Witt, Linda, Judith Bellafaire, Britta Granrud, & Mary Jo Binker. *A Defense Weapon Known to Be of Value: Servicewomen of the Korean War.* Lebanon, N.H.: University of New England Press/Military Women's Press, 2005, pp. 192–3.
11. Higgens, Marguerite. *War in Korea: The Report of a Woman Combat Correspondent.* New York: Doubleday Books, 1951.
12. O'Connor, Rev. Patrick. "Catholic Nurse Describes Life on Korean Battlefield." The New World (NCWC News Service), 16 February 1951.
13. Witt, Linda, Judith Bellafaire, Britta Granrud, & Mary Jo Binker. *A Defense Weapon Known to Be of Value: Servicewomen of the Korean War.* Lebanon, N.H.: University of New England Press/Military Women's Press, 2005, pp. 192–3.
14. O'Connor, Rev. Patrick. "Catholic Nurse Describes Life on Korean Battlefield." The New World (NCWC News Service), 16 February 1951.
15. Clements, Glen. "Epic Hungham Evacuation Ends; 200,000 Taken Off Beachhead." *Pacific Stars and Stripes,* 6(333); 16 December 1950.
16. Margaret Brosmer, interview by Scott Baron, 29 May 2005, transcript, The Women's Memorial Arlington, VA.
17. Author. *Oxford Companion to American Military History.* New York: Oxford University Press, 1999.
18. Margaret Brosmer, interview by Scott Baron, 29 May 2005, transcript, The Women's Memorial Arlington, VA.
19. Ibid.
20. Richard Hooker was a pseudonym for Richard Hornberger, who as a captain and surgeon for the 8055th MASH performed "Meatball Surgery" in Korea. The novel is based on his experiences.

Col. Ruby Grace Bradley, USA

Many of the women who served in Korea from 1950 to 1953, were not serving in their first war. Many military nurses had served in harm's way during World War II, although few had actually served at actual sites.

On 30 November 1951, as the Eighth Army prepared to withdraw from Pyongyang in the face of one hundred thousand Chinese and North Korean soldiers intent on recapturing the capital, nurses and medics of the 171st Evacuation Hospital scrambled to evacuate the sick and wounded.

Maj. Ruby Grace Bradley moved from ambulance to plane and back on the improvised landing strip as she supervised loading of the last of the wounded onto the plane. As chief nurse, she'd refused evacuation until the last patients were loaded aboard. As she returned from one last visit to the ambulance and dodged snipers' bullets on her way back to the plane, the ambulance exploded, victim of a direct hit from an enemy shell.[1] Years later, in an interview, Bradley would remark, "You got to get out in a hurry when you have somebody behind you with a gun."

Bradley could speak with authority. The first time she found herself in similar circumstances was in the Philippines in December 1941. She hadn't been quick enough, and had spent thirty-seven months as a POW of the Japanese.[2]

Ruby Grace Bradley was born on a farm in Spencer, West Virginia, on 19 December 1907 and dreamed of being a teacher. After high school, she

Photo courtesy of The Women's Memorial

attended Glenville State Teachers' College and graduated in 1926. She taught elementary students for four years in Spencer's one-room schools until 1930, when she changed direction and entered the Philadelphia General Hospital School of Nursing.

After graduation from nursing school in 1933, she accepted a position as a nurse for the CCC at Walter Reed Hospital in D.C. Her first exposure to the military must have been favorable, as she enlisted in the ANC nine months later, on 16 October 1934.[3] With the relative rank of second lieutenant, she served as a general duty nurse at Walter Reed until transferred to the station hospital at Fort Mills in the Philippine Islands. She reported for duty at Fort Mills on 14 February 1940.

Many military personnel favored serving in the Philippines in 1940, and Bradley enjoyed the dances and parties in the warm tropical evenings. But storm clouds were gathering on the horizon, and most observers believed that war with Japan was a matter of when rather than if. On 14 February 1941, Bradley assumed the duties of surgical and head nurse at the station hospital, Camp John Hay, in the mountains of Baguio, Luzon. She was on duty the morning of 8 December, preparing for a routine hysterectomy, when she was summoned to headquarters and informed that the Japanese had bombed the American fleet at Pearl Harbor, Hawaii. As she reported back to the operating room to assist in the surgery, bombs began to fall.[4]

That morning, eighteen Japanese planes, seventeen of them in formation, dropped 128 bombs on the post, many of which, luckily for the Americans, failed to explode. Lieutenant Bradley and her fellow nurse, Lt. Beatrice Chambers, along with Soldiers and civilians, fled into the mountains and tried to get to Manila but found all roads blocked. The retreating Americans had destroyed bridges over the rivers, and the Japanese aircraft had targeted major highways. When they were captured, along with others, on 28 December 1941, they became the first nurses seized by the Japanese.[5]

For the next three months, Bradley and Chambers remained at the hospital at Camp John Hay, treating prisoners as best they could, lacking both instruments and medicine. Several missionary and civilian nurses assisted them. Whatever instruments and medicines they possessed had to be smuggled into the camp.

In April 1943, they were transferred to the civilian internment camp, Camp Holmes, in Baguio, where they remained until 20 September when Bradley was moved to the Santo Tomas Internment Camp in Manila. Chambers elected to remain behind, a move she would later regret.

During her time in captivity, Bradley and the other "Angels in Fatigues" not only improvised medical supplies (using hemp for sutures and sheets for bandages) but smuggled in food and medicine to give to starving children, a violation that could have resulted in their execution. Credited with assisting in

230 covert operations, including the delivery of thirteen American babies, Bradley weighed a scant eighty pounds when American forces liberated the camp on 3 February 1945.[6]

Returning from the Pacific to a hero's parade in Spencer, West Virginia, Bradley was promoted to first lieutenant after eleven years in the Army, and after taking leave, reported to the station hospital at Fort Meyer, Virginia, as assistant chief nurse on 4 July 1945. One month later, on 12 August, she assumed the same duties at McGuire General Hospital in Richmond, Virginia, where she was promoted to captain on 27 October.

On 1 March 1946, she took over as principal chief nurse of the station hospital at Fort Eustis, Virginia. Assignments rotated rapidly; a year at Letterman General Hospital in San Francisco (starting in August 1947), seven months at Walter Reed in D.C., and then ten months at a naval air station in Cocoa, Florida.

On 17 July 1950, Bradley, newly promoted to major as of the previous May, volunteered for assignment as chief nurse of the 171st Evacuation Hospital at Fort Bragg, North Carolina, and was ordered to prepare for immediate movement to the FEC. Like Bradley, the hospital had seen service during World War II. Bradley arrived with her unit at Camp Hakata, Japan on 27 August, and landed at Taegu, Korea, on 21 September, less than a week following the Marines' landing at Inchon.[7]

On 28 October, the 171st moved north to Pyongyang in support of the U.S./UN offensive, but the unexpected entry of two hundred sixty thousand Chinese troops changed the equation and by late November, the hospital was scrambling to withdraw in the face of an advancing enemy. The 171st withdrew to Yongdongpo, arriving on 6 December, and ten days later moved to Camp Kokura, Kyushu, Japan. Bradley remained with the 171st until July 1951, when she was posted as a nursing consultant to Headquarters, Eighth U.S. Army, Korea. She was promoted to chief nurse of the Eighth Army on 1 August; she remained with the Eighth Army until 20 June 1953.

Following the Korean War, on 15 June 1955, Bradley was awarded the Florence Nightingale Medal, the highest award of the International Red Cross, for her service as a POW in World War II, and as a combat nurse in Korea.

She remained in the Army and served at Fort McPherson, Georgia, as chief nurse, Headquarters U.S. Army-Europe at Heidelberg, Germany, and later as director of nurses, Brooke Army Medical Center at Fort Sam Houston, Texas. Bradley retired as a full colonel on 31 March 1963.[8]

After leaving the Army, Bradley continued nursing until she retired at the age of eighty. She died of a heart attack on 28 May 2002 in Hazard, Kentucky, at the age of ninety-four, and was buried at Arlington National Cemetery with full military honors, which included a twenty-one-gun salute, riderless horse and caisson, and a U.S. Army Band. She is the most decorated woman in the history of the U.S. Army.[9]

Bradley was frequently heard to recall the words of her recruiters when she'd enlisted in 1934: "Now don't worry, you won't be in a war." Then she'd laugh and smile. "Here I was in two of 'em."[10]

ENDNOTES

1. Senator John D. Rockefeller IV, statement on the Senate floor, in memory of Col. Ruby Bradley, 7 July 2002.
2. Bradley, Ruby G. "Prisoners of War in the Far East." ANC Web site: http://history. amedd.army.mil/ANCWebsite/bradley.htm
3. Ibid.
4. Norman, Elizabeth. *We Band of Angels–The Untold Story of American Nurse Trapped on Bataan by the Japanese.* New York: Pocket Books, 1999, pp. 6–7.
5. Bradley, Ruby G. "Prisoners of War in the Far East."
6. Johnson, Laura Kendall. "One of the Most Decorated Women in Military History Laid to Rest." *Knight Ridder/Tribune News Service*, 9 July 2002.
7. Bradley, Ruby G. "Prisoners of War in the Far East."
8. Ibid.
9. U.S. Army Center for Military History.
10. NBC Nighty News with Tom Brokaw Feb. 23, 2000 or (www.west-point.org/family/ Adbc/Media/Boston Bradley.htm.)

PART IV

★ ★ ★

World War II

There is a story that at the signing of the peace treaty at Versailles on 23 June 1919, a German delegate, upset with the harsh terms imposed on Germany by the Allies, remarked to a reporter, "We'll see you again in 20 years. "[1] If true, it was prophetic. Twenty years, two months, and seven days later, on 1 September 1939, Germany invaded Poland, initiating World War II.

The period between the first and second world wars has frequently been called "The Long Armistice," and in many ways the second war was just a continuation of the first, in the sense that events resulting from the end of World War I directly influenced events that led to World War II.

The end of World War I was accompanied by the fall of three great empires: the Romanov Empire in Czarist Russia, the Austro-Hungarian Empire in Eastern Europe, and the Ottoman Empire in Turkey. Into the power vacuum thus created, nationalistic movements emerged in Japan, Italy, Spain, France, and Germany, enhanced both by a worldwide economic depression and lethargy on the part of democracies exhausted from war, resulting in policies of appeasement and isolationism.

World War I caused 400 billion dollars in property damage and destroyed much of Europe's infrastructure. More than 65 million men and women took part in World War I; 13 million of them were killed or later died from their injuries. This number exceeded the number killed in all the wars between 1790–1913, including the Napoleonic Wars, the Crimean War, the Danish Prussian War, the Austro-Prussian War, the American Civil War, the Franco-Prussian War, the Boer War, the Russo-Japanese War, and the Balkan Wars. [2]

English women served extensively in the military during wartime for the first time, beginning in 1914 with FANY. Created in 1907 as a link between frontline fighting units and the field hospitals, FANYs ran field hospitals, drove ambulances, and set up soup kitchens and troop canteens, often close to the front under extremely dangerous conditions. FANYs were awarded many decorations for bravery, including seventeen Military Medals, one Legion d'Honneur, and twenty-seven Croix de Guerre.

In 1915, female volunteers were allowed to serve overseas in hospitals at the Western Front, Mesopotamia, and Gallipoli as part of VADs. During the war, approximately thirty-eight thousand VADs worked as assistant nurses, ambulance drivers, and cooks, and VAD hospitals were opened in most large towns in Britain.

The British WAAC was established in January 1917, and women served as drivers, clerks, telephone operators ("telephonists"), cooks, and instructors. When the Royal Flying Corps and Royal Naval Air Service merged in March 1918 to form the Royal Air Force, a female branch, the WRAF, was immediately created. More than one hundred thousand British women served in the uniformed services during 1914–18, nearly half as nurses.[3]

World War I was the first war in which American women were able to partic-ipate in the military. Two hundred twenty civilian women of the Army Signal Corps served overseas in England and France as operators called "Hello Girls." (They were finally recognized as veterans in 1979.) Only American Army nurses saw service in France, and by the end of the war, some ten thousand American military nurses had served overseas in field hospitals, troop transports, and in operating rooms at the front. One hundred two Army nurses died overseas, most from influenza and pneumonia. Twenty-three were awarded the DSM and three received the DSC.[4]

Despite passage of the 19th Amendment in 1919, which gave American women the right to vote—partly to acknowledge their service during the war—the prevailing attitude was against women serving in the military in general, and specifically in combat.

During the '30s, particularly the latter part of the decade, as war clouds gath-ered over Europe, the U.S. government discussed the possibility of creating a women's corps. However, it was only after Pearl Harbor that Congress authorized the creation of the WAAC, on 14 May 1942, over the objections of many members of Congress. Col. Oveta Culp Hobby was sworn in as the first director of the WAAC that same day. The WAAC was changed on 1 July 1943 to the Women's Army Corps, and was given full military status. By August 1942, women were authorized to enlist in the WAVES as part of the Navy, and an estimated one hundred thousand did, but women in the WAVES were prohibited from serving overseas. Women Marines were authorized on 7 November 1942 and women served in the Coast Guard SPARs. More than one thousand women also ferried aircraft as part of the WASP. Thousands of other women served with the ANC and the NNC. There are no exact figures on how many women served in the Army and Army Air Corps during the war, but there were close to one hundred thousand women serving in April 1945, with a little more than sixteen thousand overseas.[5] In all, it is estimated that as many as four hundred thousand women served in uniform during World War II.[6] This was the greatest utilization of women, from the greatest number of countries, in the history of the world.

Even though American women were not allowed to serve in combat units, the idea was considered. Even before America entered the war, Gen. George C. Marshall studied the performance of European women soldiers, especially the British women in Anti-Aircraft Artillery (AAA) units, and after America's entry into the war, he asked Eisenhower to investigate the effectiveness of British mixed-gender units. After Eisenhower's favorable report, Marshall determined to conduct his own experiment.[7]

Operating under severe security, twenty-one WAAC officers and 374 enlisted servicewomen were assigned to two AAA batteries and searchlight units of the 36th Coast Artillery, assigned to the Military District of Washington. Between 12 December 1942 and 15 April 1943, men and women trained together in antiaircraft units, and the commanding officer of the experimental unit, Col. Timberlake, found that the women "met the physical, intellectual and psychological standards" and were "superior in efficiency," an opinion shared by the district commander, Maj. Gen. John T. Lewis. They recommended to Marshall that the experiment be expanded and continued.[8]

General Marshall weighed the various considerations. How would the public respond? What about the conservative members of Congress who had opposed the women's corps itself? How would this impact Marshall's plan to expand the WAC? How would the change impact existing legislation? Would women continue to volunteer? Would they be drafted?

Even though Marshall's experiment was considered a success, two factors played significantly into his decision not to continue the experiment: (1) There was no real threat from the air to the continental United States and AAA positions could be filled by men on limited duty; (2) There was a much greater need for WAACs in clerical and administrative positions. The experiment was ended, the women were reassigned, and Marshall ordered that the results should be kept confidential. "It is not believed that national policy or public opinion is yet ready to accept the use of women in field force units." At least for World War II, American servicewomen would not be sent into combat.

ENDNOTES

1. Snyder, Louis. *The Long Armistice 1919–1939: Europe between Wars*. New York: Franklin Watts, Inc., 1964, p. 1.
2. Ibid.

3. Caddick-Adams, Peter. *Oxford Companion to Military History.* UK: Royal Military College of Science, Cranfield University, 2001.
4. "Military Nurses in World War I." The Women's Memorial, Arlington, Va. http://www.womensmemorial.org/historyandcollections/history/lrnmrewwinurses.html
5. U.S. Army Women's Museum, Ft. Lee, Va, Strength of the Army Reports, STM 30, 1942–1945; Treadwell, Mattie E. *The US Army in World War II, Special Studies, The Women's Army Corps.* Washington, D.C.: Government Printing Office, 1954.
6. Campbell, D'Ann. "Women in Combat: The World War Two Experiences in the United States, Great Britain, Germany, and the Soviet Union," *Journal of Military History*, April 1993.
7. Ibid.
8. Ibid.

2nd Lt. Frances Y. Slanger, USA

Eighteen army nurses of the 45th Field Hospital, along with those of the 128th Evacuation Hospital, landed at Utah Beach in Normandy, France, on 10 June 1944, four days after the invasion of Europe by Allied forces during World War II. Among the group of registered nurses was 2nd Lt. Frances Y. Slanger of Roxbury, Massachusetts, who would later become the first American nurse to be killed in the European theater. On D-Day, approximately ten thousand Allied soldiers were killed and wounded by German defenders as they came ashore at five beaches along a sixty-mile front. Surgeons and medics were staggered by the number of casualties and asked the Allied command in London to send nurses as soon as possible.[1]

Slanger was of Jewish descent and, during the war there was strong anti-Semitism in America, in addition to racial discrimination in America. These biases existed in the armed services and it was not unusual for American Soldiers to call a colored person a nigger or a Jew a kike. However, regarding the latter, once the wounded were tended to by nurses of all ethnic backgrounds, the Soldiers realized that they owed their lives to the professionalism and tender care given by these women who never seemed to tire while being exposed to the carnage inflicted by war.

Photo courtesy of NARA

War was no stranger to Slanger, who was born Freidel Yachet Schlanger in Lodz, Poland. She and her mother and sister endured Russian occupation during World War I when she was fifteen months old. The brutal Cossacks barricaded Lodz, often known as the stepchild of Russia, in anticipation of a German invasion. Slanger's father, Dawid, had immigrated to America two years before, seeking a safe refuge for his family. However, once the war began, steamship companies decided that it was too dangerous to send their ships across the Atlantic because of the German U-boat threat. With immigration discontinued, Dawid's wife and two daughters stayed in Lodz, living in the slums of the city where the Russians killed and maimed Jews at will. On 18 November 1914 a fierce battle for the city began. Though victorious, the Germans suffered thirty-five thousand casualties.

When the war ended, Slanger was five years old and had witnessed the horrors of war. Two years later (in 1920), she and her mother and sister immigrated to the United States, where her family began their new life in a row house in south Boston. While in America her father changed his name to David Slanger. He supported the family as a fruit peddler and each morning he would awaken his daughter before dawn to help him make his rounds. To her neighbors and people along his route she became know as the fruit peddler's daughter.

Throughout her early years, Slanger dreamed of becoming an internationally known writer. She attended Abraham Lincoln intermediate school and in her free hours wrote poems and essays. At the age of seventeen she entered the High School of Practical Arts. In addition to her writing ambition, Slanger had a natural tendency to care for the less fortunate, especially children. This led to her decision to become a nurse. When she announced this desire to her family, they were dumbfounded. They termed such work as a Christian calling and as a Jewish woman she was expected to marry a man of promise—a lawyer, doctor, or businessman. However, Slanger persisted in attempting to make this dream come true and visited the Boston City Hospital School of Nursing to apply for training. She was quickly told by the supervising nurse to come back when she had finished high school.

At about this time, the 1929 financial crash occurred and Slanger was forced to split her time between helping her father and attending school. Following her graduation she worked in the stockroom of the Massachusetts Knitting Mills. At twenty years of age and with the depression still taking its toll, the family's financial plight became worse since her father was ill and the family depended on the money she made at the mills. However, Slanger dared to pursue her undiminished dream and she filled out an application for the Boston City Hospital School of Nursing. She waited anxiously for the nursing school's reply. There were rumors that Boston nursing schools had limitations on the number of Jewish and colored students they would accept each year. In fact, only two colored applicants were allowed each term at the Boston City Hospital School of Nursing. Slanger was accepted and ordered to report for the winter session in February 1934.

Throughout her young life, Slanger kept what she called her "chapbook" (a personal diary/scrapbook). It included her writings, clippings of important world events, and—not surprisingly—her letter of acceptance to nurse's training.

When she began attending nursing school, Slanger soon found that nursing supervisors were the gods of the floor during her probationary term of training. Two supervisors gave her particular problems. She didn't know whether it was her attitude, work ethic, or the fact that she was Jewish that bothered the supervisors. One reported her as blundering, slow, irresponsible, and unable to accept criticism. She was often taken to task for spending too much time with children. All Slanger sought was fairness and justice.

Although the supervisors submitted mixed reviews of Slanger's training progress, the pros far outweighed the cons and on 23 February 1937, Slanger graduated from Boston City Hospital's School of Nursing. After passing state examinations, she became a certified registered nurse.

In 1939, Poland was invaded by Germany and fifty thousand civilians were killed. The following year, the Germans officially sealed the Lodz ghetto encampment, confining one hundred seventy thousand Jews indefinitely, a number of them relatives of the Slanger family. More Jews were herded into the ghetto, and brought in by train from other cities. Many were worked to death in factories that produced munitions for the German army.

When the Germans invaded the Soviet Union in 1941, it appeared that a world war was in the offing. Following the attack on Pearl Harbor and America's entry into the war, Slanger joined the U.S. Army Nurse Corps and was ordered to report to Lovell General Hospital at Fort Devens, Massachusetts, on or about 12 November 1941. However, in October her father suffered his second stroke; she rescinded her enlistment and the ANC placed her application in a deferred file.

News of the mass murders of Jews in Poland was first published by the *Boston Globe* in June of 1942 and this moved Slanger to officially join the ANC and in this capacity help Allied soldiers stop the Nazis. She joined the ANC in the spring of 1943 but was denied overseas duty due to defective vision in both eyes. Thus, she was limited to duty within the continental boundaries of the United States.

Slanger completed training at Fort Devens, Fort Rucker in Alabama, and Camp Gordon in Georgia. However, once her training was complete, she was determined to serve overseas and challenged the ANC policy successfully. This was a major step for the five foot one inch, introverted nurse who had to face down a medical officer. But her argument was clear and persuasive. Nurses were needed urgently on the front lines and she was ready to meet that need. She was successful in her argument and cleared to serve overseas. She was assigned to the 2nd Platoon of the 45th Field Hospital Unit and on 10 June 1944 was on board the freighter *William N. Pendleton* as it crossed the English Channel headed for the Normandy coast.

Transferred to a landing craft, the nurses struggled ashore at Utah Beach amidst the fierce sounds of warfare, something they had not experienced before. It was frightening as cannons roared and the skies were filled with Allied and German aircraft engaged in air-to-air combat. The nurses finally made it to a field hospital in a pasture near Le Grand Chemin. It was the only medical facility operating in the area. When they entered the tents the scene was almost overwhelming. The smell of the dead permeated the air, causing the nurses to hesitate before plunging into the chaotic fight to save lives in the desperation of the moment.

The nurses worked until they dropped from sheer exhaustion. When they awoke, their gruesome tasks continued and, periodically, German planes would drop bombs or strafe so close to the hospital tents that were marked by large red crosses that the medical teams had to leave their patients and race for foxholes.

Though compassionate and skillful in her care for the wounded and dying, Slanger remained a loner, often sitting by herself and writing in her chapbook. Her three tent mates liked and admired her although she appeared to them to be somewhat mysterious because she never joined them in their off-duty frolicking, preferring to remain a bit on the outside as if she thought she didn't fit in. She did make friends with other Jewish personnel, in particular Capt. Joseph P. Shoham, a dentist of the 2nd Platoon who later became the platoon's mess boss. Second platoon doctors were all Jewish except one, but a Jewish nurse, like Slanger, was a rarity. One of the doctors whom she befriended managed to figure out why Slanger was so different. It was, he believed, because everything seemed to mean much more to her than to the others.

The 45th moved five times after landing at Utah Beach, finally arriving in Elsenborn, Belgium, on 7 October 1944. The town was relatively peaceful and the unit set up an encampment near the city. The doctors, medics, and nurses finally had time to rest, write home, read their mail, and in general recuperate after five months of arduous duty. Elsenborn was considered safe from German attack because their now-weakened army was fighting to hold the city of Aachen to the north. With no apparent nearby threat, the unit relaxed; the need to dig foxholes seemed unnecessary.

The U.S. military newspaper, *Stars and Stripes*, (the paper had first been printed in France in July 1944) and the biweekly magazine, *Yank*, often printed front-page articles about the arrival and activities of WACS in Europe but gave little attention to nurses. Slanger and her tentmates were aware of the many letters printed in other periodicals about the work of the nurses but Slanger was concerned that the GIs in the foxholes who put their lives on the line every day deserved to be honored in print, not the WACs or nurses.

One night as Slanger was writing in her chapbook, she decided to send a letter to the editor at *Stars and Stripes* describing nurses' feelings for Soldiers. The letter went as follows:

It is 0200, and I have been lying awake for one hour, listening to the steady, even breathing of the other three nurses in the tent and thinking about some of the things we had discussed during the day. The rain is beating down on the tent with torrential force. The wind is on a mad rampage and its main objective seems to be to lift the tent off its pole and fling it about our heads.

The fire is burning low and just a few live coals are on the bottom. With the slow feeding of wood, and finally coal, a roaring fire is started. I can't help thinking how similar to a human being a fire is. If it is allowed to run down too low, and if there is a spark of life left in it, it can be nursed back. So can a human being. It is slow; it is gradual; it is done all the time in these field hospitals and other hospitals in the European Theater of Operations.

We have read several articles in different magazines and papers sent in by a grateful GI praising the work of the nurses around the combat zones. Praising us . . . for what? I climbed back into my cot. Lieutenant (Margaret M.) Bowler was the only one I had awakened. I whispered to her, Lieutenant (Christine) Cox and Lieutenant (Elizabeth) Powers slept on. Fine nurses and great girls to live with . . . of course, like in all families, an occasional quarrel, but these were quickly forgotten.

I'm writing this by flashlight, in this light it looks something like a dive. In the center of the tent are two poles, one part chimney, the other a plain tent pole. Kindling wood lies in disorderly confusion on the damp ground. We don't have a tarp on the ground. A French wine pitcher, filled with water stands by. The GIs say we rough it. We in our little tent can't see it. True, we are set up in tents, sleep on cots, and are subject to the temperature of the weather.

We wade ankle-deep in mud, but you have to lie in it. We are restricted to our immediate area, a cow pasture or a hayfield, but then, who is not restricted? We have a stove and coal. We even have a laundry line in the tent. Our GI drawers are at this moment doing the dance of the pants what with the wind blowing, the tent waving precariously, the rain beating down, the guns firing and me with a flashlight, writing. It all adds up to a feeling of unreality.

Sure, we rough it, but in comparison to the way you men are taking it, we can't complain, nor do we feel that bouquets are due us. But you, the men behind the guns, the men driving our tanks, flying our planes, sailing our ships, building bridges and the men who pave the way and the men who are left behind—it is to you we doff our helmets. To every GI wearing the American uniform—for you we have the greatest admiration and respect.

Yes, this time we are handing out the bouquets—but only after taking care of some of your buddies, comforting them when they are brought in bloody, dirty with the earth, mud and grime, and most of them so tired. Somebody's brothers, somebody's fathers, and somebody's sons, seeing them gradually brought back to life, to consciousness, and to see their lips separate into a grin when they first welcome you. Usually they kid, hurt as they are. It doesn't amaze us to hear one of them say, "hi' ya babe," or "holy mackerel, an American woman," or more indiscreetly "How about a kiss?"

These Soldiers stay with us but a short time, from ten days to possibly two weeks. We have learned a great deal about our American Soldier, and the stuff he is made of. The wounded do not cry. Their buddies come first.

The patience and determination they show, the courage and fortitude they have, is sometimes awesome to behold. It is we who are proud to be here. Rough it? No, it is a privilege to be able to receive you, and a great distinction to see you open your eyes and with that swell American grin say, "Hi' ya babe."

On the same day that Slanger delivered her letter to the unit's mail clerk, the 45th received word that it could expect no casualties the following day. Although guns could be heard off in the distance, this particular Saturday the personnel could relax. The 45th believed that this quiet day would be one of many to follow as the Allied forces moved toward Germany.

All was quiet that evening; after dinner many returned to their tents to write letters and play poker. And, when lulls like this happened most thought of those they'd left behind at home. Suddenly, at 2100 hours an artillery shell crashed into the ground near the tent encampment. The second shell tore into tents and personnel as they ran from their shelters in a state of confusion into a downpour. They had no idea where the shells were coming from and which way to run. Since it was a pitch-black night, they turned off the generators thinking that their lights might be giving away their position. More shells rained down on them and the screams and yelling of injured personnel began to swell. The wounded and critical casualties were rushed to the surgery tents amidst the chaos. A woman's cry, "Over here!" was heard over the din and doctors and medics rushed to one of the nurse's tents, which was badly damaged. Three nurses huddled around a small figure in the debris.

Slanger had been critically wounded, shrapnel had cut her deeply across her abdomen and she was hemorrhaging badly. From their experience, those that surrounded her knew that she wouldn't make it. She was carried to a medical tent, where she died within the hour. Many of her comrades, both men and women, sobbed at her passing. Frances Slanger was thirty-one years old.

American guns positioned to the west behind the 45th finally countered the German artillery. After firing twenty shells, the German batteries ceased their barrage. The night was silent once again.

Around midnight, members of the 2nd Platoon held a brief service for those lost during the attack: Slanger; Maj. Herman Lord, doctor in charge of the 2nd Platoon; and Pvt. Vincente Rivas. Three days after the incident Frances Y. Slanger, Slanger, #752108, was buried at the U.S. Cemetery at Henri-Chapelle, which is approximately twenty miles northwest of Elsenborn. Two thousand graves of American Soldiers dot the Belgian hillside in the cemetery.

Seventeen days after Slanger mailed her letter, *Stars and Stripes* printed it, not as a letter to the editor, but as an editorial titled, "A Nurse Writes the Editorial." Her poignant words lauding American GIs struck a chord with Soldiers and civilians alike. The article, published posthumously, drew hundreds of letters from American Soldiers and civilians from around the world. In author Bob Welch's book, *American Nightingale: The Story of Frances Slanger, Forgotten Heroine of Normandy,* he quotes a typical letter written by an Army Air Force air gunner, which was also signed by eight other airmen.

Inspiration is difficult to discover. We discovered it. Amid the roar and thunder of war emerges at one time or another the genuine, worth-living-for thoughts of a human being. Only few people can put it on paper—but all of us have that singular, infinite thought deep in our minds and hearts. Frances Slanger put it on paper—so overwhelmingly beautiful yet so much from the heart. She captured the distinguishable characteristic of human love and understanding which has become so latent in our speedy world. She portrayed modesty in the nth degree—looking for no praise, but gathering the hearts of millions of GIs into

Army nurses of the 45th Field Hospital pay homage at the grave of 2nd Lt. Frances Y. Slanger USA at Henri-Chapelle Cemetery in Belgium. *Courtesy of NARA*

her possession and then losing them. Losing them in this life to her memory, but retaining them in that unknown world to come.

Frances Slanger is a great woman. We say it because her memory in our minds will linger steadfastly long after the final gun is fired in this war. Why? Because Frances Slanger pointed out the only genuine rule for peace on earth: human love and understanding.[2]

In addition to being awarded the Purple Heart Medal posthumously, a newly built hospital ship was named *Frances Y. Slanger,* American airmen displayed painted images of her on the sides of their aircraft, often with the words, In Memory of Lt. F. Slanger, USANC.

In October 1947, Slanger's body was brought back to America aboard the Liberty ship, *Joseph V. Connolly.* That year the U.S. Army offered the parents of those lost in the war and buried in overseas cemeteries the option of having their loved ones returned to America. Slanger's relatives wanted her remains to be returned home. On 21 November 1947 Slanger was finally laid to rest at Independent Pride of Boston, a Jewish cemetery, in West Roxbury, Massachusetts. She was buried with full military honors. On the upper part of her gravestone (which was etched with flowers and the symbol of the Army Nurse Corps) are words taken from her letter:

U.S. ARMY NURSE CORPS
The wounded do not Cry,
Their Buddies Come First.

The lower half of the stone reads:

Lt. Frances Y. Slanger
Beloved Daughter and sister
Killed in Belgium Oct. 21, 1944

ENDNOTES

1. The main reference for writing this chapter was Bob Welch's book, *American Nightingale: The Story of Frances Slanger, Forgotten Heroine of Normandy*. New York: Atria Books, 2004. Welch's work is probably the most comprehensive story written to date regarding the life, wartime experiences, and death of Frances Slanger. It is extremely well researched and written with accuracy and completeness seldom found in such war stories. In reviewing his Bibliography it appears that it is the only book solely written about this heroic nurse. It is a book that vividly grasps the carnage of war and the sacrifices made by our young men and women who have fought for our nation in past wars and those of today.
2. Excerpted from Welch, Bob. *American Nightingale*, p. 224. The letter was written by Sgt. George W. Fritton, an air gunner with the Army Air Force's 647th Bomb Squadron, 410 Bomb Group.

Ens. Jane Louise Kendiegh
Cheverton, USN

It was only through an accident of fate that Ens. Jane Louise "Candy" Kendiegh Cheverton achieved the distinction of being the first flight nurse to land on a battlefield during World War II.[1]

Described as 108 pounds of green-eyed charm and efficiency, Jane Louise Kendiegh was born in Henrietta, Ohio, in 1922 (although numerous articles give Oberlin, Ohio, as her birthplace). She grew up on an apple orchard farm and was an honor student and valedictorian of Henrietta High School in 1940. She graduated from the St. Luke School of Nursing in Cleveland in 1943, achieving a childhood dream of becoming a nurse. Shortly after her graduation, she joined the U.S. Naval Nurse Corps.[2]

Commissioned an ensign, Cheverton was trained at the Great Lakes Naval Training Station, Illinois, and then was sent to the Naval Hospital at Treasure Island before being assigned to the NATS. She was one of twenty-four nurses who made up the first group to volunteer and be selected for training as air evacuation flight nurses.[3]

Cheverton was sent to the Naval Air Station at Alameda, California, in December 1944 for the basic air evacuation course. There she attended lectures on how high altitudes affected skull fractures or severe concussions, the expansion of gases in abdominal tracts, and other peculiarities of flight medicine.[4] Other classes were more practical in nature, such as flight operations, maintenance of medical equipment, water survival training, use of oxygen masks in flight, and how to safely evacuate patients from the aircraft under emergency conditions.

Upon completion of a six-week phase of classroom training, the nurses gained practical experience on transcontinental flights transferring wounded and ambulatory patients between stateside hospitals.[5]

After she graduated on 22 January 1945, and following her practice flights, Cheverton was assigned to the newly formed VRE-1 (Evacuation Transport Squadron) comprised of twenty-four flight nurses, twenty-four corpsmen (all pharmacist mates), a flight surgeon, and twenty-two twin-engine R4D Douglas Skytrains, the Navy version of the venerable Army C-47 or civilian DC-3.[6]

VRE-1 arrived in Guam in early February 1945, putting in place an evacuation system that would transport combat casualties directly from the battlefield to forward hospitals in Guam, then on to Pearl Harbor in Hawaii, ultimately arriving in the continental United States, where every effort was made to place the wounded in hospitals as close to home as possible.[7]

Initially, there was speculation as to whether or not nurses would be allowed to fly onto the actual battlefields, a concern that increased with the invasion of Iwo Jima on 19 February 1945. However, the military did decide to allow flight nurses into combat areas, and preparations were made to document and record the event. Navy Lt. Gill Dewitt was assigned to accompany the mission and "photograph the first navy nurse in action."[9]

Dewitt reported to Agana Airfield on Guam at 0200 hours on 3 March 1945 with orders to accompany Lt. (jg) Ann Purvis, only to discover upon arrival that Purvis' plane had already departed. Disappointed, he boarded the second plane for the fifteen-hundred-mile trip. Dewitt went aft, where he joined Ensign Cheverton; her corpsman; and a cargo of cots, blankets, and medical supplies.[10]

When they arrived at Iwo Jima, an offshore bombardment was in progress and the plane was ordered to circle the field, which continued for ninety minutes. Dewitt recalled, "We circled and circled the small island and watched the bursting shells beneath us like firecrackers on the Fourth of July."[11]

It was only after landing and reporting in that they learned that the first plane, with Lieutenant Purvis on board, had become lost, and thus Cheverton was afforded the distinction of being the first Navy nurse on a Pacific battlefield.[12]

Cheverton immediately reported to the hospital—a sandbagged tent beside the airfield—and set to work. There were sixteen critically wounded waiting on stretchers, ready to be loaded aboard; the flight surgeon gave her the rundown on each patient and indicated what treatment they would need. She recalled, "We took the worst. Others would be evacuated on hospital ships."[13]

First Navy nurse who saw action on a battlefield, Ens. Jane Kendiegh Cheverton attends a wounded man on Iwo Jima before taking off with casualties on a Navy evacuation plane. *Courtesy of NHC*

Their takeoff path was downwind to avoid flying over Japanese lines, and Cheverton worked without rest until her patients were safely delivered to ambulances in Guam. It was the first of what would become routine missions for the nurses of VRE-1, and Cheverton returned to Iwo Jima several more times, with three days off between missions. "The thing we always worried about . . . were the Japanese snipers. We were afraid of the gas tank getting hit," Cheverton recalled.[14]

Cheverton earned the additional distinction of being the first nurse to land at Okinawa, on 7 April 1945. She observed kamikaze planes at their deadly work. "They just disintegrated. They flew right into ships." When a photo of her tending the wounded made the front page of newspapers nationwide—from the *New York Times* to the *Seattle Times*—Cheverton became a media sensation, and the press followed her across the Pacific issuing dispatches regarding the "Angel of Mercy" and the "Most-whistled-at nurse in the Pacific."[15]

After three trips to Okinawa, Cheverton was ordered stateside where, accompanied by an injured Marine, she went on a month-long War Bond tour, speaking at shipyards and businesses. Soon, however, she returned to the Pacific where she was assigned the Guam-to-Honolulu leg of the evacuation route. Just about this time, she began dating one of the squadron's pilots, Lt. Robert E. Cheverton, whom she married on Valentine's Day (14 February) 1946.

Following the war and her discharge (married women were not allowed to serve), she followed her husband through his twenty-four-year Navy career, retiring to Point Loma, near San Diego, California, in 1963. She worked as an R.N. until her retirement in 1985. She died at home from cancer on 19 July 1987.[16]

Cheverton, as well as each of the first twelve nurse pioneers of VRE-1, received commendations from the Commander, Forward Area-Central Pacific, which read:

"For excellent service as a flight nurse in the Forward Area–Central Pacific, during the first quarter of 1945, for participation in numerous areas of the Pacific Ocean and contributing materially in the successful evacuation of wounded from the battle area of Iwo Jima. The skill care of patients, and devotion to duty throughout were worthy of the highest praise."[17]

ENDNOTES

1. Dewitt, Lt. Gill. *The First Navy Flight Nurse on a Pacific Battlefield: A Picture Story of a Flight to Iwo.* Fredericksburg, Tx.: The Admiral Nimitz Foundation, 1983.
2. Ibid.
3. Sutter, Janet. "'Angel of Mercy' Kept Wings: WWII Nurse Still Dotes on Patients," *The San Diego Union,* 24 March 1985.
4. Cooper, Page. *Navy Nurse.* New York: McGraw-Hill Book Company, 1946, pp. 171–72.
5. *American Journal of Nursing,* Volume 45, Number 6, June 1945.
6. Cooper, Page. *Navy Nurse,* pp. 174–75.
7. Frachette, Joseph. "Flight Nurse," *Navy Medicine,* March–April 1945.
8. *U.S. Navy Department BUMED (Bureau of Medicine) Newsletter Aviation Supplement,* 5(1), 20 July 1945.
9. Dewitt, Lt. Gill. *The First Navy Flight Nurse on a Pacific Battlefield.*
10. Ibid.
11. Ibid.
12. Ibid.
13. Sutter, Janet. "Angel of Mercy Kept Wings".
14. Ibid.
15. Ibid.
16. Ibid.
17. *U.S. Navy Department BUMED (Bureau of Medicine) Newsletter Aviation Supplement.*

Cpl. Barbara Lauwers
Podoski, USA

Cpl. Barbara Lauwers Podoski arrived for her interview with Kate Scott at The Women's Memorial dressed in a skirt and tunic, to which was attached with great pride her World War II miniature medals. Among those medals were three Slovakian ribbons, a U.S. Bronze Star, and a small circular ribbon which surrounded a button with the letters OSS on it. The diminutive corporal (she appeared to be just under five feet tall) had been born in Brno, Czechoslovakia, in 1914. At ninety-one, she was articulate in her recall of the war and her participation in it. She is an amazing woman.

★   ★   ★

Barbara met an American export official, Charles Lauwers, in Czechoslovakia the day after the German invasion of her country, 16 March 1939. She and her husband obtained travel documents at the American Consulate and escaped to America via the Belgian Congo aboard the SS *President Taylor*. The Lauwers settled in New York City and socialized only with their Slovak countrymen and often frequented the Czechoslovak consulate. On one occasion they attended a soccer game between the Sokol New York and the Chicago Club. Jan Masaryk, foreign minister of the

Barbara Lauwers Podoski was interviewed by Kate Scott in Arlington, Virginia, on 5 August 2005. The tape and transcript are deposited at The Women's Memorial in Arlington. *Photo courtesy of USA*

Czechoslovakian government in exile, was in the bleachers at the game and when Podoski saw him she bowed to him and he beckoned her to join him. They had met once before in London and after learning of her present limited personal activity he said to her, "Off with you to the legation in Washington. We need people like you—and *now!*"

Shortly thereafter the Japanese attacked Pearl Harbor and soon America was at war. Podoski's husband was drafted into the Army and a few days before Christmas in 1941 Podoski relocated to D.C. to work for the Czechoslovakian Legation.

Midmorning of 1 June 1943, Podoski became a U.S. citizen; a few hours later she joined the U.S. Army. She felt a strong patriotic duty to serve her new country; she hoped to be able to free up a Soldier for combat. She also hoped the service would be a great adventure. After completing three months of basic training, and a brief stint in the Army press service, she was ordered to Fort Oglethorpe, one of the two officers' schools for women in the Army.

Before Podoski started officers' school, a WAC captain arrived unexpectedly from D.C. and selected three of the officer candidates who were multilingual for very special training and Lauwers was one of the three (she was fluent in English, German, Czech, Slovak, and French). After she reported for duty in D.C. she learned that she was to be assigned to the OSS and sworn to secrecy about the agency. The OSS compound operated in several temporary buildings near the Lincoln Memorial, away from the rest of D.C.

Female GIs were dispersed throughout the agency; Podoski worked in a back room sorting out material of European origin. One coworker was a taciturn sergeant; one day she heard him hum a Czech melody and learned that it was his fraternity hymn at Harvard. Podoski treated him to the original version, the whole six stanzas in Czech, and the sergeant was ecstatic; she never learned how the melody got to the oldest American university.

In January 1944, Podoski was shipped out to the Algerian port of Oran in North Africa. She was sent to the Allied Control Commission in Algiers, where she worked with Americans, French, British, and a small detachment of Russians. Most of the men assigned to her regiment were paratroopers and were training for action behind enemy lines. Podoski was intrigued by the thought that someday she might be a part of something very significant. Since the U.S. Army did not admit women into combat she decided to prepare on her own. She convinced some French paratroopers that she would like to make a parachute jump. She landed among tree stumps, broke her collarbone, and knocked out several teeth. Her statement to hospital attendants was that she had had too much to drink and fallen into some tree stumps.

Shortly after the Allied armies entered Rome she was transferred to Italy and was used to interrogate prisoners of war. The prisoners were surprised that their interrogator was a woman and some balked at this interaction. In fact, one SS soldier—who was a perfect specimen of the Nordic race—was so furious with Podoski and humiliated that he started to vilify America and President Roosevelt. He stated, "We'll be bombarding New York soon. That Jew in the White House, we'll show him!" Podoski listened to him rant and then asked him to repeat what he had said. She became so angry with his words that she gave him "a knuckle sandwich right across the kisser!" The stunned man froze in place and was quickly removed from her tent by a sentry.

When an attempt was made on Hitler's life on 20 July 1944, the OSS was handed an opportunity to conduct a subversive propaganda operation, which proved to be highly successful. It was called Operation Sauerkraut. Because Podoski was the only one in her unit who spoke German, she was at the center of the operation. When she learned that several hundred Czech and Slovak soldiers had been attached to the German army in Italy she developed a plan targeted at these soldiers. She prepared propaganda leaflets in both Czech and Slovak to be taken across the lines by dissident German prisoners. This message was also broadcast over the BBC and directed at the Czechoslovak soldiers in Northern Italy. The leaflets read:

"Czechoslovak soldiers with the German army! In September 1938, at the Berlin Sports Palace, Hitler swore before the world that not a single Czechoslovak would serve in the German army. Yet today, our soldiers are being used by the Nazis to service their troops! On the side of the Allies in Italy, behind German lines, fighting underground with Italian partisans are men and women who left their homeland so they could one day return to Czechoslovakia and free people. You were sent to fight against this underground. You came to this battleground to protect Germans. The fate of Germany is already sealed. Hitler's armies are falling apart, beaten in Russia, Italy, France, they are now retreating to their own borders.

"There is only one command for you, soldiers. Shed this German yoke of shame, cross over to the partisans. Come at once. Only one road leads to the homeland: the road some of your countrymen chose four years ago. Remember President Masaryk's words: 'We are fighting for the freedom of Europe and mankind!' Czech and Slovak soldiers: Fulfill your obligations to a land that for 1,000 years has retained its spiritual independence. Come across to us!"

Podoski also came up with the idea for the creation of The League of Lonely German Women. Leaflets were printed and distributed behind the German lines informing German soldiers that their wives and girlfriends were sleeping with Nazi officers, soldiers on furlough, and foreign workers in the Reich. Each dissident POW was sent through front lines with a brick of three thousand sheets of propaganda material. Though there were only four such missions, some six hundred enemy soldiers surrendered to Allied forces, each carrying a propaganda leaflet.

On 6 April 1945 Corporal Podoski was presented with the U.S. Bronze Star by a Polish officer for her meritorious achievement in connection with military operations against the enemy in Italy. Behind her, standing at attention, was her MO team that supported the Sauerkraut operation.

After being discharged from the Army at the end of the war, Podoski, still linked to the OSS, was transferred from the Office of War Information (OWI) where her multilinqual skills could be utilized. The OWI was soon to move from Italy to Austria and her hope was to somehow make her way home to Brno, Czechoslovakia. Now a 1st lieutenant in the OWI, she began the search to find her family. She eventually found them; they were all well and thrilled to see Podoski resplendent in her uniform. After a week of festivities with her family, she rejoined her unit in Austria. She was then repatriated to the United States, disembarking in New York City. There was no one to meet her; her husband had divorced her during the war.

Back in the United States, Podoski worked for a time with a Voice of America broadcasting station, returned for a brief visit with her family in Brno, then traveling back to America. She subsequently held a series of jobs to make ends meet. Finally, she was hired by the Library of Congress and worked there for twenty years. During that time, luck was with her once again in the guise of Joseph Junosza Podoski, whom she met and married.

Corporal Podoski receiving the Bronze Star in Rome. *Courtesy of NARA*

Her husband died in 1984 and she returned his ashes to Poland. "Mine will—hopefully—go across the Potomac to the National Cemetery in Arlington. Resting there are Soldiers of the American Army, which was my first true home in this country. From the cemetery there is a beautiful view of the river and of Washington. And it is close to the airport that links America with old Europe."

Prisoners of War

Prior to World War II, American military history offers only one example of a female prisoner of war, that of Mary Edwards Walker during the Civil War, who as an assistant surgeon of the 52nd Ohio was captured on the field of battle and held in Richmond for four months before being exchanged in August 1864. For her valuable service and patriotic zeal, Walker was awarded the Medal of Honor, the only woman to be so honored.

Prior to the Japanese attack on Pearl Harbor, there were approximately 7,719 nurses serving on active duty worldwide in the ANC and NNC. Of these, 105 nurses were assigned to the South Pacific (88 ANC and 12 NNC in the Philippines; 5 NNC in Guam). During the war, seventy-eight women were confined as POWs; seventy-seven of them in the Pacific and one in the European Theater of Operations.[1]

The first women to be taken prisoner were five Navy nurses stationed on Guam; they were captured on 10 December 1941. Under the command of Chief Nurse Marion Olds, lieutenants (junior grade) Leona Jackson, Lorraine Christianson, Virginia Fogerty, and Doris Yetter continued working at the naval hospital on Guam as prisoners of the Japanese until 10 January 1942, when they were transported to Japan and interned at the Zentsuji Prison on Shikoku Island.

On 12 March, the nurses were transferred to Kobe. In the summer, they sailed aboard the SS *Gripsholm*, a Swedish liner chartered by the U.S. State Department as an exchange and repatriation ship under the auspices of the American Red Cross. They were taken to Mozambique, Portuguese South Africa, where they were exchanged and repatriated on 25 August 1942.[2]

The Japanese attacked the Philippines on 8 December and aggressively bombed military targets: the fighters and bombers at Clark Field and Fort Stotsenberg, and Camp John Hay to the north. Of the eighty-eight Army nurses on duty, seventy-three were assigned to Sternberg Hospital and its satellites in Manila, thirteen were at Middleside Hospital at Fort Mills on Corregidor Island, and two were at Camp John Hay, in the mountains near Baguio. There were also twelve Navy nurses assigned to Canacao Naval Hospital at Cavite, but after the base and hospital were bombed and destroyed in a raid on 10/11 December, the nurses were ordered to evacuate to Manila to assist the army nurses at Sternberg Hospital.[3]

The Japanese began an almost continuous bombing of Manila on 10 December, and the available medical facilities were overwhelmed by the enormous numbers of wounded and injured Soldiers, Sailors, and civilians. The nurses exchanged white dresses for coveralls, size 44. The quartermaster issued steel helmets and gas masks, and the women soldiered on.

On 13 December, Fort McKinley was evacuated, and its twenty nurses returned to Sternberg for other assignments. On 22 December, the same day that the majority of General Homma's troops landed at Lingayen Gulf, north of Manila, Camp John Hay at Baguio was ordered evacuated. Its two nurses, lieutenants Ruby Bradley and Beatrice Chambers, accompanied other personnel attempting to join Allied forces in Bataan, but then elected to return to care for seriously wounded Soldiers and civilians unable to make the arduous journey. They became the first Army nurses taken prisoner by the Japanese when they were captured on 28 December. They were interned at Camp John Hay, which was now being used as a Japanese POW camp.[4]

On 24 December, the military decided to evacuate the seventy-three Army nurses remaining in Manila. That day, twenty-four Army nurses, one Navy nurse, and twenty-five Filipino nurses set out by truck to Camp Limay on the southeast coast of Bataan to set up Hospital #1. The following day, twenty additional nurses departed Manila aboard the ferry *Mc E. Hyde* with orders to establish Hospital #2 at Coclaban. The nurses safely crossed the bay before Japanese planes sank the ferry, with the loss of all their medical supplies and equipment. One of the Coclaban nurses traveled to Limay, joined by seven additional Army nurses from Manila. Ten nurses were sent to Corregidor, and twelve nurses volunteered to remain behind at Sternberg to care for patients too injured or ill to be moved.[5]

As the Japanese closed in on Manila, preparations were made to evacuate the remaining Army nurses. On 29 December, eleven of the nurses were evacuated from Cavite to Corregidor. On the 31st, the last Army nurse in Manila, Lt. Floramund Felmuth, boarded the inner-island steamer *Mactan*, pressed into service as a hospital ship, in charge of three hundred seriously wounded Soldiers. The ship miraculously evaded the Japanese blockade and made it safely to Australia.

Either abandoned or forgotten, eleven Navy nurses remained in Manila at the temporary naval hospital at the Santa Scholastica Musical College (one Navy nurse, Ann Bernatitus, had evacuated to Corregidor with the Army). They witnessed General Homma's victorious entry into Manila on 2 January 1942, and were shortly afterward taken prisoner, along with twenty-seven doctors, dentists, and several dozen enlisted Sailors. They remained in place until 8 March, when the men, doctors, corpsmen, and patients were transferred to Bilibid Penitentiary, a civilian prison used for military prisoners, which would later be remembered for its brutality. The nurses were moved to Santo Tomas University, which was used as an internment camp for foreign nationals. The Navy nurses were the only medical unit for the camp until they were joined by the captured Army nurses on 25 August 1942. Together, they set up a hospital next door at the Santa Catalina Girls' School.[6]

ENDNOTES

1. American Women and the Military Gender Gap Web site. http://www.gendergap.com/military/usmil6.htm.
2. Ibid.
3. Norman, Elizabeth. *We Band of Angels–The Untold Story of American Nurses Trapped on Bataan by the Japanese.* New York: Simon and Schuster, 1999, p. 273.
4. Ibid, p. 274.
5. Ibid, pp. 23–4.
6. Cooper, Page. *Navy Nurse.* New York: McGrawHill Book Co., 1946, pp. 29–30.

Lt. (jg) Dorothy Still Danner, USN

Among the Navy nurses left behind in Manila, and perhaps typical of them, was Lt. (jg) Dorothy Still Danner. Along with chief nurse Laura Cobb and lieutenants (jg) Mary Chapman, Bertha Evans, Helen Gorzelonski, Mary "Red" Harrington, Margaret Nash, Goldie O'Haver, Eldene Paige, Susie Pitcher, and Edwina Todd, the group became known as the Sacred Eleven.[1]

Danner had joined the Navy in 1937 after having worked as a private nurse for several years. Then twenty-three, she was looking for adventure and a steady paycheck. After two years at Balboa Naval Hospital in San Diego, she received orders assigning her to the Canacao Naval Hospital in the Philippines. She remembered the languid trip across the Pacific aboard the USS *Henderson* (AP-1) as festive, and recalled being met at the dock in Honolulu by leis and hula dancers.[2]

Her first year in the Philippines was paradise, and although aware of rumors of war with Japan, "nobody thought the Japs would be silly enough to try and do anything to Uncle Sam." Even when the dependents were evacuated in early 1941, and tales emerged about the Rape of Nanking, Danner, and others, she was still confident there would be no war:

> Pearl Harbor shocked me as it did everyone else. I and the other nurses
> were awakened in the middle of the night and told that Pearl Harbor had

Photo courtesy of NBMSA

been hit. We were sent to the hospital as soon as we were dressed. Since the hospital was right in the target zone, we sent all the ambulatory patients back to duty, and the rest to Manila.... On Wednesday the tenth, the Navy Yard [at Cavite] was bombed. It was wiped out.[3]

Danner and the other Navy nurses were ordered into joint (Army–Navy) surgical teams operating all over the city, and she ran a receiving station out of the Jai Alai Club. After about two weeks, the Navy nurses were reunited at Santa Scholastica as the Army evacuated Manila and declared it an open city. In reply to the questions of when the Army was going to get them out, chief nurse Cobb replied, "We have no orders to leave so we stay put."[4]

Danner recalled her first contact with the Japanese:

At first the Japanese were not hostile and mostly left us alone. But then they started taking quinine from us. They took our beds and mattresses. They also began to slap around and beat up the men. But they ignored us—the nurses.[5]

On 8 March the nurses were separated, and sent to Santo Tomas, where they would be joined six months later by the Army nurses.

The Army nurses that had evacuated to Bataan were overwhelmed by the large number of casualties, which grew daily, and the scarcity of medical equipment, supplies, and even tents to shelter their patients. Most wards were nothing more than cots under the trees, and the nurses carried out their duties under the constant harassment of the Japanese. The nurses worked long hours doing the best they could with what they had. Capt. Rosemary Hogan was one of them.[6]

ENDNOTES

1. Sforza, Kevin. "Bethesda Nurses Honor Former POW," *Journal of the National Naval Medical Center*, 13 September 2001.
2. Danner, Dorothy Still. "Remembrances of a Nurse POW." *Navy Medicine 83*(3), May–June 1992, pp. 36–40.
3. Ibid.
4. Norman, Elizabeth. *We Band of Angels: The Untold Story of American Nurses Trapped on Bataan by the Japanese.* New York: Simon and Schuster, 1999, p. 25.
5. Danner, Dorothy Still. "Remembrances of a Nurse POW."
6. Norman, Elizabeth. *We Band of Angels*, pp. 80–81.

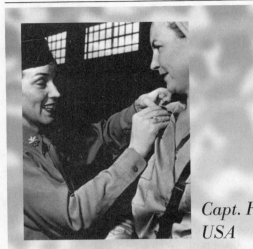

Capt. Rosemary Hogan, USA

One of the first women to be awarded the Purple Heart, Rosemary Hogan was born in Walters, Oklahoma, on 12 May 1912. She spent her childhood in Oklahoma, never leaving the state, but dreamed of seeing the world. To that end, she entered nursing school, after which she enlisted in the Army at Fort Sill, Oklahoma, on 1 August 1936, and was commissioned a second lieutenant in the ANC (although at that time it was relative rank).

Transferred to the Philippine Islands, she arrived in Manila just prior to the Japanese attack on Pearl Harbor in early December 1941, but as heavy fighting broke out in the Philippines, the nurses were evacuated on 24 December. Hogan was among the twenty-four Army nurses, one Navy nurse and twenty-five Filipino nurses sent to Camp Limay on the southeast coast of the Bataan Peninsula to set up a one-thousand-bed hospital. On 26 December, they were joined by seven other nurses.[1]

The nurses arrived in Camp Limay to find their equipment packed in a warehouse, ready to be shipped overseas. They uncrated and inventoried the equipment and set up Hospital #1, but were soon ordered to move to Little Baguio to be closer to the fighting. Since the evacuation of Manila was hurried, there was inadequate time to gather necessary supplies, and the nurses found

Lieutenant Hogan, former prisoner of war, gets new lieutenant bars from Maj. Juanita Redmond (Hipps). *Photo courtesy of ANCC* themselves caring for approximately two thousand wounded and ill men in tents, and often open jungle, with severe shortages of food, water, and medicine. Soon, malaria, dysentery, and malnutrition afflicted the troops, patients, and the medical staff itself, including the nurses.

Twice, on 31 March and 7 April, bombs fell on Hospital #1 itself, killing a total of 100 patients, and wounding 195 more, including three nurses. During the second attack, on 7 April 1942, Hogan was seriously wounded by shrapnel while she and another nurse were assisting a surgeon during an operation. Forced to huddle in foxholes, they watched as the hospital was destroyed.[2]

On 8/9 April, the nurses were ordered to evacuate Hospitals #1 and #2. At Camp Limay 2,300 evacuees fled to the southernmost base on Bataan through Japanese fire. Their arrival on Bataan put an enormous strain on a garrison already on three-eighths rations. Bataan surrendered on 9 April, and those taken prisoner endured what came to be known as the Bataan Death March, which resulted in 16,000–25,000 deaths.

Only the Rock (Corregidor) was left. As events progressed, those in the garrison on Corregidor gradually came to the realization that politically as well as strategically, it was unlikely that the island would be relieved. Cognizant of this fact, Gen. Jonathan Wainwright, in command since the departure of MacArthur to Australia on 11 March, made efforts to salvage what he could before the inevitable came to pass.

On the evening of 29 April, twenty Army nurses boarded two PBY Catalina flying boats for evacuation to Australia. Among the twenty were the three wounded nurses, including Hogan. While landing at Lake Lanao on the southern Philippine Island of Mindanao for refueling, one PBY was damaged trying to take off under cover of darkness, and the colonel in charge of the passengers, believing the plane to be beyond repair, ordered the passengers into the jungle.

The Navy crew was able to make the repairs but, unable to locate the passengers and pressured by the advancing Japanese, took off, stranding their passengers. The fifteen passengers—the colonel, a naval officer, three female civilian dependents, and ten Army nurses—evaded the Japanese for almost two weeks before surrendering on 11 May. The men were shipped off to a POW camp on Luzon, and the women remained confined in a convent at Davao until they were transferred to Santo Tomas on 9 September 1942. (The second PBY arrived safely at Port Darwin, Australia, with its ten army nurses on the evening of 1 May 1942.)[3]

On 3 May, the last eleven Army nurses to evade capture on Corregidor, as well as Navy nurse Ann Bernatitus, sailed out to sea aboard a converted yacht to rendezvous with the submarine USS *Spearfish* (SS190) which carried the nurses, along with seven senior Army and Navy officers, safely to Freemantle, Australia.[4]

With General Wainwright's surrender on 7 May 1942, the last fifty-four Army nurses in the Philippines were taken prisoner. The nurses continued providing medical care in the Malinta tunnel, and later the ruins of Middleside Hospital, until being transferred to Manila on 2 July. They were held at Santa Catalina convent, until joining the other nurses at Santo Tomas on 25 August. The ten stranded Mindanao nurses arrived on 9 September 1942. The following September, one of the two Camp Hay nurses, Lieutenant Ruby Bradley, arrived at Santo Tomas. The other nurse, Lieutenant Beatrice Chambers, would remain at Camp Hay until being liberated on 4 February 1945.[5]

ENDNOTES

1. Norman, Elizabeth, p. 33.
2. Ibid., pp. 80–81.
3. Ibid., pp. 112–14.
4. Ibid., pp. 110–11, 118–21.
5. Ibid., pp. 181–82.

Lt. (jg) Margaret "Peggy" Nash, USN

One of the greatest worries for the captured nurses was whether their families back home knew if they were alive. The Japanese, nonsignatories to the Geneva Convention, were inconsistent in notifying the Red Cross with names of prisoners. One Navy nurse's family, that of Lt. (jg) Margaret "Peggy" Nash, learned of her capture through an unlikely source.

Having joined the U.S. NNC on 28 April 1936, Nash had been serving in Guam in October of 1941 when she was ordered to report to the Canacao Naval Hospital in the Philippines. With the others, she'd endured the bombings, the capture, and the deprivations inherent in imprisonment. And like the others, she had no way of contacting her family to let them know that she was alive but a prisoner.

Interned at Santo Tomas, she became concerned that a Japanese guard, who followed her for five days, was stalking her. "The moment I came out of the building, he was right there, and when I'd get to the hospital, I'd turn around and he'd be following me. I was scared to death." Then one morning, while she was working on the ward, he took her photograph. It appeared the next day in Japanese propaganda newspapers. After the American invasion, the photo was found on a captured Japanese soldier, and Cdr. R. F. Armknect, an acquaintance of Nash's on Guam, saw the photograph. Armknect notified the Navy, who notified her family.[1]

Photo courtesy of The Women's Memorial

On 14 May 1943, due to overcrowding and disease at Santo Tomas, the Japanese opened a second internment camp at Los Banos, approximately forty-two miles southeast of Manila. The eleven Navy nurses, along with 787 of the healthiest male internees, were sent to establish the camp and hospital.[2]

The nurses endured almost three years of captivity, some longer, under conditions that could be charitably referred to as primitive. Conditions in the camp worsened as the war dragged on. The nurses worked long hours, improvising by necessity as shortages of medicine and supplies increased. The nurses risked beatings to smuggle extra food to the children, and lost weight by giving the children their rations. So great was their self-sacrifice and dedication to their patients that they became known as the "Angels of Bataan."

Things went from bad to worse in January 1944 when the administration of the camps changed from civilian to military control. Restrictions were increased and violation of minor infractions resulted in severe consequences, and on occasion, execution. Malnutrition and diseases like malaria and dysentery ravaged the prisoners, and the brutality of the guards increased as the Allies came closer.[3]

On 9 January, troops of the American Sixth Army landed at Luzon, opposed by 275,000 Japanese troops in well-prepared defensive positions. On 28 January, a raid behind Japanese lines at the POW camp at Cabanatuan, by the 6th Rangers of the 1st Cavalry (Alamo Scouts) and Philippine guerillas, freed 511 American and Allied POWs, some who were survivors of the Bataan Death March. Five hundred twenty Japanese soldiers were killed or wounded, with a loss of only two American and twenty-one Filipino lives. (The 2005 film, *The Great Raid*, was based on the event.)[4]

Intrigued by the raid, General MacArthur ordered Maj. Gen. Vernon D. Mudge, "Go to Manila! Go around the Nips, bounce off the Nips, but go to Manila. Free the internees and Santo Tomas."[5]

On 3 February 1945, elements of the 1st Cavalry liberated Santo Tomas, and its sixty-five army nurses. Nurse Bertha Dworsky recalled, "Tanks were crashing through the gates. . . . Tanks rolled up to the front door. . . . The men in the tanks looked like giants, we were so emaciated and thin.[6] Lt. Chambers rejoined her comrades at Santo Tomas the following day.

On 23 February, the 11th Airborne Division raided the Los Banos Internment Camp, liberating the internees and eleven Navy nurses. Lt. Danner recalled the liberation:

> On January 9, American troops landed at Lingayed Gulf. The Japanese awakened us in the middle of the night and told us they were leaving. They turned the camp over to the Administrative Committee and advised us not to go outside. . . . An American flag was run up the flagpole, and

we sang the national anthem. . . . Unfortunately our freedom only lasted a week. Then the Japanese came back.[7]

MacArthur was afraid, not without cause, that the Japanese might massacre the internees at Los Banos. Other massacres of prisoners had already occurred, specifically 150 POWs at Palawan Island on 14 December 1944.[8]

Paratroopers were dropped over Los Banos, and they attacked in conjunction with infantry that came ashore in amphibious armored tracked vehicles, Amtracs. One pulled up in front of the hospital and Danner recalled, "Oh we never saw anything so handsome in our lives. These fellows were in camouflage uniforms wearing a new kind of helmet, not those little tin pan things we were used to seeing. And they looked so healthy and lively."[9]

Approximately 1,500 internees were evacuated by Amtracs, the remainder overland by truck. Only two Soldiers were killed and one internee injured. In retaliation, the Japanese murdered 1,500 residents of the nearby town of Los Banos. The Japanese commander, Lieutenant Konishi, was later tried and executed as a war criminal.[10]

Remarkably, despite bombing, artillery, shrapnel, dysentery, malaria, dengue fever, malnutrition, starvation, and mistreatment, all seventy-seven nurse POWs survived three years of harsh captivity, and were promoted, given back pay, and returned to the United States for hospitalization and evaluation at Letterman and Oak Knoll Hospitals in San Francisco.[11]

Upon their return, five of the nurses had sufficient time in service to retire, nineteen were medically retired, and twenty-three remained in the service, many seeing additional service in Korea. The remainder were honorably discharged.[12]

In the European Theater of Operations, only one woman, 2nd Lt. Reba Whittle Tobiason, a flight nurse with the 813th MAES, was taken prisoner of war.

ENDNOTES

1. Margaret Nash, interviewed by Andree Marechal-Workman, September 1992, transcript, Naval Hospital Oakland, Public Affairs.
2. Norman, Elizabeth. *We Band of Angels–The Untold Story of American Nurses Trapped on Bataan by the Japanese*. New York: Simon and Schuster, 1999, p. 276.
3. Danner, Dorothy Still. "Remembrances of a Nurse POW." *Navy Medicine 83*(3), May–June 1992, pp. 36–40.
4. King, Michael J. "Rangers: Selected Combat Operations in World War II," Chapter 6 of the U.S. Army Command and General Staff College's Leavenworth Papers, No. 11.
5. Sternberg, R. *Return to the Philippines*. New York: Time-Life Books, 1979, p. 114.
6. Norman, Elizabeth. *We Band of Angels*, pp. 203–4.
7. Danner, Dorothy Still. "Remembrances of a Nurse POW."
8. King, Michael J. "Rangers: Selected Combat Operations in World War II."

9. Danner, Dorothy Still. "Remembrances of a Nurse POW."
10. Ibid.
11. Norman, Elizabeth. *We Band of Angels*, pp. 213–32.
12. American Women and the Military Gender Gap Web site: http://www.gendergap. com/military/usmil6.htm.

2nd Lt. Reba Whittle Tobiason, USA

The story of Reba Whittle Tobiason is markedly different from those of the nurses captured in the Pacific. As the only female POW in the European Theater of Operations, she was isolated and unable to share the sense of community and comradeship that developed among the women interned at Santo Tomas and Los Banos. She was the only flight nurse captured by the enemy, and the first Army nurse to be repatriated and returned home.

The Pacific nurses endured almost continuous combat conditions on Bataan and Corregidor, while Tobiason flew into combat, often landing under fire, but lived in the relative comfort and safety of England. The Pacific nurses surrendered; Whittle was captured. Most of the nurses in the Pacific endured nearly three years of captivity, some longer. Whittle was repatriated after almost four months.

Perhaps most significantly, the Pacific nurses returned to parades; celebrity and public acclaim; three books and a movie covered their experiences. Tobiason was ordered to remain quiet, and had to fight for two decades to qualify for a disability retirement due to her wartime injuries, and was only officially recognized as a POW years after her death in 1992.[1]

Reba Zitela Whittle was born in the ranchlands of Rock Springs, Texas, on 19 August 1919 to Edward and Lottie Whittle. She graduated from the Medical and Surgical School of Nursing at San Antonio, Texas, in June of 1941, and almost

Photo courtesy of Stanley Tobiason

immediately applied for an appointment in the ANC. After taking her induction physical at Fort Sam Houston, Texas, on 10 June, she was initially disqualified. At five feet, seven inches, she weighed only 117 pounds, which was below the minimum. This requirement was waived, and she was sworn in and commissioned a second lieutenant (#N734426) in the ANC on 17 June 1941.[2]

After serving at Kirkland Field, New Mexico, and Mather Field, California, Tobiason volunteered for training as a flight nurse in January 1943. Evacuation of the wounded by aircraft was a new concept at the beginning of the war. The C-47 multiengine aircraft used in the missions flew troops and supplies in to, and wounded Soldiers out of, battlefield areas. Because of this two-fold mission, these planes were not considered noncombatant. As a result, service in air evacuation was at great risk, since the unarmed planes were legitimate military targets and often came under direct fire.

Tobiason was accepted into the program in August 1943 and reported to USAAF School of Air Evacuation at Bowman Field, Kentucky, in September. Besides classes, candidates drilled and engaged in calisthenics and ten-mile hikes carrying full backpacks. They stood guard, ran the obstacle course, and crawled under barbed wire while under live machine gun fire. Tobiason completed the intense six-week training course and graduated in January 1944.[3]

Assigned to the 813th MAES, Tobiason was one of twenty-five flight nurses who boarded the *Queen Mary* on 21 January 1944, along with four flight surgeons and twenty-five enlisted men, while the band played "A Pretty Girl is Like a Melody." Upon arrival in England, the unit was based at Balderton, Nottinghamshire, and later Grove, Berkshire, attached to the 9th Air Force.[4]

For the next eight months, Tobiason flew more than five hundred hours, including eighty combat hours, on forty missions to Belgium and France, carrying supplies in and the wounded out, often under fire, without event. That changed in September 1944.

On 27 September 1944, the war was going well for the Allies. The Germans were evacuating Greece, and the Allies were liberating the Netherlands. But the war was far from over, as the 445th Bomber Group's disastrous raid over Kassel and the failure of Operation Market Garden proved. That morning, Tobiason boarded a C-47 for an evacuation flight from Paris. With her was the pilot, 1st Lt. Ralph Parker Jr.; the copilot, 2nd Lt. David Forbes; the crew chief/aerial engineer, Sgt. Harold Bonser; the radioman, Cpl. Chester Bright; and her surgical tech, T-3 Jonathan Hill.

The evacuation flight arrived in Paris to find no wounded, but they were informed that there were wounded at Liege, Belgium, but were told, "It's a combat zone, and it's hard to get in and out. We aren't going to send you. Everybody on the crew has to agree to go. It's up to you." As Sergeant Bonser later recalled, "We took a vote on it and everybody said, "Well, they need us so we'll go.""[5]

Through a miscalculation, they flew three miles over German territory, and machine guns firing incendiary bullets hit the plane and started a fire aboard. The plane barely missed a smokestack in the village of Aachen, before crash landing in a turnip field. In Bonser's words, "It just didn't want to stay in the air any longer.[6]

Tobiason recalled, "[I] was sleeping quite soundly in the back of our hospital plane until suddenly awakened by the terrific sounds of guns and crackling of the plane as if it had gone into bits. And suddenly, we hit the ground—myself landing in the navigator's compartment head first. . . . Immediately we saw soldiers not many yards away. Second glance, we recognized they were German GIs. . . . The surprised look on their faces when they saw a woman was amazing."[7]

Despite their injuries, the crew was able to exit the burning plane through the escape hatch over the pilot's compartment and get away from the aircraft. Almost immediately, they were captured by German troops. Bonser recalled of Tobiason, "It seemed she was more worried about those that were hurt and bleeding than what she was about herself."

Tobiason had suffered a head wound, and several shrapnel wounds, as well as damage to her back. The pilot had a bullet in his ankle, and the copilot's face was burned. The most seriously hurt was the medic. They were marched to the village of Aachen, while American artillery shells exploded around them. After a preliminary interrogation by English speaking German officers, during which the copilot was physically abused for being Jewish, and an examination by a doctor, the enlisted were separated from the officers, and were sent to Cologne, and in Tobiason's case, Luft Stalag IX (Camp 9C).[8]

Tobiason was given a solitary cell because there were no provisions for female prisoners. While a prisoner, she performed nursing duties for the male POWs in the camp. The morale of the camp was greatly improved by her presence, and the men made her small gifts, including stage makeup they had received from the Red Cross for theatrical productions.[9]

In the interim, Tobiason's family had been notified that she was "missing in action", and they received letters of condolences from the nurses and unit chaplain. It was only the day after the family held a memorial service in November that they learned Tobiason was a prisoner of war.[10]

Her future husband in England, Lt. Col. Stanley Tobiason, kept up to date with her affairs through an English lady, a Miss Duxbury, who corresponded with a boyfriend also interned at the same camp, Capt. William S. Holden. (As a military prisoner, Tobiason was prohibited from writing to anyone in the military.)[11]

On 25 January 1945, Whittle was part of a prisoner exchange, and was repatriated to Switzerland along with 109 other POWs. She later joked that it was because the Germans had absolutely no idea of what to do with her. She traveled home aboard the SS *Gripsholm*, the same ship which had earlier repatriated the five Navy nurses captured at Guam. She returned to D.C., and received a congratulatory telegram from President Roosevelt. She was awarded the Air Medal, a Purple Heart, and was promoted to first lieutenant. Reassigned to an air base in Miami, she was disqualified for flight status as a result of her wounds.[12]

After marrying Tobiason, she was released from active duty on 31 January 1946. They had two sons, Capt. Joel Tobiason, an Annapolis graduate and Naval aviator during Vietnam, and Stanley Tobiason, Jr. As a condition of her repatriation, Whittle was required to sign a sworn statement not to talk about her experiences, a common practice during the war (to avoid putting other prisoners at risk). As a result, she became the forgotten POW.[13]

Tobiason tried unsuccessfully for the next twenty years to qualify for a disability retirement due to her wartime injuries and the loss of her health while a prisoner of war, but she wasn't officially recognized as a POW until March 1992, years after her death from cancer on 26 January 1981. Remembering that she never seemed bitter over her lack of recognition, Colonel Tobiason, in accepting his wife's award in D.C., said simply, "She would have been very delighted."[14]

Following victory in World War II, after the bands and parades, the country put a lot of effort into returning to normal, and the commanders began to plan immediately for the demobilization of the returning vets, and the dissolution of the women's services. The priceless service rendered by women in the war, and indeed the men, was soon forgotten. It would take several decades before they would be recognized as "The Greatest Generation."

ENDNOTES

1. "Tobiason, WW II POW Finally Receives Recognition." *The Rocksprings Record and Texas Mohair Weekly*, 14 May 1992, Vol. 99, No.13.
2. File # N734426. National Personnel Records Center (NPRC), St Louis, MO.
3. Buck, Anna. "POW in Germany." *Army Magazine*, March 2000.
4. Ibid.
5. Harold Bosner, interviewed by Mary Jo Binker, 27 April 2000, Falls Church, VA. Tape and transcript are deposited at The Women's Memorial Foundation, Arlington, VA.
6. Ibid.
7. Tobiason, Reba Whittle. *Diary of 2nd Lt. Reba Whittle Tobiason*. Air Evacuation Museum, Brooks AFB, San Antonio, Texas, not published.
8. Harold Bosner interview.
9. Tobiason, Reba Whittle. *Diary of 2nd Lt. Reba Whittle Tobiason*.
10. Letter from Capt. Kyle Lawrence, Group Chaplain, Headquarters 27th Air Transport Group—APO 744, 6 December 1944.
11. "Tobiason, WW II POW Finally Receives Recognition."

12. Baron, Scott. *They Also Served: Military Biographies of Uncommon Americans.* Spartenburg, N.C.: MIE Press, 1999.
13. Grimes, Charlotte. "Women POWs of WW II." *St. Louis Post Dispatch*, 19 April 1992.
14. "Tobiason, WW II POW Finally Receives Recognition."

Epilogue

As of the writing of this book (spring 2006), the world remains an unsettled place. The war in Iraq continues and although the United States has attempted to turn over control of provinces and cities to American-trained Iraqi security forces, insurgency attacks on Iraqi police and military recruiting stations continue to take hundreds of lives. As yet there is no stabilized government in the country, although the Iraqi people elected a parliament in December 2005. Squabbling over the replacement of a new prime minister continues to set back the process of forming a stabilized governing body. U.S. forces are for the most part now kept in the background and used only to support Iraqi forces when fighting requires their presence, although U.S. troops periodically patrol the streets of major cities.

Iraq is a dangerous place for American troops and the Iraqi people. IEDs blow up on a daily basis and suicide bombers cause havoc by destroying Shiite and Sunni mosques and other sites where people gather in large numbers. It is apparent that the insurgents intend to fight the formation of an Iraqi government with any and all means at their disposal. This could eventually lead to a civil war. Presently, there appears to be no light at the end of the tunnel. Unless the Iraqis can effectively take control of their country, American forces might remain in country for years to come. At this time there are approximately 133,000 U.S. troops (Army and Marine Corps, of which 10 percent are women) on the ground in Iraq and Afghanistan, supported by U.S. Air Force, Navy, and Coast Guard units.

The question now facing the United States is whether Congress and the American people will stay in Iraq and Afghanistan for the long haul and allow our gallant young military men and women to finish their mission; that is, to support the successful establishment of a democracy in Iraq.

Postscript

It was the intention of the authors to include a vignette about the experiences of Lt.Col. Martha McSally, USAF, an extraordinary officer and leader. Colonel McSally was the first Air Force female to fly in combat, in 1994. She logged nearly 100 hours in combat, enforcing a no-fly zone over Iraq.

In August 2004 she became the first Air Force woman to take command of a fighter squadron, the 354th, home based at Davis-Monthan Air Force Base. Her command, known as the "Bulldogs," comprises twenty-two A/OA-10 aircraft and fifty-five pilots and crew members.

Unfortunately, Colonel McSally and her squadron had just returned from an overseas deployment as we were completing this book. There simply was not enough time in her postdeployment schedule for us to interview her and ready her story for publication. We regret we could not include this worthy hero in *Women at War*.

Courtesy of USAF

APPENDIX A

Women of Arlington

It is not known exactly how many servicewomen are buried at the Arlington National Cemetery, and with funerals on the average of twenty-five each workday, it is unlikely that anyone ever will. As these words are being written, American sons and daughters at risk while serving overseas in Afghanistan and Iraq have ended their journey in the Virginia hills overlooking D.C., having given the last full measure of devotion.

Many of the women buried at Arlington are military wives of famous generals and admirals, as well as common foot soldiers and sea dogs, who served their country in their own fashion. There are nurses from the Civil War and the War with Spain, civilians who risked their lives on the battlefield to care for wounded comrades without military status, rank, or recognition and benefits as veterans. There are also the women who donned military dress to answer their nation's call to arms, even if they weren't allowed to bear arms, and served honorably in the Armed Forces of the United States.

Listed below are only a few of the notable military women buried at Arlington:

CAPT. JOY BRIGHT HANCOCK, DIRECTOR OF WAVES

Hancock served as a chief yeoman during World War I and is considered the Mother of the WAVES, as she was instrumental in gaining permanent status for the WAVES in the Navy. She was awarded the Legion of Merit.

LT. CDR. FLORANCE ABY BLANCHFIELD, ANC, WORLD WAR I AND WORLD WAR II

Blanchfield was the first woman commissioned into the regular Army. She was awarded the Distinguished Service Medal as Superintendent of the ANC.

LT. CDR. MARY GAVIN, ANC, WORLD WAR I AND WORLD WAR II

Gavin served with Base Hospital #42 overseas during World War I, caring for the wounded of St. Mihiel and Verdun and recruiting nurses during World War II.

COL. GERALDINE PRATT MAY, 1ST DIRECTOR, WAF, WORLD WAR II

A graduate of the WAC Officer's Candidate School at Fort Des Moines, she was among the first women assigned to the Army Air Corps during World War II. She received reserve commission in the newly created Air Force and was appointed the first WAF director with the rank of full colonel.

2ND LT. RUTH GARDINER, ANC FLIGHT NURSE, WORLD WAR II

Gardiner was the first servicewoman to die in a theater of operations during World War II when her plane crashed on an air evacuation mission at Nannek, Alaska, on 27 July 1943.

LT. CDR. JUANITA REDMOND (HIPPS), ANC, WORLD WAR II

Redmond served on Bataan after escaping from Corregidor. She wrote the 1943 best-seller *I Served on Bataan,* on which the movie *So Proudly We Hail* was based.

COL. ROSEMARY HOGAN, AFNC, WORLD WAR II

Captured by the Japanese as she and other nurses attempted to evacuate the Philippines, she was imprisoned at Santo Tomas, a civilian prison in Manila, until liberated by American forces in 1945. Hogan was among the first four women to attain the rank of full colonel.

LT. KATHRYN GEORGETTE VAN WAGNER, FLIGHT NURSE, WORLD WAR II

Van Wagner was a Navy flight nurse during World War II, earning two Air Medals.

SARAH BAILY WILLIAMS, WASP, WORLD WAR II

Williams flew military domestic flights delivering newly manufactured aircraft to U.S. Naval and Air Force stateside squadrons. WASPs contributed to releasing male pilots to overseas combat squadron assignments.

MARGUERITE HIGGINS, WAR CORRESPONDENT, WORLD WAR II AND KOREA

Higgins was a Pulitzer Prize-winning female war correspondent during World War II and the only one during Korea. Higgins witnessed the liberation of Dachau and the Nuremberg Trials.

COL. RUBY BRADLEY, HIGHLY DECORATED WORLD WAR II POW AND KOREAN MASH NURSE

Bradley was a POW in the Pacific and one of the most decorated women in American History (see her profile in the Korean War section).

MAJ. THYNE NAOMI GAYLORD, ANC, WORLD WAR II AND KOREA

Gaylord saw duty in the China-Burma-India theater in World War II. She returned to duty in 1950 and served in the Korean War.

MAJ. EVELYN STAPLES, USAAF/WAC, WORLD WAR II AND KOREA

Enlisting in the USAAF/WAC, Staples was recruited by the OSS during World War II. She parachuted behind enemy lines into occupied France and was twice recalled to active duty, working intelligence assignments during the Korean War and the Cuban Missile Crisis.

MAJ. EDNA MARIE NELSON EDWARDS, ANC, WORLD WAR II AND KOREA

Edwards served in the Pacific during World War II, helping to liberate the Philippines, and served in Korea. She was awarded the Bronze Star and a Korean Service Medal with three battle stars.

LT. CDR. ANNIE RUTH GRAHAM, ANC, WORLD WAR II, KOREA, AND VIETNAM

Graham, who served overseas during World War II, Korea, and Vietnam, is one of eight women named on the Vietnam Memorial.

COL. ELIZABETH BLOOMER, ANC, WORLD WAR II, KOREA, AND VIETNAM

Bloomer landed at Normandy Beach, served with a MASH unit in Korea, and rode a gunboat along the Mekong Delta in Vietnam.

COL. LILIAN HARRIS, WAC, WORLD WAR II, KOREA, AND VIETNAM

Harris was a member of the first class of graduating WACs and served on General Eisenhower's staff in North Africa, Italy, and Northern Europe. She was awarded the Legion of Merit and a Bronze Star. She saw service during Korea and Vietnam.

BRIG. GEN. MADELYN PARKS, ANC, WORLD WAR II, KOREA, AND VIETNAM

Parks served her country for more than 30 years during three wars and was awarded the Distinguished Service Medal. She was the fifteenth chief of the ANC, and she served overseas during World War II and Vietnam.

SPC. CHIN SUN PAK WELLS, USA, KOREA

After serving with the 8th Army in Korea, Wells returned to the United States, assigned as a personnel specialist in the Office of the Deputy Chief of Staff for Personnel. She died in the line of duty on 11 September 2001, when terrorists hijacked a commercial airliner and flew it into the northwest side of the Pentagon.

REAR ADM. GRACE HOPPER, INVENTOR OF COBOL (Computer Programming Language)

The oldest officer on active duty (80) before her death, Hopper was known as "Amazing Grace" for her pioneering work in data processing and computer science.

LT. KARA HULTGREEN, FIRST WOMAN TO QUALIFY AS AN F-14 COMBAT PILOT

A member of the Black Lions VF-213, Hultgreen was practicing to deploy to the Persian Gulf and was approaching the flight deck of the USS *Abraham Lincoln* on 25 Oct 1994, when her aircraft began losing altitude and crashed into the sea.

CAPT. MARGARET FREEMAN, USAF, VIETNAM

Served in Ubon AFB, Thailand, during the Vietnam War and assigned to the Defense Intelligence Agency at the Pentagon.

LT. COL. ELVIRA E. COOK, AFNC, VIETNAM

Cook served as the chief nurse of Aeromedical Evacuation in Vietnam.

LT. CDR. BARBARA ANN ALLEN (RAINEY), USN, FIRST FEMALE NAVAL AVIATOR

Accepted into the U.S. Naval Flight Training School, she became the first female naval aviator in American history when she graduated at Corpus Christi, Texas, on 22 February 1974. She was killed on 13 July 1982 while assigned as a flight instructor, practicing touch-and-go landings with a student at Middleton Field, Alabama.

VICE ADM. FRAN McKEE, USN

McKee was the first female commanding officer of the Naval Security Group at Fort Meade, Maryland. In 1976 she became the first female line officer to be promoted to flag rank. She received her second star when she became the director of human resource management in the Office of the Chief of Naval Operations in D.C.

MAJ. MARIE ROSSI-CAYTON, ONE OF THE FIRST U.S. FEMALE PILOTS IN COMBAT

Credited on her Arlington tombstone as the "first female combat commander to fly into combat," Marie Therese Rossi-Cayton was one of the first officers to fly into enemy territory at the start of Operation Desert Storm. On 1 March 1991, Major Rossi and three of her four-man crew were killed when her helicopter hit an unlit tower at night during Desert Storm flight operations.

TECH. SGT. CHERYL-ANN TURNAGE, USAF

Turnage served as a flight steward for the 76th Airlift Squadron. Sergeant Turnage died in a CT 43 crash on 3 April 1996 near Dubrovnik, Croatia. The aircraft carried Commerce Secretary Ron Brown and his staff.

CAPT. KATHLEEN McGRATH, USN, GULF WARS

McGrath was the first of the five women selected in 1998 to command Navy combat ships. She commanded USS *Jarrett*, a 453-foot frigate and stopped smugglers in the Persian Gulf. She was the first woman to take a U.S. warship to sea.

STAFF SGT. ANISSA ANN SHUTTEWORTH SHERO, USAF

First Air Force American woman to die in Afghanistan during Operation Enduring Freedom. She was serving aboard an MC-130H combat Talon II when it crashed and caught fire after taking off from an airstrip in southeast Afghanistan.

STAFF SGT. MADLYN WHITE, USA

White died while on duty at the Pentagon on 11 September 2001, when terrorists hijacked a commercial airliner and flew it into the northwest side of the Pentagon.

CW5 SHARON T. SWARTWORTH, USA, IRAQI FREEDOM

Swartworth died when the UH-60 Blackhawk helicopter she was in was shot down by unknown enemy ordnance in Tikrit, Iraq, 7 November 2003.

PFC. SAM WILLIAMS HUFF, USA, IRAQI FREEDOM

Huff was killed while returning from the Al Dora police station in Iraq when the vehicle in which she was traveling was struck by an IED, 17 April 2005.

SPC. TOCCARA R. GREEN, IRAQI FREEDOM

Green was killed when multiple improvised explosive devices detonated near her unit during convoy operations near Al Asad, Iraq, 14 August 2005.

Purple Heart Medals Awarded, World War II to Iraqi Freedom

Last Name	First	Middle	Served	Branch	Rank	Reason for Medal
Abretske	Lois	T.	Desert Storm	USAR	Sgt.	Injured when SCUD missile hit barracks
Ahrendson	Frances	Wallace	WWII	ANC	Lt.	Severely injured by German antipersonnel mine on the French Riviera in 1945
Ainsworth	Ellen		WWII	ANC	Lt.	Killed when German aircraft bombed the 56th Evacuation Hospital at Anzio on 2-12-1944
Albertassi	Mary	H.	WWII	ANC	Capt.	Wounded on Okinawa
Aleman-Guzman	Nelly		1980s	ANC	Maj.	Injured in El Salvador 21 November 1989 when a sniper attacked the house in which she was living. The sniper was part of a larger, coordinated terrorist attack on foreign military personnel in the city.
Allen	Dorothy		1970s	USN	RM3	Injured in Puerto Rico when terrorist guerillas attacked a Navy bus outside of Sebeca on 3 December 1979
Andrews	Ruth	E.	WWII	ANC	Maj.	Injured while serving with the 107th Evacuation Hospital
Atkins	Julia	V.	Iraqi Freedom	USA	Sgt.	Killed 10 December 2005 while on patrol in Baghdad (an IED detonated near her HMMWV)
Awner	Heather		Iraqi Freedom	USAR	Pvt.	Assigned to 94th Military Police Battalion in Iraq. Wounded when her HUMVEE hit a land mine.
Bailey	Helen	E.	WWII	ANC	Lt.	Wounded when German aircraft bombed the 77th Evacuation Hospital near Cherbourg on 3 October 1944

(continued)

Last Name	First Name		Conflict	Branch	Rank	Description
Baker	Ethel	Coffee	WWII	ANC	Capt.	Wounded by shrapnel when German aircraft bombed the 77th Evacuation Hospital near Cherbourg on 3 October 1944
Balch	Laura	Hundman	WWII	ANC	Capt.	Injured when the hospital ship *St. David* was bombed by the Germans off Italian coast 24 January 1944
Barnes	Melissa	Rose	War on Terror	USN	YN2	Killed when terrorists flew an aircraft into the Pentagon on 11 September 2001
Baumann	Theresa	Mitchison	WWII	ANC	Lt.	Injured when German aircraft bombed the tented 16th General Hospital near Aachen, Germany, in 1945
Beaudoin	Cindy		Desert Storm	USAR	Spc4	Killed by a land mine 28 February 1991
Benfield	Stacy		1990s	USAF	SA	Injured when terrorists bombed the Khobar Tower complex in Dharan, Saudi Arabia, on 25 June 1996
Benyas	Evelyn	Balter	WWII	ANC	Lt.	Injured during Buzz Bomb attacks in London
Best	Carla		Iraqi Freedom	USA	Sgt.	Injured when a roadside bomb exploded in Baghdad October 2004
Billings	Margaret	May	WWII	ANC	Lt.	Killed when Japanese suicide bomber hit hospital ship *Comfort* 28 April 1945
Bishop	Margaret	F.	WWII	ANC	Lt.	Received shrapnel wounds when 15th General Hospital was bombed 10 November 1944
Bohn	Lisa	K.	Enduring Freedom	USAR	Maj.	Wounded in terrorist bombing in Islamabad, Pakistan, 17 March 2002
Bonner	Barbara	Wooster	Vietnam War	NNC	Lt.	Wounded in Brinks BOQ Bombing in Saigon Christmas Eve 1964

Last	First	Middle	War	Branch	Rank	Description
Bosveld	Rachel		Iraqi Freedom	USA	Pfc.	Wounded 12 September 2003 when HUMVEE blown up; killed 26 October 2003 during mortar attack on a Baghdad Police Station
Bowler	Margaret	McIntyre	WWII	ANC	Lt.	Wounded when 45th Field Hospital bombed in France on 21 October 1944
Braddy	Alayna		Iraqi Freedom	USA	Spc.	Wounded twice while serving in Iraq with the 230th Military Police Company
Brady	Ruth	M.	WWII	WAC	Pvt.	Wounded when the building where she worked in England was bombed by the Germans
Brenner	Matilda		WWII	ANC	Lt.	Dietitian wounded when Army Hospital in Belgium was hit by a V-2 rocket bomb in December 1944
Broadwell	Teresa		Iraqi Freedom	USA	Pvt.	Wounded when 194th MPs were attacked by Shiites in Karbala, Iraq, on 16 October 2003
Buckley	Deloris	Ruth	WWII	ANC	Lt.	Wounded at Anzio Beachhead when 95th Evacuation Hospital was bombed
Burford	Tanya		War on Terror	USAF	SRA	Wounded during the Khobar Towers terrorist bombing
Burgeson	Blanche		WWII	WAC	Sgt.	Wounded when the building at which she worked in England was bombed by the Germans
Burke	Mary	Theresa	WWII	WAC	Sgt.	Wounded while on assignment at Bushy Park, London
Burral	Mary		Iraqi Freedom	USA	Spc	Truck hit by RPG in Iraq on 3 May 2003
Butler	Leona	Gaylon	WWII	WAC	Pfc.	Hit by flying glass in July 1944 when V-2 bomb hit building in southern England where she worked

(continued)

Byrne	Virginia	T.	WWII	ANC	Lt.	Wounded by shrapnel when 15th General Hospital was bombed 10 November 1944
Campbell	Jamie	L.	Iraqi Freedom	ARNG	Lt.	Killed when the Blackhawk helicopter she was piloting crashed near Tal Afar, Iraq, on 7 January 2006
Cardile	Diane		Iraqi Freedom	MC	Pfc.	Wounded when a suicide car bomber hit her convoy vehicle 23 June 2005 near Fallujah
Carr	Patricia	Reiss	Vietnam War	ANC	Lt.	Wounded while assigned to 3rd General Hospital in South Vietnam
Carrillo	Josephine		Joint Guard	USAF	TSGT	Injured while participating in Operation Joint Guard in Bosnia 1997
Cawvey	Jessica		Iraqi Freedom	NG	Spc.	Killed when her cargo truck convoy was attacked 6 October 2004 near Fallujah, Iraq
Chambers	Anita	Foss	Korean War	ANC	Maj.	Wounded while serving in Korea
Charette	Holly	A.	Iraqi Freedom	MC	LPL	Killed when suicide car bomber hit her convoy vehicle 23 June 2005 near Fallujah, Iraq
Chaulk	Gracia	Ann	WWII	WAC	TCH4	Wounded while serving with 5th Army in Italy
Chesley	Frances	Olive	WWII	ANC	Lt.	Killed when Japanese suicide bomber hit hospital ship Comfort 28 April 1945
Chicone	Thelma	Dow	WWII	WAC	Pfc.	Injured during Buzz Bomb attack while in Great Britain
Clark	Beverly	S.	Desert Storm	USAR	Spc	Killed 26 February 1991 when SCUD missile hit barracks in Al Khobar, Saudi Arabia
Clark	Lelia		WWII	ANC	Lt.	Wounded when 5th Evacuation Hospital was hit by enemy shrapnel

Clark	Regina		Iraqi Freedom	USN	CPO	Killed when a suicide car bomber hit her convoy vehicle on 23 June 2005 near Fallujah, Iraq
Claxton	Bette	Geayne	WWII	ANC	Lt.	Wounded while aboard hospital ship *Hope* near Corregidor
Cole	Sarah		War on Terror	USN	PO3	Killed when terrorists flew an aircraft into the Pentagon 11 September 2001
Cook	Cordelia		WWII	ANC	Lt.	Wounded when Army hospital in Italy bombed December 1943
Cornum	Rhonda	Leah	Desert Storm	USA	Maj.	Wounded when medevac helicopter shot down in Iraq 27 February 1991. She was taken prisoner and released after five days.
Costales	Fidela		Iraqi Freedom	USAR	Sgt.	Wounded when her convoy was ambushed on 5 April 2004 near Mosul, Iraq
Cotterman	Robbie		War on Terror	USAF	MSgt.	Wounded when Khobar Towers were bombed 25 June 1996
Crippen-Dechon	Dorothy		WWII	WAC	Lt.	Wounded while serving in Southwest Pacific
Cross	Linnie		WWII	ANC	Lt.	Served as a flight nurse, aircraft shot down over Italy
Crumpton	Frances		Vietnam War	NNC	Lt.	Wounded when Brinks BOQ in Saigon bombed Christmas Eve 1964
Cruz-Cortes	Roxane		War on Terror	USA	Sgt.	Injured when terrorists flew an aircraft into the Pentagon 11 September 2001
Dana	Jamie		Iraqi Freedom	USAF	TECH	Injured when bomb exploded under her HUMVEE July 2005

(continued)

Last	First	Middle	Conflict	Branch	Rank	
Daniels	Shelly		Iraqi Freedom	USA	Pfc.	Injured when grenade was thrown through door of Army vehicle she was driving
Davis	Betty	Jane	WWII	ANC		Injured 1 January 1945 during Battle of the Bulge; assigned to the 150th Evacuation Hospital
Delvaux	Nicole	J.	Iraqi Freedom	NG	Sgt.	Member of the 32nd Military Police Company wounded 16 December 2003 by shrapnel from a rocket-propelled grenade
Doyle	Claudine	Glidewell	WWII	ANC	Lt.	Was on HMS *Newfoundland* when ship was bombed, was at the 95th Evacuation Hospital on Anzio when it was bombed, transferred to 300th General Hospital, Naples, which was bombed
Duckworth	Ladda	Tammy	Iraqi Freedom	NG	Maj.	RPG hit the helicopter she was piloting in Iraq on 12 November 2004
Dudley	Rachel		WWII	ANC	Lt.	Injured while serving at an Army hospital in China-India-Burma
Duff	Keisha		Iraqi Freedom	USA	Spc.	Member of the 299th Engineer Battalion in Tikrit who made daily trips with water and rations to Soldiers assigned two miles away; on 10 August 2003 while driving a hemmit she hit a mine and was injured but eventually returned to active duty in Iraq
Dumas	Frances	Nash	WWII	ANC	Lt.	Wounded when open-air hospital on Corregidor was bombed by Japanese
Echols	Denise		Iraqi Freedom	USA	Sgt.	Wounded by shrapnel from exploding mortar shell that hit the 915th Forward Surgical Support Team's bivouac site 3 July 2003

Eckert	Evelyn	WWII	ANC	Lt.	Killed when Japanese suicide bomber hit hospital ship *Comfort* 25 April 1945
Edwards	Cynthia	1970s	USN	CT2	Injured in Puerto Rico when Navy bus attacked by terrorists 3 December 1979
Elder	Casey	Iraqi Freedom	ANG		Injured April 2004 while on patrol in Baghdad and a convoy the unit was escorting was hit by a roadside bomb
Elseck	Blanche	WWII	ANC	Lt.	Aboard hospital ship *St David* when it was bombed 25 January 1944
Espinoza	Natasha	Iraqi Freedom	USA	Spc.	Injured when convoy hit a land mine
Esposito	Aida	Genevieve	WWII	WAC	Lt.	Wounded when the building at which she worked in England was bombed by the Germans
Fallon	Jamie	Lynn	War on Terror	USN	SK3	Killed when terrorists flew aircraft into Pentagon 11 September 2001
Farquhar	LaVerne	WWII	ANC	Lt.	Killed when the 33rd Field Hospital at Anzio Beachhead was bombed on 10 February 1944
Felder	Tyanna	Avery	Iraqi Freedom	USA	Spc.	Killed 4 April 2004 in Balad, Iraq, when her vehicle convoy was hit by an IED
Flannery	Theresa	Lynn	Iraqi Freedom	USAR	Spc.	Assigned to 350 Civil Affairs Command; injured during firefight at Najaf, Iraq, 2 April 2004
Floyd	Rosetta	Iraqi Freedom	USA	Spc.	Medic attached to Headquarters Company, 1st Battalion, 12th Regiment, 1st Cavalry Division hit by enemy mortar round at compound in Sadr City, Iraq

(continued)

Ford	Renada		Iraqi Freedom	USA	Spc.	Medic with the 70th Engineer Battalion injured in a RPG attack
Foreman	Kristi		War on Terror	USAF	E4	Injured when the Khobar Tower, Dharan, Saudi Arabia, was bombed on 25 June 1996
Fox	Annie	G.	WWII	ANC	Maj.	First woman awarded Purple Heart for meritorious service on 7 December 1941 at Pearl Harbor
Francis	Lakeina	Monique	War on Terror	USN	M.Sgt.	Killed in terrorist-induced explosion on USS *Cole*, Yemen, 12 October 2000
French	Carrie	L.	Iraqi Freedom	ANG	Spc.	Killed when her convoy vehicle was hit by an IED near Kirkuk, Iraq, on 5 June 2005
Frye	Nichole		Iraqi Freedom	USAR	Pfc.	Killed when roadside bomb exploded near her convoy 35 miles north of Baghdad
Gallop	April		War on Terror	USA	Spc.	Injured when terrorists flew aircraft into Pentagon 11 September 2001
Garcia	Adele		Iraqi Freedom	NG	Sgt.	Injured 25 May 2004 when a roadside bomb exploded near the truck she was driving in downtown Baghdad
Gasiewicz	Cari		Iraqi Freedom	USA	Sgt.	Died 4 December 2004 in Baqubah, Iraq, when two explosive devices detonated near her convoy
Gasvoda	Christine	Annette	WWII	ANC	Lt.	Killed when the medevac aircraft to which she was assigned crashed on 13 April 1945
Gaylon	Leona	J.	WWII	WAC	Pvt.	Received head wounds from flying glass when bomb hit a building in southern England where she was working on 16 July 1944

Last Name	First Name	Middle	Conflict	Branch	Rank	Description
Gibbons	Effie Mae	Thorber	WWII	WAC	Pfc.	Injured in southern England when building in which she was working was hit by a buzz bomb on 16 July 1944
Gilbert	Mary		War on Terror	USAF	SSG	Injured when terrorists bombed Khobar Towers, Dharan, Saudi Arabia, 25 June 1996
Gonzales	Aleina	Ramirez	Iraqi Freedom	USA	Spc.	Killed 15 April 2005 when a mortar struck her forward operating base in Tikrit, Iraq
Goodman	Valerie	Alice	WWII	ANC	Lt.	Injured when suicide bomber hit the hospital ship Comfort 28 April 1945
Grander	Patricia		WW II	WAC	Pfc.	Injured when a buzz bomb hit in her vicinity when she was on assignment in England
Grant	Mariana	Raba	Vietnam War	USAF	Capt.	Physician injured when MASH was mortared by the enemy 1968
Grant	Regina		War on Terror	USA	Maj.	Injured when terrorists flew an aircraft into the Pentagon 11 September 2001
Green	Danielle		Iraqi Freedom	USA	Spc.	Member of the 571st Military Police Company hit by rocket from a homemade missile launcher on 25 May 2004
Green	Sheron		Vietnam War	WAC	Spc.	Injured in 1968 on assignment in Vietnam
Green	Toccara	R.	Iraqi Freedom	USA	Spc.	Motor transport operator killed in an ambush of convoy near Al Asad on 14 August 2005
Greenwood	Ida	M.	WWII	ANC	Lt.	Killed aboard hospital Ship Comfort by Japanese suicide bomber 28 April 1945

(continued)

Surname	First	Middle	Conflict	Branch	Rank	Description
Grewer	Florence	Taylor	WWII	ANC	Lt.	Killed aboard hospital Ship *Comfort* by Japanese suicide bomber 28 April 1945
Gutierrez	Analaura	Esparza	Iraqi Freedom	USA	Pfc.	Killed 1 October 2003 near Tikrit, Iraq, when HUMVEE was hit by grenades and rocket
Hahn	Alice	Powers	WWII	ANC	Lt.	Wounded when Japanese bombed hospital on Bataan
Hajek	Helen	Yaroschak	WWII	WAC	Sgt.	Wounded while in London, England, with WAC
Halfaker	Dawn		Iraqi Freedom	USA	Capt.	Wounded when rocket grenade hit a truck she was riding in; the truck was on its way to help American soldiers under attack in northeast Baghdad June 2004
Hammond	Natasha		Desert Storm	USA	Sgt.	Wounded during Operation Desert Storm
Hampton	Kimberly		Iraqi Freedom	USA	Capt.	Kiowa helicopter she was piloting shot down by Iraqis near Fallujah, Iraq, 2 January 2004
Hansen	Isabelle	Wheeler	WWII	ANC	Lt.	Injured when hospital ship *Newfoundland* was bombed by enemy planes and sank off the coast of Salerno
Hanson	Anne		Iraqi Freedom	USAR	Spc.	Injured when bomb hit her truck 6 August 2005 on road between Tikrit and Kirkuk, Iraq
Harding	Alisha		Iraqi Freedom	USMC	Cpl.	Injured during a suicide car-bombing in Iraq 22 June 2005
Harrison	Debra		Iraqi Freedom	USAR	Lt. Col.	Injured when her vehicle was ambushed and a bullet hit her windshield, sending glass into her face and mouth
Harrison	Mary	W.	WWII	ANC	Lt.	Injured when 95th Evacuation Hospital was bombed at Anzio Beachhead 7 February 1944

Last	First	Conflict	Branch	Rank	Description
Harvey	Nicola	Iraqi Freedom	USAR	Spc.	Member of a convoy carrying supplies for the 101st Airborne Division injured June 2003 by a roadside explosive device
Hauer	Audra	Iraqi Freedom	USA	Spc.	Member of the 1161st Transportation Company injured 12 June 2003 when vehicle hit a land mine
Hawkins	Jahala	Iraqi Freedom	USA	Spc.	Communications specialist with the 70th Engineer Battalion was injured 4 June 2003 in Baghdad when homemade bomb exploded and the windshield of her vehicle shattered leaving glass fragments in her face
Henderson	Bianca	Iraqi Freedom	USA	Spc.	Injured by a roadside bomb
Henderson	Jeanne	WWII	ANC	Lt.	Received shrapnel wounds when 15th General Hospital was bombed 10 November 1944
Henderson	Mekelle	Iraqi Freedom	USA	Capt.	Injured when military vehicle hit a land mine in Baghdad on 8 May 2003
Herbert	Angeline	War on Terror	USAF	A1C	Injured when terrorists bombed Khobar Tower Complex, Dharan, Saudia Arabia, 25 June 1996
Hermes	Stephanie	Iraqi Freedom	USAR	Spc.	HUMVEE rolled when hit by an IED, she was ejected onto the road
Herrera	Mary	Iraqi Freedom	NG	MP	Wounded when 855th MP Company was attacked outside of Fallujah, Iraq, 9 November 2003
Hinshaw	Esther	WWII	ANC	Lt.	Injured when hospital ship St. David was bombed off coast of Italy 11 January 1944
Hipps	Juanita	WWII	ANC	LTC	Wounded on Bataan by enemy bombers while on duty at military hospital

(continued)

Hogan	Rosemary	Luciens	WWII	ANC	Lt.	Wounded when Japanese bombed open-air hospital on Bataan
Hoppe	Ruby		WWII	ANC	Lt.	Wounded at Anzio when 95th Evacuation Hospital was bombed 7 February 1944
Housby	Jessica	M.	Iraqi Freedom	NG	Sgt.	Killed when a roadside bomb exploded near her convoy on 9 February 2005
Howard	Kelli		Iraqi Freedom	USAR	Sgt.	Wounded while serving in a support fueling unit caught in an ambush Easter Sunday 2004
Huff	Sam	W.	Iraqi Freedom	USA	Pfc.	Died 18 April 2005 in Baghdad of injuries sustained the previous day, when an IED detonated near her HMMWV
Hufnagel	Michelle	A.	Iraqi Freedom	USA	Sgt.	Wounded in Baghdad 26 April 2004 in an explosion
Humphrey	Christina	J.	Iraqi Freedom	USMC	LCP	Wounded in a suicide bomb attack 23 June 2005
Innes	Jeanne	Henderson	WWII	ANC	Lt.	Injured at a military hospital in Belgium
Jackson	Leslie	D.	Iraqi Freedom	USA	Pfc.	Killed 20 May 2004 when vehicle hit IED en route to Camp Eagle, Iraq
Jacobson	Elizabeth	N.	Iraqi Freedom	USAF	A1C	Killed when an IED detonated near her convoy vehicle near Camp Bucca, Iraq, 28 September 2005
Jaenke	Jaime	S.	Iraqi Freedom	USN	PO2	Killed when her HUMVEE was struck by IED in Aubor province, west of Baghdad, 5 June 2006
Jameson	Tricia		Iraqi Freedom	NG	Sgt.	Nebraska National Guard medic died when her HUMVEE ambulance moved to the aid of Marines who had been wounded in an attack on their convoy near Trebil, Iraq, 14 July 2005
Janek	Dorothy		WWII	WAC	Pfc.	Injured by buzz bomb while assigned to Bushy Park, England

Last Name	First Name	Middle	Conflict	Branch	Rank	Circumstances
Jiminez	Angelica		Iraqi Freedom	USMC	LCP	Injured in suicide bombing attack in Fallujah, Iraq, 23 June 2005
Johnson	Margaret		WWII	WAC	Pvt.	Injured when buzz bomb hit building where she was working in southern England
Johnson	Orpha	L.	WWII	ANC	Lt.	Wounded when German aircraft bombed 95th Evacuation Hospital at Anzio
Johnson	Shoshana		Iraqi Freedom	USA	Spc.	Wounded and taken POW when the 507th Maintenance unit became isolated from its convoy and was attacked by Iraqi soldiers on 23 March 2003; rescued 13 April 2003
Jones	Tina		Iraqi Freedom	USA	Spc.	Injured when her convoy, a part of the 515th Transportation Company, was attacked outside of Baghdad on 29 October 2003
Kaempfer	Irene		WWII	ANC	Lt.	Wounded when an enemy shell fell on the tented Army hospital where she was working on 10 April 1944 at Anzio Beachhead
Kidd	Jacqueline	Fleck	War on Terror	USA	Spc.	Injured while working as air traffic controller at Pentagon helipad 11 September 2001 when terrorists flew aircraft into the Pentagon
King	Stacey	L.	Desert Storm	USA	CPL	Injured when barracks hit by Iraqi SCUD missile 25 February 199
Knox	Mary		WWII	WAC	Sgt.	Injured when a buzz bomb hit in her vicinity when she was on assignment in England
Krupiczowicz	Julia		Iraqi Freedom	NG	Spc.	Injured in Iraq

(continued)

Surname	Given Name	Middle	War	Branch	Rank	Description
Kurth	Agatha		WWII	ANC	Lt.	Injured while working at the 24th Evacuation Hospital
LaBeau-O'Brien	Cheryl	Raus	Desert Storm	USA	Sgt.	Killed when Blackhawk helicopter on which she was a door-gunner was shot down by enemy fire 27 February 1991
Lacey	Dorothy		WWII	WAC	Pfc.	Injured when buzz bomb hit in her vicinity while she was on assignment in England
LaFave	Thelma		WWII	ANC	Lt.	Died when the plane she was on crashed into the ocean on 25 January 1945
LaFontaine	Elizabeth	Sanchez	War on Terror	USN	PO3	Injured while serving aboard the USS *Cole* when the ship was bombed by terrorists at the Port of Yemen on 12 October 2000
Lane	Sharon		Vietnam War	ANC	Lt.	Killed when an enemy rocket hit the ward to which she was assigned at the 312th Evacuation Hospital in Chu Lai
Langdeau	Laura		Iraqi Freedom	USMC	Cpl.	Severely injured in mortar attack on air base near Fallujah, Iraq
Lau	Karina		Iraqi Freedom	USA	Pvt.	Killed in Iraq 2 November 2003 when Chinook Helicopter she was on was shot down by enemy fire
Leer	Mary	Duncan	WWII	ANC	Capt.	Wounded when the 65th General Hospital, England, was bombed by the enemy
Lelacheur	Lauretta		WWII	ANC	Capt.	Wounded twice during Mediterranean-European Campaign
Lewis	Anna	B.	WWII	ANC	Lt.	Wounded when the 42nd Field Hospital was bombed by the enemy on 24 November 1944

Lewison	Katrina	Gier	Iraqi Freedom	USA	Lt.	Wounded in Iraq when grenade thrown at HUMVEE she was riding in
Liberty	Erin		Iraqi Freedom	USMC	LCP	Wounded 23 June 2005 when suicide bomber rammed into seven-ton truck with 20 Marines aboard
Lo	Gaozoua	D.	Iraqi Freedom	MC	Cpl.	Wounded 26 August 2004 when an explosive device hit her transport vehicle
Loftus	Michelle		Iraqi Freedom	USA	Pfc.	Received injuries from a remotely detonated land mine while serving as a door gunner while on patrol in a military vehicle on 26 July 2003
Lopez	Margaret		War on Terror	USN	GSM1	Received burns when USS Cole was attacked by terrorists on 12 October 2000 in the Port of Yemen
Lozinski	Abby		Iraqi Freedom	USA	Pfc.	Injured when a roadside bomb detonated near her patrol vehicle September 2003
Lucas	Latoya		Iraqi Freedom	USA		Seriously injured when her military vehicle was hit by an RPG while traveling in a supply convoy in Mosul, Iraq, in July 2003
Lynch	Jessica		Iraqi Freedom	USA	Pfc.	Severely injured when her unit became separated from its convoy and was attacked by Iraqi soldiers 23 March 2003; captured and held POW in hospital for nine days
MacIntyre	Margaret	Bowler	WWII	ANC	Lt.	Injured by German artillery shell 21 October 1944
Mahan	Violet	R.	WWII	ANC	Lt.	Received shrapnel wounds when enemy bombed the 77th Evacuation Hospital on 3 October 1944
Maravillosa	Myla	L.	Iraqi Freedom	USA	Sgt.	Died when her HMMWV was attacked by enemy forces using rocket grenades on 24 December 2005 near Al Hawijah, Iraq

(continued)

Last Name	First Name	Middle	War	Branch	Rank	Description
Markley	Rosalie		WWII	ANC	Capt.	Injured when the 9th Field Hospital was bombed during the Battle of the Bulge
Marquis	Rea	B.	WWII	WAC	T5	Injured by buzz bomb while on assignment to England
Marshall	Michelle		War on Terror	USAF	A1C	Wounded during the Khobar Towers bombing 25 June 1996
Mason	Ruth	A.	Vietnam War	NNC	Lt.	Wounded when living quarters bombed by terrorists 24 December 1964
May	Candace		Iraqi Freedom	USA	Pvt.	Wounded while on patrol in Iraq early June 2003
Mayes	Christine	L.	Desert Storm	USAR	Spc.	Killed when SCUD missile hit barracks in Saudi Arabia 26 February 1991
McConnell	Amy		Korean War	ANC	Lt. Col.	Served in 8076 MASH and 171st Evacuation Hospital
McCullough	Helen	Agnes	WWII	ANC	Lt.	Wounded while enemy bombed the 56th Evacuation Hospital at Anzio Beachhead
McGeogh	Holly		Iraqi Freedom	USA	Pfc.	Killed when roadside bomb exploded hitting her convoy
Mella	Marguerite		WWII	ANC	Lt.	Wounded when hospital ship St. David was bombed and sunk off the coast of Italy 24 January 1944
Menzie	Mary	Brown	WWII	ANC	Lt.	Wounded during the bombing of Corregidor during the late spring of 1942
Michels	Grace	Bradshaw	WWII	ANC	Capt.	Wounded when 24th Evacuation Hospital was bombed by the enemy
Mitchell	Adrienne		Desert Storm	USAR	Pvt.	Killed when SCUD missile hit barracks in Al Khobar, Saudi Arabia, 26 February 1991

Last Name	First Name	Middle	War/Operation	Branch	Rank	Details
Mitchell	Michele		Iraqi Freedom	USA	SSgt.	Wounded by a roadside bomb in Iraq on 25 April 2004
Mohon	Amanda		Iraqi Freedom	USA	Pfc.	Wounded in the 21 December 2004 mess tent bombing
Montgomery	Tamara	O.	Iraqi Freedom	USAR	Lt.	Injured 11 April 2004 in Iraq while acting as machine gunner while under small-arms and machine gun fire; sustained multiple wounds
Moore	Henrietta	Burnhart	WWII	USA	Lt.	Wounded while on duty at the 51st Evacuation Hospital during the Battle of the Bulge
Morgan	Stacy		War on Terror	USAF	Spc.	Injured when Khobar Towers were bombed 25 June 1996
Morrison	Shawna		Iraqi Freedom	NG	Sgt.	Killed 5 September 2004 in a mortar attack on her base in Iraq
Morrow	Marjorie	Gertrude	WWII	ANC	Lt.	Killed when enemy bombs hit the 33rd Field Hospital at Anzio Beachhead on 7 February 1944
Nagel	Deanna		Iraqi Freedom	NG	Spc.	Wounded when an RPG exploded in front of her HUMVEE outside of Baghdad International Airport on 13 June 2003
Navarro	Arellano Juana		Iraqi Freedom	USMC	LCP	Killed during firefight in Aubor province, west of Baghdad; 8 April 2006
Neill	Connie		Iraqi Freedom	USA	Pfc.	Wounded by a roadside bomb on 8 January 2004 near Mosul, Iraq
Nolan	Agnes		WWII	ANC	Lt.	Injured when a German aircraft bombed and sank the hospital ship she was on; 13 September 1943

(continued)

Nolan	Madonna	WWII	ANC	Lt.	Injured when a German aircraft bombed and sank the hospital ship she was on; 13 September 1943
O'Connell	Nora	WWII	ANC	Lt.	Received shrapnel wounds when the 108th Evacuation Hospital was bombed on 10 November 1944
Ogle	Cecilia Haas	WWII	ANC	Lt.	Wounded during an air raid on Santo Tomas, February 1945
Olds	Sherry Lynn	War on Terror	USAF	SMS	Killed at the U.S. Embassy in Nairobi, Kenya, 7 August 1998
Oravec	Ann Marie	Iraqi Freedom	NG	Sgt.	Wounded by shrapnel September 2003 when her vehicle ran over an explosive
Osbourne	Pamela	Iraqi Freedom	USA	Sgt.	Killed 10 October 2004 when two rockets hit her camp near Baghdad, Iraq
Oswald-Lackey	Hope	Vietnam War	ANC	Maj.	Served in a MASH unit in Vietnam
Otis	Dorothea Murphy	WWII	ANC	Lt.	Wounded by enemy sniper 23 May 1945 in Susice, Czechoslovakia
Pak	Chin Sun	War on Terror	USA	Spc4	Killed when terrorists flew an airplane into the Pentagon 11 September 2001
Palmer	Lakiba Nicole	War on Terror	USN	SR	Killed when the USS Cole was attacked by terrorists in the port of Yemen 12 October 2000
Palmer	Rita Glidden	WWII	ANC	Lt.	Wounded when Japanese aircraft bombed Hospital #1 on the Bataan Peninsula, Philippines
Picou	Ora	WWII	ANC	Lt.	Wounded by enemy fire on the island of Luzon in the Philippines in April 1945
Piestewa	Lori	Iraqi Freedom	USA	Spc.	Killed in a firefight in Iraq on 23 March 2003 when her unit was attacked by the enemy

Piper	Laura	A.	Iraq 1994	USAF	Lt.	Accidentally shot down by U.S. fighter pilots 14 April 1994
Pitzel	Mary Pat	Mulcay	WWII	ANC	Lt.	Served in European Theater on troop transport
Powers	Elizabeth		WWII	ANC	Lt.	Wounded when German aircraft bombed the 45th Field Hospital in Belgium
Price	Amber	R.	Iraqi Freedom	MC	L. Cpl.	Wounded 13 August 2005 while riding in a supply convoy from Camp Taqaddum to Camp Fallujah
Putman	Tiffany		War on Terror	USN	PO1	Wounded when the USS Cole was attacked by terrorists in the port of Yemen 12 October 2000
Ratchford	Marsha	Dianah	War on Terror	USN	1ST	Killed when terrorists flew an airplane into the Pentagon 11 September 2001
Rathbun-Nealy	Melissa	Coleman	Desert Storm	USA	Spc4	Wounded and captured by enemy forces in Iraq on 31 January 1991 and held as POW for 33 days
Reali	Regina	C.	Iraqi Freedom	USAR	Sgt.	Killed when an IED exploded near her HMMWV 23 December 2005 in Baghdad, Iraq
Redmond	Juanita	Hipps	WWII	ANC	Lt.	Wounded when Japanese aircraft bombed Hospital #1 on the Bataan Peninsula, Philippines
Reed	Tatjana		Iraqi Freedom	USA	Sgt.	Killed when homemade bomb detonated near her convoy in Samarra, Iraq, on 22 July 2004
Rendon	Connie		Iraqi Freedom	USAR		Wounded in ambush while driving a truck north of Baghdad
Reynolds	Ann	Darby	Vietnam War	NNC	Cat.	Wounded in Saigon when guerillas bombed the Navy BOQ on 24 December 1964

(continued)

Rhoades	Mary	A.	Desert Storm	USAR	Sgt.	Wounded when SCUD missile hit her unit's barracks in Saudi Arabia on 25 February 1991
Rice	Chelsea		Iraqi Freedom	USA	Spc.	Wounded from shrapnel from a mortar shell while driving supplies to frontline troops
Richards	Andrea	D.	War on Terror	USAF	SSG	Wounded when terrorists bombed the Khobar Towers in Dharan, Saudi Arabia, on 25 June 1996
Richards	Esther		WWII	RC		Killed by enemy bomb at Anzio Beachhead 7 February 1944 (appears to have been issued a special Purple Heart by Franklin Delano Roosevelt although she was not in uniform at the time of her death)
Ritter	Monique	Alexander	War on Terror	USN	CTR	Severely wounded when Puerto Rican terrorists attacked a Navy bus near Sabana Seca on 3 December 1979
Roders	Catherine		WWII	ANC	Lt.	Hit by shrapnel during evening air raid while stationed in Caserta, Italy
Rodgers	Audrey	McDonald	WWII	ANC	Lt.	Wounded during attack by Japanese aircraft
Rozelle	Dana		War on Terror	USAF	M. Sgt.	Injured when terrorists bombed the Khobar Towers in Saudi Arabia on 25 June 1996
Rubalcava	Isela		Iraqi Freedom	USA	Spc.	Killed when a mortar round struck near her in Mosul, Iraq, on 8 May 2004
Rubenstein	Matilda		WWII	ANC	Lt.	Severely wounded when the 15th General Hospital in Leige, Belgium, was bombed by enemy aircraft
Sal	Mary		WWII	WAC	Pvt.	Wounded by a buzz bomb while on assignment to England

Last Name	First Name	Middle	Conflict	Branch	Rank	Description
Sanchez	Tracie		Iraqi Freedom	USA	Pvt.	Wounded by shrapnel from an RPG that hit near her during a firefight in Karbala, Iraq, on 16 October 2003
Saunders	Michelle		Iraqi Freedom	USA	Pvt.	Wounded in attack on HUMVEE on duty in Iraq
Saychen	Sophie		WWII	WAC	Sgt.	Wounded by buzz bomb while on assignment to England
Scott	Antoinette		Iraqi Freedom	NG	Spc.	Wounded in IED attack in November 2003
Seaton	Sandra		War on Terror	USN	CTO	Wounded when Navy bus was attacked by Puerto Rican terrorists near Sabana Seca on 3 December 1979
Sheets	Carrie	Thompson	WWII	ANC	Lt.	Killed when the 95th Evacuation Hospital at Anzio Beachhead was bombed by German aircraft on 7 February 1944
Shirley	Clio	E.	WWII	ANC	Lt.	Wounded when the 77th Evacuation Hospital was shelled by the enemy in Belgium on 3 October 1944
Shute	Frances	Rice	WWII	WAC	Maj.	Wounded during the Normandy Campaign of 1944
Sigman	Blanche	Fay	WWII	ANC	Lt.	Killed when the 95th Evacuation Hospital at Anzio Beachhead was bombed by German aircraft on 7 February 1944
Silewiez	Janina		WWII	WAC	Pvt.	Wounded by buzz bomb while on assignment in England
Skinner	Sara		Iraqi Freedom	USA	Lt.	Wounded in mortar attack in Iraq in November 2004
Slanger	Frances	Y.	WWII	ANC	Lt.	Killed when Germans bombed the 45th Field Hospital in Belgium on 21 October 1944

(continued)

Slaybaugh	Laura		WWII	ANC	Lt.	Wounded when the hospital ship *Newfoundland* was bombed by the enemy and sank during the invasion of Salerno
Snyder	Gladys	M.	WWII	ANC	Lt.	Wounded by enemy fire on 21 October 1944 and again on 10 November 1944
Sonnheim	Susan		Iraqi Freedom	USA	Sgt.	Injured when a police station in Iraq was bombed; credited with saving four Iraqi policemen
Sopper	Marie	Rose	War on Terror	USNR	Lt.	Killed when aircraft she was on was hijacked by terrorists and flown into Pentagon on 11 September 2001
Speiser	Sherry		WWII	ANC	Capt.	Wounded while serving aboard a hospital ship in the Mediterranean Theater
Spelhaug	Glenda	Thomas	WWII	ANC	Lt.	Killed when German aircraft bombed the 56th Evacuation Hospital on Anzio Beachhead on 10 February 1944
Spinks	Connie		Iraqi Freedom	USAR	Spc.	Injured when suicide bomber in pickup truck drove into her HUMVEE 22 October 2004
Spors	Rachelle		Iraqi Freedom	NG	Spc.	Injured by a roadside bomb while responding to an emergency call of another bombing 14 July 2005
Sprunk	Margaret	R.	WWII	WAC	Sgt.	Wounded when a buzz bomb hit in her vicinity during her assignment to England
Stanke	Dorothy	M.	WWII	ANC	Lt.	Killed when a Japanese suicide bomber hit the hospital ship *Comfort* on 28 April 1945

			War	Branch	Rank	Description
Stidham	Kesha		War on Terror	USN	SA	Wounded when terrorists bombed the USS *Cole* in the port of Yemen on 12 October 2000
Stockwell	Melissa	J.	Iraqi Freedom	USA	Lt.	Wounded when an IED exploded, throwing HUMVEE she was driving into a guardrail 13 April 2004
Sullivan	Mary	A.	WWII	ANC	Lt.	Wounded when the 15th General Hospital was bombed on 10 November 1944
Swartworth	Sharon	T.	Iraqi Freedom	USA	WO5	Killed in Iraq when the UH-60 Blackhawk Helicopter on which she was a passenger was hit by enemy fire and crashed near the Tigris River on 7 November 2003
Talboy	Helen		WWII	ANC	Lt.	Wounded when HMS *Newfoundland* was bombed and sunk off the coast of Salerno
Tarango-Griess	Linda	Ann	Iraqi Freedom	USA	Spc.	Killed when an IED detonated near her convoy vehicle on 11 July 2004 near Samsarra, Iraq
Taylor	Brandy		Iraqi Freedom	USAR	Spc.	Wounded by mortar fire on 20 March 2003, the day her unit, the 296th Transportation Company, arrived in Iraq
Thurman	Tamara		War on Terror	USA	Sgt.	Killed when terrorists flew an aircraft into the Pentagon on 11 September 2001
Tinges	Anne	W.	WWII	WAC	Lt.	Wounded by a buzz bomb while on assignment to England; first WAC to receive PH
Todd	Iona		WWII	ANC	Lt.	Wounded by shrapnel when the 298th General Hospital was bombed on 10 November 1944

(continued)

Last	First	Middle	Conflict	Branch	Rank	Description
Tsui	Amy		Iraqi Freedom	ANG	Sgt.	Wounded by grenade when convoy was ambushed
Valdez	Ramona	M.	Iraqi Freedom	MC	Cpl.	Killed when a suicide car bomber hit her convoy vehicle on 23 June 2005 near Fallujah, Iraq
Vega	Frances		Iraqi Freedom	USA	Spc.	Killed in Iraq when the Chinook helicopter she was on was shot down on 2 November 2003
Veit	Mildred		WWII	WAC	Cpl.	Wounded by a buzz bomb while stationed at 8th AF HQ at High Wyckham, England
Voelz	Kimberly	Fahnestock	Iraqi Freedom	USA	SSG	Killed while responding to an explosive ordnance disposal call in Iskandaria, Iraq, on 14 December 2003
Wagner	Camilla		Vietnam War	USAF	Capt.	Injured by a terrorist explosive device in 1969 while serving in Vietnam as an accounting officer
Wagner	Karen	J.	War of Terror	USA	Lt. Col.	Killed when terrorists flew an aircraft into the Pentagon on 11 September 2001
Walker	Laura	M.	Enduring Freedom	USA	Lt.	Killed when a roadside bomb exploded under her HUMVEE near Delak, north of Kandahar on 18 August 2005
Walsh	Gladys	Marie	WWII	ANC	Capt.	Wounded by shrapnel in Holland on 31 December 1944 while serving with the 100th Semi-Mobile Evacuation Hospital and the 5th Auxiliary Surgical Group
Walsh	Jessica		Iraqi Freedom	NG	Sgt.	Injured by explosive device detonated under her HUMVEE 27 December 2003
Warchol	Helen	Elaine	Korean War	AFNC	Lt.	Injured in attack on MASH unit

Surname	Given		War	Branch	Rank	Circumstances
Weathers	Sarah		WWII	WAC	Spc.	Wounded by buzz bomb while on assignment in England
Weeks	Lois		Vietnam War	WAC	M. Sgt.	Injured when grenade was thrown at a jeep she was riding in
Wharton	Helen		WWII	ANC	Maj.	Wounded when the hospital ship *Newfoundland* was bombed off the Italian coast on 13 September 1943
White	Maudlyn		War on Terror	USA	SSG	Killed when terrorists flew an aircraft into the Pentagon on 11 September 2001
White	Sonya	L.	War on Terror	USAF	SRA	Injured when terrorists bombed the Khobar Towers in Saudi Arabia, 25 June 1996
Whitfield	Dorothy	Chisholm	WWII	WAC	Pfc.	Injured when a V2 rocket bomb hit the building in southern England where she worked on 16 July 1944
Whitehurst	Debra	J.	War on Terror	USN	RM2	Wounded when a Navy bus was attacked by terrorists in Puerto Rico on 3 December 1979
Whittle	Reba	Tobiason	WWII	ANC	Lt.	Wounded when medical evacuation aircraft was shot down behind German lines; held as POW for four months
Williams	Imogene		WWII	WAC	Cpl.	Wounded by buzz bomb while on assignment in England
Williamson	Sandra		Iraqi Freedom	USA	Sgt.	Wounded when an Iraqi mortar shell exploded near the 915th Forward Surgical Support Team's bivouac in Iraq on 3 July 2003
Wills	Marilyn		War on Terror	USA	Lt. Col.	Wounded when terrorists flew an aircraft into the Pentagon on 11 September 2001

(continued)

Wilson	Juanita		Iraqi Freedom	USA	SSG	Wounded in attack on HUMVEE on a convoy mission north of Baghdad on 21 August 2004
Wilson	Ruth	Ann	Vietnam War	NNC	Ens.	Wounded when terrorist guerillas bombed her BOQ in Saigon on 24 December 1964
Windham	Emma	Jane	WWII	WAC	Pfc.	Wounded in bombing raid in England in July 1944 and later killed in aircraft collision
Wing	Genevieve	Flood	WWII	ANC	Capt.	Wounded by flying shrapnel on 31 December 1944 while serving with the 5th Auxiliary Surgical Group, a frontline surgical hospital
Wingerd	Fern	H.	WWII	ANC	Lt.	Wounded on Anzio Beachhead during enemy bombing
Witmer	Michelle		Iraqi Freedom	ANG	Spc.	Killed when her HUMVEE was ambushed in Baghdad, Iraq, on 9 April 2004
Wright	Elizabeth	U.	WWII	ANC	Lt.	Injured by a buzz bomb on 24 November 1944 in Liege, Belgium; injured by a second bomb 11 January 1945
Yancey	Vicky	Costanzo	War on Terror	USN		Killed when terrorists flew an aircraft into the Pentagon on 11 September 2001
Yniestra	Gwen		WWII	ANC	Lt.	Wounded when the 15th General Hospital was bombed on 10 November 1944
Zuhoski	Selena	P.	War on Terror	USAF	TSGT	Wounded when terrorists bombed the Khobar Towers in Saudi Arabia on 25 June 1996

Source: Judith Bellafaire, Ph.D., Chief Historian, Women in Military Service for America Memorial Foundation, Inc., Arlington, Virginia

APPENDIX C

The Women In Military Service For America Memorial Foundation, Inc.

The Women In Military Service For America Memorial Foundation, Inc., is the nation's only major memorial to honor the some 2.5 million uniformed women who have served in the nation's defense. Its primary mission is to chronicle the history of women's service in the military and tell the story of the women who have served. Located at the gateway to Arlington National Cemetery, the memorial and its 33,000-square-foot education facility features an exhibit gallery, 196-seat theater, bookstore, never-before-seen artifacts, period uniforms, and rare photographs and memorabilia, beginning with the American Revolution.

At the heart of the memorial is the Register, the computerized database of past and present servicewomen. This interactive system, which includes the pictures, awards and decorations, and memorable experiences of nearly 250,000 uniformed women, is accessible by visitors and is designed to grow as women continue to register.

The Women's Memorial Foundation, the nonprofit organization that built and now maintains the memorial, presides over the world's largest archive related to women's military service. The foundation also manages a vigorous oral history program and maintains an extensive library of books by and about military women. The archive, library, and oral history files are available to scholars, researchers, and journalists. To learn more about the Memorial, its programs and activities, membership eligibility and how to join, visit the Web site at www.womensmemorial.org, or call 800-222-2294/703-533-1155.

Bibliography

Pfc. Teresa Broadwell Grace, USA

Teresa Broadwell Grace, interview by Scott Baron, 19 April 2006, transcript, The Women's Memorial, Arlington, VA.

Loeb, Vernon, "Combat Heroine: Teresa Broadwell Found Herself in the Army—Under Fire in Iraq," *Washington Post,* 23 November 2003.

Pfc. Michelle Loftus Fisher, USA

Michelle Loftus Fisher, interview by Scott Baron, 15 February 2006, transcript, The Women's Memorial, Arlington, VA.

Zdechlik, Mark. "Soldier Wounded in Iraq on the Mend Back Home in Minnesota." Minnesota Public Radio, 6 August 2003.

SSgt. Jessica Lee Clements, USAR

Claus, C. Todd, "Injury Fails to Impede Clements' Zeal for Life," *The Journal,* 26 August 2004.

Jessica Lee Clements, interview by Scott Baron, 27 February 2006, transcript, The Women's Memorial, Arlington, VA.

Lerner, Maura, "Back from Iraq One Step at a Time," *Minneapolis Star Tribune,* 8 August 2004.

Potter, Ned. "Female Soldier's Recovery Called a 'Miracle.'" ABC News, 28 November 2004.

Maj. Marie T. Rossi-Cayton, USA

Francke, Linda, journalist. "Hers: Requiem for a Soldier," *New York Times* Magazine, 21 April 1991. http://arlingtoncemetery.net/mariethe.htm

Army Aviation Hall of Fame 1992 Induction of Major Marie T. Rossi-Cayton, USA. http://www.quad-a.org/Hall of Fame/personnel/rossi-cayton.htm

"Marie Rossi – Gulf War Casualty." *People Weekly,* Summer 1991 p. 12.

The 15 Most Intriguing People of the War: Marie Rossi. Lexis Nexis Academic Universe Database, Spring/Summer 1991.

Vietnam Introduction

Chambers, John Whiteclay II. *Oxford Companion to American Military History.* New York: Oxford University Press, 1999.

Norman, Elizabeth. *Women at War: The Story of 50 Military Nurses Who Served in Vietnam.* Philadelphia: University of Pennsylvania Press, 1990.

Powell, Mary Reynolds. *A World of Hurt: Between Innocence and Arrogance in Vietnam.* Chesterfield, OH: Greenleaf Ent., 2000.

Monthly Rpts, WAC Det, USARV, to WAC Staff Adviser, Mar 70, Jan 71, Jan 72, ODWAC Ref File, Vietnam, CMH.

Morden, Col. Bettie J. The Women's Army Corps during the Vietnam War: Special series by office of the chief of Military History. Washington, D.C.: Government Printing Office, 1990.

Staff Adviser, USARPAC, Historical Rpts, 1972 and 1973, ODWAC Ref File, USARPAC, CMH. The last two WAC officers to leave Vietnam (Mar 73) were Maj. Georgia A. Wise and Capt. Nancy N. Keough.

Lt. Col. Anne Marie Doering, USA

Bob and Anne Jamison, informal interviews by Scott Baron, November 2005.

Lt. (jg) Ann Darby Reynolds, USN

Horne, Al. N. H. "Navy Nurse Tells of Viet Raid," *Boston Record American,* 9 January 1965.

Hovis, Bobbi. *Station Hospital Saigon: A Navy Nurse in Vietnam, 1963–1964.* Annapolis, Md.: Naval Institute Press, 1992.

Ann D. Reynolds, interview by Kate Scott, 19 August 2004, transcript, The Women's Memorial, Arlington, VA.

Spc5 Sheron Lee Green, USA

Sheron Lee Green, interview by Scott Baron, 13 November 2005 transcript, The Women's Memorial, Arlington, VA.

Chronological Record of Medical Care (SF600) dated 10 June 1968, Surgeon, 1st Aviation Brigade, APO SF 96384.

Spc5 Karen Irene Offutt, USA

Karen Irene Offutt, interview by Scott Baron, 18 November 2005 transcript, The Women's Memorial, Arlington, VA.

Steinman, Ron. *Women in Vietnam: The Oral History.* New York: TV Books LLC, 2000.

Korea Introduction

Blair, Clay. *The Forgotten War.* New York: Random House, 1988.

Chambers, John Whiteclay III. *Oxford Companion to American Military History.* New York: Oxford University Press, 1999.

Samda, Andrea Matles, editor. The Korean War (1950–1953). The Library of Congress Country Studies. Washington: The Library of Congress, Federal Research Division, Call #DS 932 N662: US Government Printing Office, 1994.

The Korean War in Brief. Office of Public Affairs, Veterans Administration, June 2000.

Walker, Jack D. "A Brief Account of the Korean War." Korean War Educator. http://www.koreanwar-educator.org/topics/brief/brief_account_of_the_korean_war.htm.

Lt. Margaret Fae Perry, USAF

Stump, Shelly. Flight Nurse Honored with Scholarship Fund. Morgantown, WV. West Virginia University Magazine, Vol. 27, Number 1, Spring, 2004.

Col. Margaret Brosmer, USA

Margaret Brosmer, interview by Scott Baron, 29 May 2005 transcript, The Women's Memorial, Arlington, VA.

Chambers, John Whiteclay III. *Oxford Companion to American Military History.* New York: Oxford University Press, 1999.

Clements, Glen. "Epic Hungham Evacuation Ends; 200,000 Taken Off Beachhead." *Pacific Stars and Stripes,* 6(333); 16 December 1950.

Higgins, Marguerite. *War in Korea: The Report of a Woman Combat Correspondent.* New York: Doubleday Books, 1951.

O'Connor, Rev. Patrick. "Catholic Nurse Describes Life on Korean Battlefield." The New World (NCWC News Service), 16 February 1951.

Strait, Sandy. *What Was it Like in the Korean War.* New York: Royal Fireworks Press, 1999.

Summers, Col. Harry G. The Korean War: A Fresh Perspective. *Military History Magazine,* April 1996.

Witt, Linda, Judith Bellafaire, Britta Granrud, & Mary Jo Binker. *A Defense Weapon Known to Be of Value: Servicewomen of the Korean War.* Lebanon, N.H.: University of New England Press/Military Women's Press, 2005, pp. 192–3.

Col. Ruby Grace Bradley, USA

Bradley, Ruby G. "Prisoners of War in the Far East." ANC Web site. http://history.amedd.army.mil/ANCWebsite/bradley.htm

Johnson, Laura Kendall. "One of the Most Decorated Women in Military History Laid to Rest." *Knight Ridder/Tribune News Service,* 9 July 2002.

Norman, Elizabeth. *We Band of Angels: The Untold Story of American Nurse Trapped on Bataan by the Japanese.* New York: Pocket Books, 1999.

Senator John D. Rockefeller IV, statement on the Senate floor, in memory of Col. Ruby Bradley, 7 July 2002.

U.S. Army Center for Military History.

World War II Introduction

Caddick-Adams, Peter. Oxford Companion to Military History. UK: Royal Military College of Science, Cranfield University, 2001.

Campbell, D'Ann. "Women in Combat: The World War Two Experiences in the United States, Great Britain, Germany, and the Soviet Union," *Journal of Military History,* April 1993.

"Military Nurses in World War I." The Women's Memorial, Arlington, VA. http://www.womensmemorial.org/historyandcollections/history/lrnmrewwinurses.html

Snyder, Louis. *The Long Armistice 1919–1939: Europe between Wars.* New York: Franklin Watts, Inc., 1964.

Treadwell, Mattie E. *The US Army in World War II, Special Studies, The Women's Army Corps.* Washington, D.C.: Government Printing Office, 1954.

U.S. Army Women's Museum, Fort Lee, VA, Strength of the Army Reports, STM 30, 1942–1945

Women In Military Service For America Memorial.

2nd Lt. Frances Y. Slanger, USA

Anderson, Lydia. "Forgotten Hero," *NurseWeek,* 18 June 2004. www.nurseweek.com/news/features/04-06/normandy_print.html

Boule, Margie. "Oregonians help remember forgotten heroine of Normandy," *The Oregonian,* 6 June 2004. www.twliterary.com/nightingale_oregonian.html

Chaganti, Shruti. "2LT Frances Slanger, ANC," Army Historical Foundation, Army History Research. www.armyhistory.org/armyhistorical.aspx?pgID=868&id=143&exCompID=32

Welch, Bob, *American Nightingale: The Story of Frances Slanger, Forgotten Heroine of Normandy.* New York: Africa Books, 2004

Ens. Jane Louise Kendeigh Cheverton, USN

Cooper, Page. *Navy Nurse.* New York: McGraw-Hill Book Company, 1946.

Dewitt, Lt. Gill. *The First Navy Flight Nurse on a Pacific Battlefield–A Picture Story of a Flight to Iwo.* Fredericksburg, Texas: The Admiral Nimitz Foundation, 1983.

Frachette, Joseph. "Flight Nurse," *Navy Medicine,* March–April 1945.

Sutter, Janet. "'Angel of Mercy Kept Wings: WWII Nurse Still Dotes on Patients," *The San Diego Union,* 24 March 1985.

American Journal of Nursing, 45(6), June 1945.

U.S. Navy Department BUMED (Bureau of Medicine) Newsletter Aviation Supplement, 5(1), 20 July 1945.

Prisoners of War

Baron, Scott. *They Also Served: Military Biographies of Uncommon Americans.* Spartenburg, N.C.: MIE Press, 1999.

Harold Bosner, interviewed by Mary Jo Binker, 27 April 2000, Falls Church, Virginia. Tape and transcript are deposited at The Women's Memorial, Arlington, VA.

Buck, Anna. "POW in Germany." *Army Magazine,* March 2000.

Cooper, Page. *Navy Nurse.* New York: McGraw-Hill Book Co., 1946.

Danner, Dorothy Still. "Remembrances of a Nurse POW." *Navy Medicine 83*(3), May–June 1992, pp. 36–40.

Grimes, Charlotte. "Women POWs of WW II." *St. Louis Post-Dispatch,* 19 April 1992.

King, Michael J. "Rangers: Selected Combat Operations in World War II," Chapter 6 of the U.S. Army Command and General Staff College's Leavenworth Papers, No. 11.

Letter from Capt. Kyle Lawrence, Group Chaplain, Headquarters 27th Air Transport Group—APO 744, dated 6 December 1944.

Margaret Nash, interviewed by Andree Marechal-Workman, September 1992, transcript, Naval Hospital Oakland, Public Affairs.

Norman, Elizabeth. *We Band of Angels: The Untold Story of American Nurses Trapped on Bataan by the Japanese.* New York: Simon and Schuster, 1999, p. 273.

Sforza, Kevin. "Bethesda Nurses Honor Former POW," *Journal of the National Naval Medical Center*, 13 September 2001.

Sternberg, R. *Return to the Philippines*. New York: Time-Life Books, 1979, p. 114.

"Tobiason, WW II POW Finally Receives Recognition." *The Rocksprings Record and Texas Mohair Weekly*, 14 May 1992, Vol. 99, No.13.

File # N734426. National Personnel Records Center (NPRC), St Louis, MO.

Tobiason, Reba Whittle. *Diary of 2nd Lt. Reba Whittle Tobiason*. Air Evacuation Museum, Brooks AFB, San Antonio, Texas, not published.

Norman, Elizabeth. *We Band of Angels: The Untold Story of American Nurses Trapped on Bataan by the Japanese*. New York: Simon and Schuster, 1999.

Sforza, Kevin. "Bethesda Nurses Honor Former POW," *Journal of the National Naval Medical Center*, 13 September 2001.

Sternberg, R. *Return to the Philippines*. New York: Time-Life Books, 1979.

Tobiason, Reba Whittle. *Diary of 2Lt. Reba Whittle Tobiason*. Air Evacuation Museum, Brooks AFB, San Antonio, TX.: Not published.

"Tobiason, WW II POW Finally Receives Recognition." *The Rocksprings Record and Texas Mohair Weekly*, 14 May 1992, Vol. 99, No.13.

File # N734426. National Personnel Records Center (NPRC), St Louis, MO.

Recommendations for Further Reading

Baron, Scott. *They Also Served: Military Biographies of Uncommon Americans*. Military Information Enterprises. (1998)

Bartimus, Tad et al. *War Torn: Stories of War from the Women Reporters Who Covered Vietnam*. Random House (2002)

Bellafaire, Judith, Granrud, Britta and Binker, Mary Jo. *A Defense Weapon Known to Be of Value-Servicewomen in the Korean War Era*. Military Womens Press (2005)

Bigler, Philip. *Hostile Fire: The Life and Death of First Lieutenant Sharon Lane*. Vandamere Press (1996)

Burgess, Lauren Cook. *An Uncommon Soldier: The Civil War Letters of Sarah Rosetta Wakeman alias Private Lyon Wakeman, 153rd Regiment, New York State Volunteers*. Oxford University Press (1996)

Cornum, Rhonda. *She Went to War*. New York: Ballantine Books, 1992; Presidio Press edition (1993).

Cummings, Mary Lou and Missy, Cummings. *Hornet's Nest*. Writers Showcase Press (2000).

D'Amico, Francine and Weinstein, Laurie. *Gender Camouflage: Women and the US Military*. New York University Press (1999)

Dean, Donna. *Warriors Without Weapons: The Victimization of Military Women*. Minerva Center (1997)

Depauw. Linda Grant. *Battle Cries and Lullabies*. University of Oklahoma Press (1988)

Dever, John Patrick. *Women and the Military: Over 100 Notable Contributions* McFarland and Co. (1994)

Dickman, Diane. *Navy Greenshirt: A Leader Made, Not Born*. Alturia Pub. (2001)

Doyne, Holly. *Kuwait Diary*. Iuniverse Inc. *(2006)*

Ebbert, Jean. *Crossed Currents: Navy Women in a Century of Change*. Potomac Books (1999)

Fessler, Diane Burke. *No Time For Fear: Voices of American Nurses in WW II*. Michigan State University Press (1996)

Fiqueroa, Denise. *The Most Qualified: A Nurse Reservist's Experience in the Persian Gulf War.* New York: Vantage Press, 2002.

Fischer, Linda. *Ultimate Power: Enemy Within the Ranks.* Unlimited Inc. (1999)

Flinn, Kelly. *Proud To Be: My Life, The Air Force, The Controversy.* Random House (1997)

Fortin, Noonie. *Women at Risk: We Also Served.* Writers Club Press (2002)

Francke, Linda Bird. *Ground Zero: The Gender Wars in the Military.* Simon and Schuster (1997)

Freedman, Dan and Rhoads, Jacqueline. *Nurses in Vietnam: The Forgotten Veterans.* Texas Monthly Press (1987)

Gavin, Lettie. *American Women in World War One: They Also Served.* Univ. of Colorado Press (2006)

Gruhzit-Hoyt, Olga. *They Also Served: American Women in World War II.* Carol Publishing Group (1995)

———. *A Time Remembered: American Women in the Vietnam War.* Presidio Press (1999)

Hall, Richard. *Patriots in Disguise: Women Warriors and the Civil War.* Marlowe and Company (1994)

Hodgson, Marion Stegeman. *Winning My Wings: A Woman Airforce Service Pilot in World War II.* Annapolis, Md.: Naval Institute Press, 1996.

Holm, Jeanne M. *In Defense of a Nation: Servicewomen in World War II.* Vandamere Press (1998)

———. *Women in the Military: An Unfinished Revolution.* Presidio Press (1992)

Holm, Jeanne M., Maj. Gen. USAF (Ret.). *In Defense of a Nation: Servicewomen in World War II.* Washington, D.C.: Military Women's Press, 1998.

Holm, Jeanne M., Maj. Gen. USAF (Ret.). *Women in the Military: An Unfinished Revolution.* Novato, Calif.: Presidio Press, 1982.

Hovis, Bobbi. *Station Hospital Saigon: A Navy Nurse in Vietnam 1963-1964.* Naval Institute Press (1992)

Jones, David E. *Women Warriors: A History.* Dulles, Va.: Brassey's (1997); Potomac Books edition (2000).

Karpinski, Janis. *One Woman's Army: The Commanding General of Abu Gharib Tells Her Story.* Miramax Books (2005)

Kassner, Elizabeth. *Desert Storm Journal: A Nurse's Story.* Lincoln Center, Mass.: The Cottage Press, 1993.

Kuhn, Betsy. *Angels of Mercy.* Atheneium Books (1999)

Leonard, Elizabeth. *All The Daring of a Soldier.* Penguin Books (2001)

Lewis, Brenda. *Women at War: The Women of WW II at Home, At Work, On the Front Line.* Amber Books Ltd. (2002)

Lewis, Vicki. *Side by Side: A Photographic History of American Women in War.* Stewart, Tabori and Chang (1999)

McIntosh, Elizabeth P. *Sisterhood of Spies: The Women of the OSS.* New York: Dell Publishing, 1998.

Monahan, Evelyn and Neidel-Greenlee, Rosemary. *All This Hell.* Univ. of Kentucky Press (2003)

———., and Rosemary, Neidel-Greenlee. *And If I Perish: Frontline U.S. Army Nurses in World War II.* New York: Alfred A. Knopf, 2003.

Morden, Bettie. *Women's Army Corps 1945-1978.* US Government Printing Office

Nathan, Amy. *Count on Us: American Women in the Military.* Washington, D.C.: National Geographic Society, 2004.

Norman, Elizabeth. *We Band of Angels: The Untold Story of American Nurses Trapped on Bataan by the Japanese.* Atria Publishing (2000)

———. *Women at War- The Story of Fifty Military Nurses Who Served in Vietnam.* University of Pennsylvania Press (1990)

Omori, Frances. *Quiet Heroes: Navy Nurses of the Korean War 1950-1953 Far East Command.* Smith House Press (2000)

Pennington, Reina. *Amazons to Fighter Pilots: A Biographical Dictionary of Military Women.* Greenwood Press (2003)

Powell, Mary Reynolds. *A World Of Hurt: Between Innocence and Arrogance in Vietnam.* Greenleaf Enterprises (2000)

Schorer, Avis D. *A Half Acre of Hell: A Combat Nurse in WW II.* Lakeville, Minn.: Galde Press, Inc., 2002.

Sherrow, Victoria. *Women and the Military: An Encyclopedia.* ABC-CLIO Inc. (1996)

Skaine, Rosemarie. *Women at War: Gender Issues of Americans in Combat.* McFarland and Company (1999)

Spears, Sally. *Call Sign Revlon: Lt. Kara Hultgreen.* Naval Institute Press (1998)

Stahe, Mary E. *Diary From the Desert.* Jona Books (2003)

Steinman, Ron. *Women in Vietnam: The Oral History* TV Book LLC (2000)

Sterner, Doris M., Capt. NC USN (Ret.). *In and Out of Harm's Way: A History of The Navy Nurse Corps.* Seattle: Peanut Butter Publishing, 1996.

Tomblin, Barbara Brooks. *G.I. Nightingales: The Army Nurse Corps in World War II.* Lexington: The University Press of Kentucky, 1996, 2004.

Treadwell, Mattie B. *The US Army in World War Two: Special Studies – The Women's Army Corps.* US Govt. Printing Office (1954)

Walker, Keith. *A Piece of My Heart: The Stories of 29 Women Who Served in Vietnam.* Presidio Press (1997)

Welch, Bob. *The Story of Frances Slanger.* Atria Books (2004)

Index

About the Authors

James E. Wise Jr., became a naval aviator in 1953 following graduation from Northwestern University. He served as an intelligence officer aboard USS *America* (CVA-66) and later as the commanding officer of various naval intelligence units.

Since his retirement from the Navy in 1975 as a captain, Wise has held several senior executive posts in private sector companies. In addition to *Stars in Blue: Movie Actors in America's Sea Services, Stars in the Corps: Movie Actors in the United States Marines,* and *Stars in Khaki: Movie Stars in the Army and the Air Services,* he coauthored *International Stars at War* and *Soldiers Lost at Sea* with Scott Baron. Additionally, he coauthored *Shooting the War: The Memoir and Photographs of a U-Boat Officer in World War II* with Otto Giese. He is also the author of many articles published in naval and maritime journals. He lives in Alexandria, Virginia.

Scott Baron served with the U.S. Army during the Vietnam War. He has a BA in constitutional law/criminal procedures from California State University—Northridge and a master's in teaching from Chapman University. He worked for more than a decade in law enforcement and taught at the Police Academy and at a community college in Aptos, California. He currently lives on the California coast and teaches U.S. history in Salinas.

Baron is the author of *They Also Served: Military Biographies of Uncommon Americans,* as well as *International Stars at War* and *Soldiers Lost at Sea,* both with James Wise. Baron has also written articles for *Stars and Stripes, GI Jobs,* and *Military.com.*